The Good Co
and other sto

Longman Imprint Books
General Editor: Michael Marland

Titles in the series
There is a Happy Land Keith Waterhouse
Nine African Stories Doris Lessing
The Experience of Colour *edited by* Michael Marland
The Human Element and other stories Stan Barstow
The Leaping Lad and other stories Sid Chaplin
Z Cars Four television scripts
Steptoe and Son Four television scrips
Conflicing Generations Five television scripts
A Sillitoe Selection *edited by* Michael Marland
Late Night on Watling Street and other stories Bill Naughton
Black Boy Richard Wright
The Millstone Margaret Drabble
Fair Stood the Wind for France H.E. Bates
Scene Scripts Seven television plays
The Experience of Work *edited by* Michael Marland
Breaking Away *edited by* Marilyn Davies *and* Michael Marland
The Kraken Wakes John Wyndham
A Hamingway Selection *edited by* Dennis Pepper
Friends and Families *edited by* Eileen *and* Michael Marland
Ten Western Stories *edited* by C.E.J. Smith
The Good Corn and other stories H.E. Bates
The Experience of Sport *edited by* John L. Foster
Loves, Hopes, and Fears *edited by* Micheal Marland
The African Queen C.S. Forester
A Casual Acquaintance and other stories Stan Barstow
Eight American Stories *edited by* D.L. James
Cider with Rosie Laurie Lee
The L-Shaped Room Lynne Reid Banks
Softly, Softly Five television scripts by Elwyn Jones
The Pressures of life Four television plays
The Experience of Prison *edited by* David Ball
Saturday Night and Sunday Morning Alan Sillitoe
A John Wain Selection John Wain
Jack Schaefer and the American West Jack Schaefer
Goalkeepers are Crazy Brian Glanville
A James Joyce Selection James Joyce
Out of the Air Five radio plays, *edited by* Alfred Bradley
Could it be? *edited by* Michael Marland
The Minority Experience *edited by* Michael Marland *and* Sarah Ray
Scene Scripts Two Five television plays
Caribbean Stories *edited by* Michael Marland
An Isherwood Selection *edited by* Geoffrey Halson
A Thomas Hardy Selection *edited by* Geoffrey Halson
While They Fought *edited by* Michael Marland *and* Robin Willcox
The Wave and other stories Liam O'Flaherty
Irish Short Stories *edited by* Frances Crowe

Companion cassettes, with readings of some of the key stories are available for the following:

The Leaping Lad and other stories; The Human Element; A Sillitoe Selection; Late Night on Watling Street; A Casual Acquaintance; Loves, Hopes and Fears; A John Wain Selection

LONGMAN IMPRINT BOOKS

The Good Corn

and other stories by
H.E. Bates

selected and edited by
Geoffrey Halson, M.A.
Formerly Head of the English Department at Hounsdown School

Longman

LONGMAN GROUP LIMITED
London

Associated companies, branches and representatives throughout the world

First published 1974
Third impression 1980
ISBN 0 582 23335 6

Acknowledgements
We are grateful to the Authors' Agents for permission to reproduce a number of extracts from *The Vanished World* by H.E. Bates,published by Michael Joseph Limited.

Printed in Hong Kong by
Yu Luen Offset Printing Factory Limited

Contents

Editor's Introduction

In the story "The Little Jeweller", Elisha Peacock, the little jeweller, after a night of fear in which heart pains have made him feel that he might be dying, is visited by his solicitor. Thoughts of making a will make him more conscious of his illness—indeed, perhaps the thoughts have helped to produce the illness. And so Elisha Peacock angrily sends his solicitor away. Immediately afterwards he feels ashamed at his uncharacteristic anger. Why had he behaved so? H. E. Bates explains: "He then discovered that he was lonely. He felt suddently a great need for companionship, for some objective event or circumstance that would make him forget his fear."

All the stories in this collection illustrate in some way every individual's "great need for companionship", and each story is in some way concerned not just with the telling of a tale but with the sensitive and compassionate exposing of ordinary people in situations where the need for communicating feelings and developing personal relationships is a vital part of the process of experiencing the fullness of life. A person's happiness or unhappiness often depends on his ability or inability to establish a successful relationship with another person.

H.E. Bates shows us in many of his stories the sad loneliness of individuals who just can't explain their feelings to others and who are unable to see others' strong feelings for themselves.

Mr Penfold, in the story of that name, is in this dilemma. He is a "travelling draper and haberdasher" and he's always "on the verge of folding himself up and putting himself away". A lonely man, he is unable to see the loneliness of the war-widow, Mrs Armitage, one of his regular customers. She needs him, yet he has dreams of marriage to her ripening daughter, and all ends in confusion. He is "kept... by great shyness from any entry into a single great experience". Colonel Gracie, in "Where The Cloud Breaks", has also a great need for companionship. His neighbour in the country, Miss Wilkinson, is lonely, too, but the need of each for each is never put positively into words and a row over Miss Wilkinson's acquisition of a television set, which the Colonel very much disliked, condemns them both to separate lives once more. On the other hand, the elderly Colonel Julian, in the story "Colonel Julian", comes to terms with the changed conditions of war and enjoys a serene relationship in his very old age with the young airmen living in his home, which had been commandeered by the R.A.F. early in the Second World War.

Sometimes the great need for companionship occurs, sadly, when people *are* married. Mrs Thurlow, in "The Ox", endures life with a war-demented husband for the sake of her two sons. She worships the money which she saves for her sons' futures. Her husband murders a man and takes the money. Her sons go to live with her brother and his wife, refusing to return to her after the trial. For Mrs Thurlow the creed of money leads to her finally facing life alone, as impassive as an ox, unable to express her feelings any more, unable to defend her need to keep her boys with her. The money-grubbing instincts of James Pypper in "The Loved One" make him utterly unaware of his wife's need to be loved and in her one search for the love of another man tragedy strikes. In "Time To Kill" a journalist, killing time waiting for a train, pays a visit to a girl he'd once been fond of, and finds her lonely in her marriage, unfulfilled, plenty of time to kill, unable to talk about her dilemma. In "The Station" a married woman sits alone in the darkness, waiting for customers to arrive at her all-night café in the depths of the country, and pity, amusement, sexual desire, tenderness, loneliness all muddle together in her furtive encounter with a callow youth as they pick plums in the garden, at night, at the back of the Station.

Louise Bowen, a school-teacher, becomes engaged to escape the feared future drabness of a spinster teacher's life but discovers, on a French holiday with her materialistic fiancé Arthur Keller, "chief assistant, Moore's Drapery, sure to become manager", that an even greater drabness, "the constant and never-changing material of her life cut up by a pair of draper's scissors", lay ahead of her if she were to marry. Able to understand herself, Louise, in "Château Bougainvillaea", gains herself perhaps another chance of happiness. She at least has seen the dangers of a faulty fulfilment of "a great need for companionship".

A mother's jealousy of her daughter frustrates her daughter's need for the companionship of young adults in the story "Every Bullet Has Its Billet". In contrast, the old mother and aging son in "The Maker of Coffins" fulfil a need in each other on Sunday evenings when the son visits his mother to play the tunes on the violin that he had learned in his childhood. A son is mothered still and a mother still has her child.

Children are aided in their maturing by contact with the feelings and relationships of the adult world. The young boy whose experiences are recalled in "Love In a Wych Elm" finds his child's attitudes to a girl of his own age changed by an encounter with one of her elder sisters who, for a brief moment, treats him as an adult—"It's nice to have a man's opinion". The six year old boy in "Let's Play Soldiers" catches, in the midst of his war games, a glimpse of real-life war tragedy when news of the death in the First World War of Mrs Strickland's son Albie is received.

In these stories one can experience the isolation of the individual where communication breaks down. With the compassion that is always present in H. E. Bates's writing one is able to see underlined the need to make effective communication the basis for establishing human relationships in a society which is, ironically, increasingly isolating the individual in its concern for the community as a whole.

In Arnold Wesker's play *Roots*, Beatie Bryant, quoting the words of the young man who has enabled her to become articulate, Ronnie Kahn, says that "Language is words. It's bridges, so that you can get safely from one place to another". The only story in this collection not so far mentioned in this introduction is the title story: "The Good Corn". Here a marriage is saved by a breakthrough in communication at a critical moment. Mrs Mortimer, unable to have a child, and faced with her husband's admission that he is the father of the farm girl's expected child, saves and deepens her marriage relationship with an admission: "Come here to me . . . Come close to me. I'm sorry. It was me. It was my fault . . . Listen to me . . . Listen to what I say . . . Listen, Joe, if I ask her perhaps she'll give it to us . . . we could do it properly—make it legal—so that it was ours." The Mortimers are able to communicate their "great need" and their lives are finally fulfilled.

Geoffrey Halson

Love in a Wych Elm

When I was a boy the Candleton sisters, seven of them, lived in a large gabled house built of red brick that gave the impression of having been muted by continual sunlight to a pleasant shade of orange-rose. The front face of it had a high, benign open appearance and I always felt that the big sash windows actually smiled down on the long gravel terrace, the iron pergola of roses and the sunken tennis lawn. At the back were rows of stables, all in the same faded and agreeable shade of brick, with lofts above them that were full of insecure and ancient bedsteads, fire-guards, hip-baths, tennis rackets, croquet hammers, rocking horses, muscle-developers, Indian clubs, travelling trunks and things of that sort thrown out by Mr and Mrs Candleton over the course of their fruitful years.

I was never very sure of what Mr Candleton did in life; I was not even sure in fact if he did anything at all except to induce Mrs Candleton, at very regular intervals, to bear another daughter. In a town like Evensford there were at that time very few people of independent means who lived in houses that had stables at the back. The Candletons were, or so it seemed to me, above our station. There was at one time a story that Mr Candleton was connected with wine. I could well believe this. Like his house, Mr Candleton's face had toned to a remarkably pleasant shade of inflammable rose. This always seemed perhaps brighter than it really was because his eyes were so blue. They were of that rare shade of pale violet blue that always seems about to dissolve, especially in intoxication. This effect was still further heightened by hair of a most pure distinguished shade of yellow: a thick oat-straw yellow that was quite startling and remarkable in a male.

All the Candleton sisters too had their father's pale violet dissolving eyes and that exceptional shade of oat-straw hair.

At first, when they were very small children, it was white and silky. Then as they grew up its characteristic shining straw-colour grew stronger. A stranger seeing them for the first time would have said that they were seven dolls who had been dipped in a solution of something several shades paler than saffron. The hair was very beautiful when brushed and as children they all wore it long.

On hot days in summer Mr Candleton wore cream flannel trousers with a blue pin stripe in them, a blazer with red and orange stripes, and a straw hat with a band of the same design. Round his waist he wore a red silk cummerbund. All his shirts were of silk and he always wore them buttoned at the neck. In winter he wore things like Donegal tweeds: roughish, sporting, oatmeal affairs that were just right for his grained waterproof shooting brogues. He wore smart yellow gloves and a soft tweed hat with a little feather in the band. He always seemed to be setting off somewhere, brisk and dandyish and correct, a man of leisure with plenty of time to spare.

It was quite different with Mrs Candleton. The house was big and rambling and it might well have been built specially to accommodate Mrs Candleton, who was like a big, absent-minded, untidy, roving bear. My mother used to say that she got up and went to bed in a pinafore. It wasn't a very clean pinafore either. Nor were her paper hair-curlers, which were sometimes still in her rough unruly black hair at tea-time. She always seemed to be wearing carpet-slippers and sometimes her stockings would be slipping down. She was a woman who always seemed to be catching up with life and was always a day and a half behind.

The fact was, I suppose, that with seven children in something like a dozen years Mrs Candleton was still naturally hazy in some of her diurnal calculations. Instead of her catching up with life, life was always catching up with her.

Meals, for example, made the oddest appearances in the Candleton household. If I went on a school-less day to call on Stella—she was the one exactly of my own age, the one I knew best—it was either to find breakfast being taken at eleven-thirty, with Mr Candleton always immaculate behind the silver toast-rack and Mrs Candleton looking like the jaded mistress of a rag-and-bone man, or dinner at half-past three or tea at seven. In a town like Evensford everybody was rigidly governed by factory hours and the sound of factory hooters. At various times of the day silences fell on the town that were a hushed indication that all honest people were decently at work. All this meant that breakfast was at seven, dinner at twelve-thirty and tea at half-past five. That was how everybody ate and lived and ran their lives in Evensford: everybody, that is, except the Candletons.

These characteristics of excessive and immediate smartness on the one hand and the hair-curler and pinafore style on the other had been bequeathed by him and Mrs Candletown in almost exactly equal measure to their children. The girls were all beautiful, all excessively dressy as they grew up and, as my mother was fond of saying, not over clean.

"If they get a cat-lick once a week it's about as much as they do get," was one of her favourite sayings.

But children do not notice such things very acutely and I cannot say that I myself was very interested in the virtues of soap and water. What I like about the Candletons was not only a certain mysterious quality of what I thought was aristocracy but a feeling of untamed irresponsibility. They were effervescent. When the eldest girl, Lorna, was seventeen she ran off with a captain in the Royal Artillery who turned out to be a married man. I thought it might well have been the sort of thing that would have ruined a girl, temporarily at least, in Evensford, but Stella simply thought it a wild joke and said:

"She had a wonderful time. It was gorgeous. They stayed at a marvellous hotel in London. She told us all about it. I thought Mother would die laughing."

Of laughing, not shame: that was typical of the Candleton standard, the Candleton approach and the Candleton judgement on such things.

The four eldest girls, two of them twins, were called Lorna, Hilda, Rosa and Freda. This habit of giving names ending in the same letter went on to Stella, with whom I played street-games in winter in front of the gas-lit windows of a porkpie and sausage shop and games in summer in the Candleton garden and among the muscle-developers and bedsteads of the Candleton loft, and then on to the two youngest, who were mere babies as I knew them, Wanda and Eva. Mrs Candleton's Christian name was Blanche, which suited her perfectly.

It was a common tendency in all the Candleton girls to develop swiftly. At thirteen they were filling out; at fifteen they were splendidly and handsomely buxom and were doing up their hair. Hilda appeared to me to be a goddess of marbled form long before she was eighteen and got engaged to a beefy young farmer who bred prize cattle and called for her in a long open sports car.

Hilda had another characteristic not shared by any of the rest of the family except her mother. She sang rather well. At eighteen she began to have her pleasant, throaty, contralto voice trained.

Mr Candleton was a strict Sunday morning churchgoer in pin-stripe trousers, bowler hat and spats, and Hilda went with him to sing in the choir. Her voice was trained by a Mr Lancaster, a rather bumptious pint-size tenor who gave her lessons three evenings a week. It was generally known that Mr Lancaster was, as a singer at any rate, past his best, but it was not long before the engagement between Hilda and the farmer was broken.

At that time Stella and I were nine. I, at least, was nine and Stella, physically, was twelve or thirteen. What I liked about her so much in those days was her utter freedom to come and go as she pleased. Other children had errands to run, confirmation classes to attend, catechisms to learn, aunts to visit, restrictive penances like shoes to clean or knives to rub up with bath-brick.

In the Candleton way she had never anything to do but play, enjoy herself, indulge in inconsequential make-believe and teach me remarkable things about life and living.

"What shall we do? Let's be married. Let's go up to the loft and be married.'

"We were married the day before yesterday."

"That doesn't matter. You can be married over and over again. Hilda's going to be, Come on, let's be married."

"All right. But not in the loft. Let's have a new house this time."

"All right. Let's be married in the wych elm."

The Candleton garden extended beyond the stables into a rough orchard of old damson trees, with a few crooked espalier pears. A pepper-pot summer house in rustic work with a thatched roof stood in one corner, almost obliterated by lilac trees. In summer damsons and pears fell into the deep grass and no one picked them up. A sense of honeyed rotting quietness spread under the lurching trees and was compressed and shut in by a high boundary line of old, tapering wych elms.

Rooks nested in the highest of the elms and when summer thickened the branches the trees were like a wall. The house was hidden and shut away. On a heavy summer day you would hear nothing there but the sound of rooks musing and croaking and fruit falling with a squashy mellow plop on the grass and paths.

Up in the wych elms the peculiar structure of boughs made a house for us. We could walk about it. We crawled, like monkeys, from tree to tree. In this paradise we stayed for entire afternoons, cocooned with scents, hidden away in leaves. We made tea in ancient saucepans on flameless fires of elm twigs and prepared dinners of potatoes and gravy from fallen pears. And up here, on a soft August afternoon, we were married without witnesses and Stella, with her yellow hair done up for the first time, wore a veil of lace curtains and carried a bunch of cow-parsley.

But before that happened I had caught, only the day before, another glimpse of the Candleton way of living.

I had called about six o'clock in the evening for Stella but although the door of the house was open nobody, for some time at any rate, answered my ring at the bell. That was not at all unusual at the Candleton household. Although it never seemed possible for nine such unmistakable people to disappear without trace it was frequently happening and often I went to the door and rang until I was tired of ringing and then went away without an answer.

I remember once ringing the bell and then, tired of it, peeping into the kitchen. It was one of those big old-fashioned kitchens with an enormous iron cooking range with plate racks above it and gigantic dressers and vast fish-kettles and knife-cleaners everywhere. In the middle of it all Mrs Candleton sat asleep. Not normally asleep, I could see. A quarter-full bottle of something for which I had no definition stood on the table in front of her, together with a glass and, beside the glass, most astonishing thing of all, her false teeth.

Blowsily, frowsily, comfortably, toothlessly, Mrs Candleton was sleeping away the afternoon in her hair-curlers and her pinafore.

But on the evening I called for Stella the kitchen was empty. I rang the bell four or five times and then, getting no answer, stepped into the hall.

"Hullo," someone said.

That very soft, whispered throaty voice was Hilda's. She was standing at the top of the stairs. She was wearing nothing but her petticoat and her feet were bare. In her hands she was holding a pair of stockings, which she had evidently been turning inside out in readiness to put on.

"Oh! it's you," she said. "I thought I heard someone."

"Is Stella here?"

"They're all out. They've all gone to the Robinsons' for tea. It's Katie's birthday."

"Oh! I see," I said. "Well, I'll come again tomorrow—"

"I'm just going to a dance," she said. "Would you like to see my dress? Would you?—come on, come up."

Standing in the bedroom, with the August sunlight shining on her bare shoulders, through the lace of her slip and on her sensational yellow Candleton hair, she was a magnificent figure of a girl.

"Just let me put my stockings on and then you can see my dress."

She sat down on the bed to put on her stockings. Her legs were smooth and heavy. I experienced an odd sensation as the stockings unrolled up her legs and then were fastened somewhere underneath the petticoat. Then she stood up and looked at the back of her legs to see if her stockings were straight. After that she smoothed the straps of her petticoat over her shoulders and said:

"Just wait till I give my hair one more brush."

I shall never forget how she sat before the dressing-mirror and brushed her hair. I was agreeably and mystically stunned. The strokes of the brush made her hair shine exactly, as I have said before, like oat-straw. Nothing could have been purer and more shining. It was marvellously burnished and she laughed at me in the mirror because I stood there so staring and speechless and stunned.

"Well, do I look nice? You think I shall pass in a crowd?"

"Yes."

"That's good. It's nice to have a man's opinion."

She laughed again and put on her dress. It was pure white, long and flouncy. I remember distinctly the square low collar. Then she put on her necklace. It was a single row of pearls and she couldn't fasten it.

"Here, you can do this," she said.

She sat on the bed and I fastened the necklace. The young hair at the nape of her neck was like yellow chicken down. I was too confused to notice whether she had washed her neck or not and then she said:

"That's it. Now just a little of this and I'm ready."

She sprayed her hair, her arms and the central shadow of her bosom with scent from a spray.

"How about a little for you?"

She sprayed my hair and in a final moment of insupportable intoxication I was lost in a wave of wallflowers.

"That's the most expensive scent there is," she said. "The most difficult to make. Wallflowers."

Perhaps it was only natural, next day, as I came to be married to Stella high at the altar of the wych elms, that I found myself oppressed by a sensation of anticlimax. Something about Stella, I felt, had not quite ripened. I had not the remotest idea as to what it could be except that she seemed, in some unelevating and puzzling way, awkward and flat.

"What do you keep staring at me for?"

"I'm just going to spray you with scent," I said. "There—piff! pish! piff—"

"Whatever made you think of that?"

I was afraid to speak of Hilda and I said:

"All girls have to have scent on when they're married."

"Do I look nice?"

She didn't really look nice. The lace curtain was mouldy in one corner and had holes down one side. I didn't like the odour of cow-parsley. But the soft golden oat-straw hair was as remarkable as ever and I said:

"You look all right."

Then we were married. After we were married she said:

"Now you have to make love to me."

"Why?"

"Everybody has to make love when they're married."

I looked at her in utter mystification. Then suddenly she dropped the cow-parsley and pushed back her veil and kissed me. She held me in an obliterating and momentary bondage by the trunk of the wych elm, kissing me with such blistering force that I lost my cap. I was rather upset about my cap as it fell in the nettles below but she said:

"Sit down. We're in bed now. We have to be in bed now we're married. It's the first thing people do."

"Why?"

"Don't you know?"

I did not know; nor, as it happens, did she. But one of the advantages of being born one of a family of seven sisters is that you arrive much earlier at the approximation of the more delicate truths than you do if you are a boy. Perhaps in this respect I was a backward boy, but I could only think it was rather comfortless trying to make love in a wych elm and after a time I said:

"Let's go and play in the loft now."

"What with?"

"I don't know," I said. "Let's have a change. We've been married an awful lot of times—"

"I know," she said. "We'll play with the chest-developers."

While we played in the loft with the chest-developers she had an original thought.

"I think if I practise a lot with these I shall get fat up top more quickly."

"You will?"

"I think I shall soon anyway."

Like Hilda, I thought. A renewed sensation of agreeable and stupefying delight, together with a scent of wallflowers, shot deliciously through me and I was half-way to the realisation of the truth that girls are pleasant things when she said:

"One day, when we're big, let's be really married, shall us?"

"All right."

"Promise?"

"Yes," I said.

"You know what you'll be when you're married to me, don't you?" she said.

I couldn't think.

"You'll be a viscount," she said.

"What's a viscount?"

"It's the husband of a viscountess."

"How shall I come to be that?"

"Because a viscountess is the daughter of a lord."

"But," I said, "your father isn't a lord."

"No," she said, "but his brother is. He lives in a castle in Bedfordshire. It has a hundred and forty rooms in it. We go there every summer. And when he dies my father will be a lord."

"Is he going to die?"

"Soon."

"Supposing your father dies before he does?"

"Oh! he won't," she said. "He's the youngest son. The oldest always die first."

She went on to tell me many interesting things about our life together. Everything in that life would be of silk, she said, like her father's shirts. Silk sheets on the bed, silk pillows, silk table-cloths, silk cushions. "And I shall always wear silk drawers," she said. "Even on week-days."

Altogether, it seemed, we should have a marvellous life together.

"And we shall drink port wine for supper," she said. "Like my father does. He always drinks port wine for supper."

"Is it nice?"

"Yes," she said. "I'm allowed to have it sometimes. You'll like it. You can get drunk as often as you like then. Like my father does."

"Does he get drunk?"

"Not as often as my mother does," she said, "but quite a lot."

I suppose I was shocked.

"Oh! that's all right," she said. "Lords always get drunk. That's why people always say 'drunk as a lord'. That's the proper thing to do."

Armed with the chest-developers, we spent an ecstatic afternoon. I was so filled with the golden snobbery of being a viscount that it was a cold and dusty sort of shock when she told me that anyway we couldn't be married for years and years, not until she was fatter, like Hilda was.

The recollection of Hilda, all burnished and magnificent and intoxicating and perfumed, inflamed and inspired me to greater efforts with the chest-developers.

"We must work harder," I said.

I wanted so much to be a lord, to live in a castle, to drink port wine and to be married to someone with silk drawers that I was totally unprepared for the shock my mother gave me.

"The little fibber, the little story-teller, the little liar," she said.

"But she said so," I said. "She told me."

"I went to board school with Reggie Candleton," she said. "He was in my class. They came from Gas Street."

Nothing in the world was worse than coming from Gas Street. You could not go lower than Gas Street. The end of the respectable world was Gas Street.

"It's she who had the money," my mother said. "Mrs Candleton. Her father was a brewer and Reggie Candleton worked there. He was always such a little dandy. Such a little masher. Always the one for cutting such a dash."

I decided it was wiser to say nothing about the prospect of marrying, or about Stella's urgent efforts with the chest-developers, or the silk drawers.

"All top show," my mother said. "That's what it is. All fancy fol-di-dols on top and everything dropping into rags underneath. Every one of them with hair like a ten-guinea doll and a neck you could sow carrots in."

I don't suppose for a moment that Stella remembers me; or that, on an uncomfortable, intimate occasion, we were married in a wych elm. It is equally unlikely that Hilda remembers me; or that, with her incomparable yellow hair, her white dance dress, her soft blonde flesh and her rare scent of wallflowers, she once asked me to give her my opinion as a man. I believe Stella is married to a bus-conductor. The rest of the Candletons have faded from my life. With the summer frocks, the summer straw-hats and the summer flannels, the cummerbunds, the silk shirts, the elegant brogues, the chest-developers and the incomparable yellow hair they have joined Mr Candleton in misty, muted. permanent bankruptcy.

Love in a wych elm is not an easy thing; but like the Candletons it is unforgettable.

Let's Play Soldiers

The yellow strings of laburnum flower had already faded that afternoon when I stood on sentry for the 1st Battalion Albion Street Light Infantry and Mrs Strickland came out of her kitchen door wearing a sack apron and a man's check cap pinned on her spindly curling rags by a long black hat pin and started shaking mats against the garden fence, not three yards from the tent made of split sacks and old lace curtains where we of the battalion held councils of war before going into battle.

Upstairs across the yard Mrs Rankin was sitting at a window with a bottom like a pumpkin hanging over the sill, huffing energetically on glass already as pure as crystal and then scrupulously polishing the vapour off again with a spotless yellow rag.

The face of Mrs Rankin, smooth and clean as porcelain, looked as if it had been polished too but the face of Mrs Strickland, like her curl-ragged hair, had nothing but greyness in it, a dopey salty greyness at the same time hard so that the skin looked like scoured pumice stone.

I was only six at the time and still a private; but I thought I detected a smell of parsnip wine in the air. Mangled dust and shreds of coco-matting rose in dense brown clouds as Mrs Strickland beat the decaying mats against the fence but I stood unshakably at attention under the laburnum tree, head up, eyes straight ahead, right hand firmly on the umbrella we were using as a rifle because Jeddah Clarke, our Captain, had the air gun, the only other weapon we possessed.

I knew that if I stood firm on guard and didn't flinch and saluted properly and challenged people and didn't let them pass until they gave the password, I might become, in time, a lance-corporal. There was nothing on earth I wanted more than to be a lance-corporal: except perhaps to kill a soldier.

"I wisht Albie was here," Mrs Strickland said. "I wisht Albie was here."

It wasn't only that morning that her voice had that pumice-dry melancholy in it. It was always there, like the curling rags. Sometimes Mrs Strickland didn't take out the curling rags until after Bill Strickland came home for his bloater tea at six o'clock and sometimes she didn't take them out at all.

"Ain't got a spare Daisy Powder, gal, I reckon?"

Mrs Strickland, staring with diffused and pleading eyes through the dust she had raised, groping up towards the sumptuous pumpkin of Mrs Rankin on the window sill, ran a dreary hand several times across her aching brow.

"Ain't got nivry one left," Mrs Rankin said. "You had the last one yisty."

Daisies were a brand of headache powder guaranteed to refresh and free you from pain in five minutes. Mrs Strickland was taking them all day.

"Ain't Bill a-workin' then?"

"Bad a-bed. Can't lift 'isself orf the piller. I wisht Albie was here."

I knew Albie couldn't be there. Albie, who was eighteen, a private too like me, was in France, fighting the Germans. I liked Albie; he had a ginger moustache and was my friend. Every other day or so I asked Mrs Strickland if and when Albie was going to become a lance-corporal, but somehow she never seemed to think he was.

"Ain't you got nivry one tucked away, gal, somewheer?"

"Nivry one," Mrs Rankin said. "Nivry one."

Despair wrapped Mrs Strickland's face in a greyer, dustier web of gloom.

"Me 'ead's splittin'. It'll split open. I wisht Albie was here.'

"Won't the boy nip and get y' couple? Ask the boy."

Mrs Strickland, seeming to become aware of me for the first time, turned to my impassive sentinel figure with eyes of greyest supplication.

"Nip down the shop and fetch us a coupla Daisies, there's a good boy. Nip and ask your mother to lend us a thrippenny bit, there's a good boy. I left me puss upstairs."

It was funny, my mother always said, how Mrs Strickland was always leaving, losing or mislaying her purse somewhere.

"And a penn'orth o' barm too, boy, while you're down there. Gotta make a mite o' bread, somehow," she called up to Mrs Rankin. "Aain't got a mite in the place, gal. Not so much as a mossel."

Mrs Rankin, who would presently be hurrying down to the yard to scour and white-wash the kitchen steps to blinding glacier whiteness and who, as my mother said, almost polished the coal before putting it on the fire, merely turned on Mrs Strickland a rounder, blanker, completely unhelpful pumpkin.

I didn't move either; I was on guard and Jeddah Clarke said you could be shot if you moved on guard.

"Nip and ask your mother to lend us a thrippenny bit, boy. Tanner if she's got it, boy—"

"I can't go, Mrs Strickland. I'm on sentry," I said. "I'll get shot."

"Kids everywhere," Mrs Strickland said, "and nivry one on 'em to run of arrant for you when you want. I wisht Albie was here."

Mrs Strickland dragged the decaying mats to the middle of the yard. The smell of parsnip wine went with her and she called up to Mrs Rankin:

"Ain't got 'arf a loaf I can have for a goin' on with gal, I reckon? Jist till the baker gits here? Jist 'arf? Jist the top?"

"You want one as'll fit on the bottom I lent you the day afore yisty? or will a fresh 'un do?"

Fiery, tempestuous white curds seemed to fly suddenly out of Mrs Strickland's mournful, aching head.

"What's a matter wi' y'? Askt y' a civil question, dint I? Askt y' civil question. What's a matter wi' y' all of a pop?"

"Sick on it," Mrs Rankin said. "About sick to death on it."

"Go on, start maungin'! Start yelpin'!"

"Yelpin'," Ain't got nothing to yelp about, I reckon, have I? When it ain't bread it's salt. When it ain't salt it's bakin' powder. Enough to gie y' the pip. When it ain't—"

"Keep on, keep on!" Mrs Strickland said. "It'll do your fat gullet good. And me with 'im in bed. And the damn war on. And Albie not here."

Suddenly she dropped the mats, picked up a bucket from the kitchen drain and started beating and rattling it like a war gong. In a flash Mrs Rankin's pumpkin darted through the window, dragging the sash down behind it. Behind the crystal glass Mrs Rankin's face remained palely distorted, mouthing furiously.

Down below in the yard, Mrs Strickland rattled the bucket again, shaking her curling rags, and yelled:

"Mag, mag. Jaw, jaw. That's all folks like you are fit for. Mag, jaw, mag, jaw—"

Mrs Rankin's face, ordinarily so polished and composed, splintered into uncontrollable furies behind the glass as Mrs Strickland started to fill the bucket with water from the stand-pipe in the yard.

In a second Mrs Rankin had the window up with a shrilling squeak of the sash and was half leaping out:

"And don't you start your hanky-pankies. Don't you start that! —I oiled and polished my door!—"

An arc of white water struck Mrs Rankin's back door like a breaker. Mrs Rankin slammed down the window and started beating the panes with her fists. Mrs Strickland screamed that she wisht Albie was here, Albie would let some daylight into somebody, and threw the bucket with a crashing roll across the yard.

A moment later a bedroom window shot open in the Strickland house and an unsober chin of black stubble leaned out and bawled:

"What the bloody 'ell's going on down there? If you two don't shut your yawpin' chops I'll come down and lay a belt acrosst the pair on y'—"

"I wisht Albie was here!" Mrs Strickland said. "I wisht Albie was here!"

Drearily she slammed away into the house and after that it was silent for some minutes until suddenly from the street beyond the yard I could hear the inspiring note of war cries. A minute later the first battalion Albion Street Light Infantry came triumphantly pounding down the path between the cabbage patches, led by Jeddah Clarke, carrying the air-gun, Wag Chettle, bearing the standard, a red handkerchief tied to a bean-pole, and Fred Baker, beating a drum he had had for Christmas.

Fred and Jeddah were actually in khaki uniforms. Jeddah, besides the air-gun, wore a bandolier across his chest with real pouches and two clips of spent cartridges; Fred had a peaked khaki cap on, with the badge of the Beds & Bucks Light Infantry on one side and that of the Royal Welch Fusiliers on the other. At that time the Fusiliers were billeted in the town and we had an inspired admiration for them because they kept a white goat as mascot. The goat ate anything you gave it, even cigarettes.

What now surprised me about the battalion was not its air of triumph but its size. Usually it was no more than eight strong. Now it was twenty. Those bringing up the rear were even flying a second flag. It was a square of blue-and-white football shirt I caught the gleam of a second and even a third air-gun and then suddenly Jeddah Clarke, our Captain, raised his air-gun and yelled:

"Gas Street are on our side! They're in the battalion! Gas Street have come in with us! Charge!"

We all cheered madly and charged. The little hairs of my neck stuck up in pride, excitement and admiration as we thundered dustily into the summer street outside.

"Charge!" we all shouted. "Charge! Capture 'em! Charge!"

Heady with thought of battle, we wheeled like thunder into Winchester Street: completely unnoticed by a milk float, two bakers' carts, a chimney sweep on a bicycle and two women pushing prams.

"Charge!" I yelled, and was stunned to hear the blast of a bugle, suddenly blown at my side by a boy named Charley Fletcher, who was in the Lads' Brigade.

This new note, defiant above the roll of Fred Baker's drum, had us all in a frenzy of battle just as we surged past a railway dray loading piles of bulky leather outside a factory, where the crane swung out from its fourth storey door like a gallows and dropped its thirty-feet of rippling chain down to the shining hot pavement below.

"Charge!" I yelled, bringing up the rear with the umbrella under my arm and pointing it forward as if it had a bayonet in the end, exactly as I had seen in pictures of soldiers charging from the trenches. There was nothing we didn't know about soldiers and the trenches. We knew all about Vimy Ridge, Ypres, Hill 60 and Verdun too. We had seen them all in pictures.

The voice of our Captain, Jeddah Clarke, tore the air with fresh challenge as we whipped out of Winchester Street into Green's Alley. Continually Charley Fletcher's bugle ripped the quiet of the afternoon to shreds with raucous notes that were almost hysterical, rallying both us and the reinforcements of Gas Street, and I wondered suddenly where we were going and where the attack would be made.

Jeddah, yelling, told us all a moment later:

"Down to The Pit! We'll git 'em in The Pit!"

My heart went absolutely icy, turned sour and dropped to my stomach.

The Pit was a terrible place. You never went to The Pit. No one ever did. If you did you never came out alive. The people there, who lived in sordid back-to-back hovels with sacks at the windows, captured you, tied you up, locked you in satanic privies and let you suffocate to death. If they didn't do that they starved you, took away all your clothes and sold you naked in slavery.

They were the most awful people in the world. People like Mrs Strickland were respectable by comparison. They were always dirty, drunk and fighting. They were always stinking and they were full of bugs and fleas.

I suddenly wanted to turn back, stand guard in the cabbage patch and dream quietly about being a lance-corporal one day.

"Charge!" everyone yelled. "Charge! Git the stones ready!"

Out of Green's Alley we swung on the tide of battle into The Jetty, a narrow track of dried mud and stone. There the triumphant column broke up for a moment or two and we began to hack stones from the dust with the heels of our boss. By this time my legs and knees were shaking: so much so that all I could hack out were two pebbles and the stopper of a broken beer bottle. But Fred Baker, seeing this, took pity on me and armed me with half a brick.

The bugle sounded again, shrill as a cornet.

"Air-guns in front!" Jeddah yelled. "Git ready when I say charge!"

We thundered on. We had been joined now by a butcher's boy on a bicycle and for some reason I found myself clinging to his saddle. Suddenly in the excitement the butcher's boy started pedalling madly and I could hardly keep up with the column as it pounded along.

Less than a minute later we were facing the jaws of The Pit. They were nothing more than a gap between two rows of derelict gas-tarred fences but beyond them I could see the little one-storey hovels with sacks at their windows, the horrible squat brick prisons of outdoor privies and a few dirty flags of shirt on a washing line.

It was impossible for my heart to turn cold a second time; it was frozen stiff already. But the paralysis that kept it stuck at the pit of my stomach now affected my legs and I stopped running.

This, as it turned out, was a purely instinctive reaction. Everyone else had stopped running too.

"Charge!" someone yelled and this time it was not our Captain, Jeddah.

The order came from behind us and as we turned in its direction we found ourselves the victims of the oldest of all battle manoeuvres. We were being attacked in the rear.

This time my eyes froze. The Pit Brigade stood waiting for us: eight or ten of them, headed by a black-mouthed deaf-mute armed with five-foot two-pronged hoe. Another had an ugly strip of barrel hoop sharpend up like a sword and another a catapult with a black leather sling big enough to hold an egg. He was smoking a cigarette. Two others were manning a two-seater pram armoured with rusty plates of corrugated iron and this, we all realised, was an armament we did not possess. It was the first tank we had encountered.

The deaf-mute started showing his black teeth, gurgling strange cries. He made vigorious deaf-and-dumb signs with his hands and the snarling faces about him jabbered. The entire Pit Brigade, older, bigger, dirtier and better armed than we were, stood ready to attack.

It was too late to think about being a lance-corporal now and a moment later they were on us.

"Charge!" everyone shouted from both sides. "Charge!" and we were locked in an instant clash of bricks, stones, catapults, flags, sticks and air-guns that would not fire. Above it all the unearthly voice of the deaf mute gurgled like a throttled man, mouthing black nothings.

I threw my brick. It fell like the legendary sparrow through the air. Someone started to tear the coat off my back and I thrashed madly about me with the umbrella. I could see our two flags rocking ship-mast fashion in the centre of battle and Charley Fletcher using the bugle as a hammer. The two-pronged hoe fell like a claw among us and the armour plates fell off the pram-tank as it ran into Fred Baker and cut his legs, drawing first blood.

Soon we actually had them retreating.

"We're the English!" I heard Jeddah shouting. "We're the English! The Pit are the bloody Germans," and this stirring cry of patriotism roused us to fresh thrills of battle frenzy.

"We're the English!" we all yelled. "We're the English!"

Suddenly as if a trap door had opened the Pit Brigade, under sheer weight of pressure, fell backward into the jaws of The Pit, hastily slamming the door behind them as a barricade and leaving outside a single stray soldier armed with a rusty flat iron suspended on a piece of cord and dressed as a sergeant of the Royal Artillery, complete with spurs and puttees.

Cut off from the tide of battle, this soldier gave several rapid and despairing looks about him, dropped the flat iron and bolted like a hare.

"Prisoner!" Jeddah yelled. "Prisoner! Git him! Take him prisoner!"

In a moment Fred Baker, Charley Fletcher and myself were after him. We caught him at the top to The Jetty. At first he lay on his back and kicked out at us with the spurs, spitting at the same time, but soon I was sitting on his face, Fred Baker on his chest and Charley Fletcher, who was the eldest, on his legs. For a long time he kept trying to spit at us and all the time there was a strong, putrid, stinking, funny smell about him.

We kept him prisoner all afternoon. Then we decided to strip him. While Fred and I sat on his face and chest Charley unrolled the puttees and took off the spurs.

"You always have spoils of war when you take prisoners," Charley explained. "Soldiers call it a bit of buckshee."

We spent some time arguing about how the buckshee should be divided and finally Charley was awarded the puttees, because he was the eldest, and Fred Baker and I each had a spur. Having the spur was even better than being a lance corporal and I couldn't remember ever having had anything that made me feel more proud.

It was almost evening before Jeddah and the rest of the Battalion got back, fifty strong, from telling of our victory in far places, in Lancaster Street, Rectory Street, Bedford Row, King's Lane and those parts of the town who could not be expected to hear of our triumph other than by word of mouth and from us.

"We still got the prisoner, Captain," we said. "What shall we do with him?"

"Shoot him," Jeddah said.

Orders were orders with Jeddah and we asked if we could have the air-gun.

He handed it over.

"I leave it to you," Jeddah said. He was now wearing a forage cap, three long service stripes, a leather belt and a Welch black flash he had captured. "Charge!"

The sound of returning triumph from the fifty-strong battalion had hardly died away before we set to work to shoot the flat-iron boy.

First of all we made him stand up by the fence, among a pile of junk and nettles. By this time we had tied his hands and legs with the cord off the flat-iron and had taken off his shoes so that he found it hard to run. But he still spat at us as he stood waiting to be shot and he still had that funny, sickening smell.

Fred Baker shot him first. The unloaded air-gun made a noise rather like a damp squib. Then Charley Fletcher shot him and the gun made a noise like a damp squib a second time. Then I shot him and as I did so I made a loud, realistic noise that was more like the crack of a bursting paper bag. I aimed between the eyes of the flat-iron boy as I shot and I was very thrilled.

"Now you're dead," we said to him. "Don't you forget. Don't you move—you're dead. You can't fight no more."

He didn't look very dead when we left him but we knew he was. We told the Captain so when we rejoined the battalion in Gas Street, Fred Baker blowing the bugle and wearing the artillery puttees, Charley Fletcher and I taking turns to carry the air-gun and both of us waving a spur.

Jeddah was drunk with victory. "Tomorrow we're goin' to charge The Rock!" he said. The Rock was even worse than The Pit but now none of us was appalled and all of us cheered. There was no holding us now.

"We'll kill 'em all!" Jeddah said. "We'll burn ole Wag Saunders at the stake." Wag was their Captain. "Just like Indians. We'll win 'em. We ain't frit. Who are we?"

"We're the English!" we yelled.

It was already growing dark when I trotted home through the streets with my spur. In the back yard there were no lights in Mrs Rankin's neat, white-silled windows and in Mrs Strickland's house all the blinds were drawn although all the lights were on.

"Where have you been all this long time?" my father said.

He sat alone in the kitchen, facing a cold rice pudding. My father was very fond of cold rice pudding but tonight he did not seem to want it. Under the green gaslight the brown nutmeg skin of it shone unbroken.

"Fighting with our battalion," I said.

I told him how the battle had been won and how I had captured the spur.

"That spur doesn't belong to you," he said. "Tomorrow morning you must take it back."

I felt sick with disappointment and at the way grown-up people didn't understand you.

"Can I keep it just for tonight?"

"Just for tonight," he said. "But you must take it back tomorrow."

Then I remembered something and I told him how the boy I'd got it from was dead.

"How is that?" he said. "Dead?"

"We shot him."

"Oh! I see," he said. "Well: tomorrow you go and find the dead boy and give him back his spur."

Looking round the kitchen I now remembered my mother and asked where she was.

"She's with Mrs Strickland," my father said. "Mrs Rankin's with her too. I expect you noticed that all the blinds were drawn?"

I said I had noticed and did it mean that someone was dead?

"It's your friend—your friend Albie's not going to come back," my father said.

After that my father didn't seem to want to speak very much and I said:

"Could I go and play in the tent until mother comes home?"

"You can go and play in the tent," he said.

"With a candle?" I said. "It's dark now outside."

"Take a candle if you like," he said.

I took a candle and sat in the tent all by myself, looking at my spur. It was shaped something like a handcuff to which was attached a silver star. The candlelight shone down on the spur with wonderful brilliance and as I looked at it I remembered the voices of Mrs Strickland and Mrs Rankin squabbling with bitterness over a loaf of bread in the afternoon and how Mrs Strickland wisht that Albie would come back, and now I listened again for their voices coming from the outer darkness but all I could hear was the voice from the afternoon:

"I wisht Albie was here. I wisht Albie was here."

There is nothing much you can do with a solitary candle and a single spur. The spur can only shine like silver and the candle-light with a black vein in the heart of it.

Early next morning I took the spur back to The Pit. I ran all the way there and I was glad that no one saw me. The sun was coming up over the gas-tarred fences, the little hovels, the privies and the washing lines and all I did was to lay the spur on a stone in the sunlight, hoping that someone would come and find it there.

I ran all the way home, too, as hard as I could: afraid of the enemy we had conquered and the soldier I had killed.

Every Bullet Has Its Billet

Irma Harris was eighteen when, in 1915, Lieutenant Bronson and his wife came to be billeted on her mother. Just out of High School, a pale arch-eyed girl with great masses of reddish gold hair scrolled up behind like the twists of a golden loaf, she had got to the age when she liked sitting for long hours in her own room, alone, thinking inexpressibly sad thoughts, with her hands spread out on her lap like two pink self-conscious flowers, waiting for the dew of all sorts of confused dreams to fall on them. Lieutenant Bronson and his wife had been married six weeks, and were very happy.

Mrs Harris was a woman whose mind was done up in curling-rags: a plain, common mind which, for forty years, she had tried to frill into superiority. On a level above the neighbours, to whom she never spoke, she thanked God for Irma: thanked God that Irma's hair was rich and beautiful, that she had the aristocratic richness of a name like Irma and not the common poverty of a name like May or Flo; that Irma had been educated, was superior, had kept pure and would, by the Grace of God, still keep pure for a long time to come. Earlier, some years before the death of Harris, who had peddled hosiery on a basket bicycle from door to door and had somehow cheese-pared his way to saving money, she had shut Irma down under a glass case, and had then gone on polishing the glass until she could see in it not only Irma but her own face. Even then it was not her own plain, ordinary curl-ragged face, but a face with a great mass of loaf-gold hair and soft pure skin as pale as bread. She saw Irma: Irma was herself. The girl was the lost self of the woman, unrecapturable except through the glass dome of imagination. Whatever might happen to Irma would happen also to herself.

In a podgy kind of way, Lieutenant Bronson was handsome, heavily built, with aristocratically tender feet which suffered terribly on the route marches. He came from the real aristocracy: estates in Cornwall, a house in Grosvenor Square, and at the outbreak of the war had been toying away time, on a pretence of working at oil, in Mexico. Yet he had a quality of self-effacement about him, a retreating charm of manner that was quite humble. The men liked him. He had a way of hushing up, as it were, his aristocratic identity. His wife was a little thing, a woman of whipped cream, delicate and sweet, all pretty froth and hardly tangible. An aristocrat also, she had not quite come to her senses after the tremendous crash of war and marriage coming almost at the same time, and she painted water-colours in the Harris's front room, in the real pre-war aristocratic mode, still nursing the idea that painting was a necessary accomplishment. Bronson adored her, and she was only bored when route marches and parades and mess duty claimed him too long. Then she painted hard, or wrote letters, or, on desperate days, went into the kitchen and prepared the anchovies or mayonnaise. On still more desperate days she invited Irma into the front room, to talk to her, while she painted.

The two girls liked each other. Only the thinnest veil of breeding and self-consciousness kept them apart, sometimes miles apart. Virginal, under the glass-case, Irma looked up to the older girl, envying the strange state of marriage, in which freedom and stability were so miraculously combined. Whirling round on an axis which marriage and war had sent crazy, Mrs Bronson looked down, with slight envy, on what she felt to be Irma's state of emotional rest.

Mrs Bronson painted with timid accurate talent, creating nothing. The delicate water-colours cost her no emotion. She copied flowers, did a bowl of Gloire de Dijon roses that Irma brought in from the garden, and another of white lilies. She was always washing her hands. She used a strange soap, after which her hands gave off a remotely exotic scent. To Irma, gradually, this scent began to stand for Mrs Bronson: her frothy prettiness, her painting, the miraculous marital state.

In this way the natural heroine-worship sprang up. Just as Mrs Harris saw herself in Irma, so Irma began to wish that she could see herself in Mrs Bronson. She wanted to be able to do the things Mrs Bronson did: to paint water-colours, to mix extraordinary oils for salad, to speak with her accent, to wash with that same remarkable soap. She did her best to dress a little like Mrs Bronson. Instead of sitting with her hands outspread, like flowers, she began to sit with her arms crossed and her hands on their opposite shoulders, in the same bemused pretty attitude as Mrs Bronson did.

All the time Mrs Harris was watching. Years of financial

alertness, of swift concentration against the remote chance of mistaking sixpence for a farthing, had left her eyes virtually lidless. She missed nothing. Her concentration on money was part instinctive, part habitual, part a fear of Harris's memory. Built up on farthings, Harris's financial success, by which he had been able to invest in the rows of working-class houses from which Irma and she now drew income, reproached her. Inspired in this way, she missed less than Harris himself. Her concentration on money had become a creed.

Similarly her concentration on Irma was becoming a disease. For years it had been a kind of nervousness, some sort of chronic palsied illusion. As she saw Irma begin to model herself on Mrs Bronson, it began to grow infinitely worse, more vicious, aggravated by the fact that, for once in her life, Irma was doing something outside the rule of the glass case. Having worshipped Irma all her life, it seemed beyond her comprehension that Irma could be guilty of worship in turn.

Mrs Harris could not understand. She saw any affection between the two girls as beyond and without reason. She saw Irma captured by someone else, taken away from her. There was something unusual, fishy, not straight about it. In a fit of jealousy she tried to stop it.

"If I were you, I shouldn't bother Mrs Bronson so much. You see, well, people like to be private. I don't think she wants you in there from morning to night."

In meek obedience, Irma stopped going into Mrs Bronson's room. Mrs Bronson at once noticed it.

"Why doesn't Irma come in to see me?"

Mrs Harris was in a quandary. No use offending Mrs Bronson. She didn't want to lose the Bronsons. An officer and his wife were better than three privates. It would pay her to be nice to Mrs Bronson.

So Irma went back, and the natural friendship seemed if anything a little stronger, more easy, so that Irma tried aping Mrs Bronson not only in things like soap and dresses, but in thought and mannerisms. They naturally talked about Bronson, and once or twice Irma went in to have supper with them, and once Bronson teased her about her hair.

"You've got so much hair you ought to dish it out to the officers. One lock, one officer. You know, to put in his Bible next to his heart. It's not fair, one girl having enough hair for a regiment and keeping it."

It was just Bronson's joke, and they all enjoyed it.

Then, once or twice, Bronson and his wife took Irma for a walk after supper. They felt a little sorry for her, sensing the situation, seeing her under the domination of the mother, the scrubbed house, the fusty passages. "The poor kid's never had a chance. I feel a bit sorry for her," Mrs Bronson said. And the three of them would walk out as far as the park, in the summer dusk, under the limes, and once Mrs Bronson, who wore no hat, said she could feel the honey-dew falling from the lime leaves down on her hair. "Just trying to make it curl like Irma's," Bronson. teased.

To Mrs Harris it was all incomprehensible. Fretted by jealousy, her mind could not rest. It remained nervous, discontented, without power to do anything.

Then she saw what she took to be an extraordinary thing. Irma and the Bronsons had been for an evening walk. Five minutes after they were back, she saw Irma's straw hat and Bronson's cap lying in the same chair in the hall.

Not hung up, but thrown down, and together. Not Mrs Bronson's hat. Irma's hat. With Bronson's thrown down in a hurry. At night, under cover of darkness.

Her mind gathered the nervous power and the direction it had lacked and shot off, before she could do anything, straight to Bronson. It seemed to hit Bronson with its extraordinary charge of suspicion, and then recoil back, leaving Mrs Harris with the hot shell of staggered conviction in her hands.

It was Mr Bronson. Not Mrs Bronson. Mr Bronson. Bronson! Her mind juggled with the red-hot conviction as a man juggles with the potato too hot to hold. Tossing it up and down, lacking the nerve to hold it, she was too distraught, that night, to do anything about it, and she kept up her distressed juggling performance all night, not knowing whether to be ashamed for Irma or enraged with Bronson, or both.

In the morning she had decided. For various reasons she would speak to Irma. There was the reason of money, the necessity of not offending the Bronsons. Then there was the reason that was much nearer Irma. Something had happened to Irma and it was very likely that Irma, a young girl, did not fully understand it.

"Irma," she said. "I want to speak to you." Then at the moment of crisis she felt her courage crumble. She felt that she could not say what she had to say in bare words, all pat, like a speech.

At this moment she remembered Harris. He, like the Lord, had had a weakness for speaking in parables. She would speak in a parable, and her idea of a parable was to say:

"Irma, you want to keep yourself to yourself."

Distress unexpectedly charged her voice with passion. The girl was wide-eyed, not understanding. She did not speak.

Mrs Harris took silence for guilt. Her mind seized the hot charge of conviction and held it painfully but in spite of pain.

"Irma! Irma!"

"But mother, what's the matter?"

"What's the matter! That's a nice thing. As if you don't know. Oh! Irma, Irma. After all I've done for you, after the way I've brought you up." And then suddenly the plain accusation, final and incontrovertible, as if she needed nothing more than the two hats, Irma's and Bronson's, on a chair, and the girl's silence.

"Irma, you're running after Lieutenant Bronson! I won't have it. I've seen it! I know. I won't have it!"

The girl was still silent. To Mrs Harris it seemed only like a confession, and in a way she was glad that it was all over so simply.

"That's all I've got to say—now. But I'd be ashamed of myself, Irma Harris. I would. I'd be utterly ashamed of myself."

Irma began to go about vaguely, for the first time in her life caught up by a dream of substantial reality. Up to that time she had not thought of Bronson. It was only Mrs Bronson. She felt excitably affectionate towards Mrs Bronson, virginally, tenderly, longing to be like her. Bronson had not touched her.

She began now to think of Bronson. What had her mother seen? She must have seen something. Knowing that she had never looked at Bronson, the girl could only wonder if Bronson had looked at her.

She began to try to figure it out for herself, in bed at night. She took the false premise of her mother, the accusation, and built up about it the arguments for one side and another, singling out the moments when she felt that there might have been something in Bronson's way of looking at her. She tried to argue it out impartially with herself, trying to prove there was nothing in it. And gradually, all the time, she was aware of an increasing feeling that it would be nice if it could be proved the other way. Then she wanted it proved the other way. She wanted to feel that Bronson had looked at her. She wanted to know, and even if necessary against all reason, that there was something in it after all.

Then all at once she thought of the things Bronson had said about her hair. Said jokingly, they suddenly took on the weight of great importance. She was staggered by them. Where they had seemed very trivial, not to be taken seriously, they now began to seem not only extraordinarily important, but very beautiful. As she lay stretched out in bed, she felt that all argument had ceased to have meaning. There was now no argument, no complexity. It was all different. The street lamp was still shining on the ceiling from outside, and, looking up at it, she felt herself flooded by waves and waves of incandescent beauty. Borne on light, they were at the same time like intransient cadences of prolonged music. Sentimentally and passively she let them wash over her, and then recede, leaving her mind as clear-washed as a shore after a tide, smoothed and quiet, animated only by the faint phosphorescence of an absurd sort of rapture.

Subsequently she became almost awfully aware of Bronson's nearness. She went upstairs and met him coming down; took in the Bronsons' meals and stood while he took the dishes from her, almost touching her. She was aware on those occasions of flashes of extraordinarily electric emotion, part pleasure, part pain, and at nights she put on, in her mind, the gramophone record of things he had said to her or about her, letting herself be passively swirled away from the eternal revolutions of repeated thought.

Then Mrs Harris noticed something else: the soap. Irma's soap was the same, she suddenly discovered, as Mrs Bronson's soap.

That could only mean one thing.

It was an awful, outrageous thing. Soap, scent, the scent of hands and body and face: together they drove her to the edge of impossible conjecture.

She rushed straight up to Irma's bedroom, only to find the girl standing there by the window, looking at Bronson, drilling No. 3 Platoon farther down the street. For a moment Mrs Harris could not speak. It was a moment of both humiliation and triumph. She felt enraged and yet quite strengthless. Then, before she could speak, Irma turned away from the window, lifted up her head and walked out of the room. She was a little flushed, but quite calm, and she did not speak.

Irma's look of unsubmissive tranquillity, her air of touch-me-not complacency, so beautiful and self-conscious and infuriating, aroused in Mrs Harris a curious sort of enmity. Her synonymity with Irma was shattered. Irma had become another being, separate, unacknowledgeable, behaving with a self-confessed awful immorality that was a condemnation of Mrs Harris herself.

Going downstairs, she followed Irma about, arguing, basing everything on that point. "What about me? What do you think I feel? After all I've done for you. Don't you see how I must feel? Don't you ever think of me? Don't you see how it affects me?"

The girl could not say anything. In so intangible an affair, where so much was only the fiction of the mind, there was nothing much she could do except be silent.

It was in silence that Mrs Harris saw guilt. She blamed Irma bitterly, but only Irma, seeing her part in the affair as active, not passive. Irma was committing—staring out of the window, aping Mrs Bronson, using the same soap—a wilful and stupid folly, a slight against parental decency. "Your father would have been *ashamed* of you." But it had not occurred to her that the lieutenant might be condoning it.

Pushed farther into secrecy, Irma enlarged in her mind the small fiction of herself and Bronson. She was pushed back into an inward loneliness, in which she made a structure of one improbability built on another. These improbabilities, as they grew up pagoda-fashion, she began to see as solid truths, lighting them up with the shimmering adolescent light of her own fancy. In this beautiful abstract fashion, she persuaded herself into an intense belief in the reality of Bronson's affection for her, suffering with a certain pleasure, believing in the aspects of its tragedy as readily as she believed in its extraordinary ecstasy.

In the Bronsons' room downstairs there was a large black tin case. Here Bronson kept his full-dress uniform, sword and various accoutrements. One night Irma cut off some of her hair and went downstairs, intending to put the hair into the breast-pocket of one of Bronson's tunics. In the darkness the lid of the box slipped out of her hands and crashed.

The Bronsons' bedroom was immediately above, and Bronson heard the crash and came downstairs. He switched on the electric light and saw Irma standing beside the box, in her nightgown. He had come down hurriedly, without a dressing-gown, and for a moment he was too embarrassed to speak. Irma stood trembling. Then just as he was going to speak he heard a door open upstairs, and he knew Mrs Harris was coming down.

Something made him put out the light. In complete silence, he and the girl stood in the darkness, trying to deny each other's existence. They heard Mrs Harris shuffle downstairs in her carpet slippers, and after about thirty seconds Bronson felt her hand stab at the light.

The words were ready on Mrs Harris's lips, like bullets waiting to be fired. They exploded straight at Bronson, rapid-firing: "I got you, I caught you. I got you, I caught you."

Neither Bronson nor Irma could speak. Mrs Harris took silence for guilt. She swivelled round and fired a double shot upstairs:

"Mrs Bronson! Mrs Bronson!"

Bronson stood white, tragically silent. He heard his wife's voice in reply and her movements as she came downstairs. He stood quiet, more nervous than Irma, still not saying anything, aware of his predicament and yet doing nothing, seeing himself only as the victim of some unhappy and apparently unchaste circumstance over which he had no control.

Mrs Harris fired a fusillade of bitter triumph as Mrs Bronson came and stood in the light of the doorway:

"They ain't moved, they ain't said nothing. That's how I found 'em. In their nightgowns. That's how I found 'em. I knew it had been going on for a long time, but not like this, not like this!"

Irma began to cry. Bronson and his wife stood with a kind of pasteboard rigidity, stiffened by some inherent aristocratic impulse not to give way before people out of their class. They knew they had nothing to fear, yet they saw themselves confronted by the iron suspicion of Mrs Harris as by a firing squad. In Mrs Harris's small distracted grey eyes there was a touch of madness, inspired by triumph. She spoke with the rapid incoherence of someone sent slightly insane by a terrible discovery. "I don't know what you're going to do, but I know what I'm going to do. I know and I'm going to do it. If you're not ashamed, I am. I'm ashamed. I'm—"

At this moment Irma fainted.

"No wonder! No wonder! Gettin' her down here in her nightgown, on the sly. Gettin' her down here—"

The insane dangerous stupidity of it all only struck the Bronsons into dead silence. And in silence, as never before, Mrs Harris saw guilt.

The next afternoon the Bronsons moved to other quarters. Irma, shut up in her room, heard Lieutenant Bronson's large tin box go clanking out of the hall like a coffin.

In less than a month there was hardly a soldier left in the town. In the papers Irma read about the regiment going to the Dardanelles, and read Bronson's name, a little later, among the killed.

More than two years later she read how Mrs Bronson too had been killed. In Mexico, where she had gone to clear up some of Bronson's affairs, she had been hit, while sitting in a café, by a stray bullet in a local revolution.

Irma envied Mr and Mrs Bronson, the dead. She began to feel that she was going about with a bullet in her own heart, and was only gradually beginning to understand, by the pain of longer silences between herself and her mother, who had fired it.

The Station

For thirty seconds after the lorry had halted between the shack and the petrol pumps the summer night was absolutely silent. There was no wind; the leaves and the grass stalks were held in motionless suspense in the sultry air. And after the headlights had gone out the summer darkness was complete too. The pumps were dead white globes, like idols of porcelain; there was no light at all in the station. Then, as the driver and his mate alighted, slamming the cabin doors and grinding their feet on the gravel, the light in the station came suddenly on: a fierce electric flicker from the naked globe in the shack, the light golden in one wedge-shaped shaft across the gravel pull-in. And seeing it the men stopped. They stood for a moment with the identical suspense of the grass and the trees.

The driver spoke first. He was a big fellow, quite young, with breezy blue eyes and stiff untrained hair and a comic mouth. His lips were elastic: thin bands of pink india-rubber that were for ever twisting themselves into grimaces of irony and burlesque, his eyes having that expression of comic and pained astonishment seen on the painted faces of Aunt Sallies in shooting galleries.

His lips twisted to the shape of a buttonhole, so that he whispered out of the one corner. "See her? She heard us come. What'd I tell you?"

The mate nodded. He too was young, but beside the driver he was boyish, his checks smooth and shiny as white cherries, his hair yellow and light and constantly ruffled up like the fur of a fox-cub. And unlike the driver's, his lips and eyes were quite still; so that he had a look of intense immobility.

He could see the woman in the shack. Short white casement curtains of transparent lace on brass rods cut across the window, but above and through them he could see the woman clearly. She was big-shouldered and dark, with short black hair, and her face was corn-coloured under the light. She seemed about thirty; and that surprised him.

"I thought you said she was young," he said.

"So she is." The driver's eyes flashed white. "Wait'll you git close. How old d'ye think she is?"

"Thirty. More."

"Thirty? She's been here four year. And was a kid when she was married, not nineteen. How's that up you?"

"She *looks* thirty."

"So would you if you'd kept this bloody shack open every night for four year. Come on, let's git in."

They began to walk across the gravel, but the driver stopped.

"And don't forgit what I said. She's bin somebody. She's had education. Mind your ups and downs."

When they opened the door of the shack and shuffled in, the driver first, the mate closing the door carefully behind him, the woman stood behind the rough-carpentered counter with her arms folded softly across her chest, in an attitude of unsurprised expectancy. The counter was covered with blue-squared oilcloth, tacked down. By the blue alarum clock on the lowest of the shelves behind it, the time was four minutes past midnight. At the other end of the shelf a flat shallow kettle was boiling on an oil-stove. The room was like an oven. The woman's eyes seemed curiously drowsy, as though clouded over with the steam and the warm oil-fumes. And for half a minute nothing happened. She did not move. The men stood awkward. Then the driver spoke. His india-rubber mouth puckered comically to one side, and his eye flicked in a wink that was merely friendly and habitual.

"Well, here we are again."

She nodded; the drowsiness of her eyes cleared a little. All the same there was something reserved about her, almost sulky.

"What would you like?" she said.

"Give me two on a raft and coffee," the driver said.

"Two on a raft and coffee," the woman said. She spoke beautifully, without effort, and rather softly. "What's your friend going to have?"

The mate hesitated. His eyes were fixed on the woman, half-consciously, in admiration. And the driver had to nudge him, smiling his india-rubber smile of comic irony, before he became aware of all that was going on.

"Peck up," the driver said.

"That'll do me," the mate said.

"Two on a raft twice and coffee," the woman said. "Is that it?"

Though the mate did not know it for a moment, she was addressing him. He stood in slight bewilderment, as though he were listening to a language he did not understand. Then as he became aware of her looking at him and waiting for an answer the bewilderment became embarrassment and his fair cherry-smooth cheeks flushed very red, the skin under the short golden hairs and his neck flaming. He stood dumb. He did not know what to do with himself.

"I'm afraid I don't know your friend's name or his tastes yet," the woman said. "Shall I make it two poached twice and coffee?"

"Just like me. Forgot to introduce you," the driver said. His mouth was a wrinkle of india-rubber mocking. "Albie, this is Mrs Harvey. This is Albert Armstrong. Now mate on Number 4, otherwise Albie."

The woman smiled and in complete subjection and fascination the boy smiled too.

"Are you sure that's all right?" she said. "Poached and coffee? It sounds hot to me."

"Does me all right," the driver said.

"I could make you a fresh salad," she said. And again she was speaking to the mate, with a kind of soft and indirect invitation. "There would be eggs in that."

"I'll have that," the mate said.

"What?" the driver said. His eyes were wide open, his mouth wide also in half serious disgust, as though the mate had committed a sort of sacrilege. "You don' know what's good."

"So you'll have the salad?" the woman said.

"Yes, please."

"I can give you the proper oil on it, and vinegar. You can have fruit afterwards if you'd like it."

"Fruit?" the driver said. "What fruit?"

She took the kettle from the oil-stove and poured a little hot water into the coffee-pot and then a little into each of the egg-poachers. "Plums," she said.

"Now you're talking," the driver said. "Plums. Some sense. Now you *are* talking."

"Go and get yourself a few if you like them so much."

"Show me. Show me a plum tree within half a mile and I'm off."

"Go straight down the garden and it's the tree on the left. Pick as many as you like."

The driver opened the door, grinning. "Coming, Albie?"

"You're not afraid of the dark, are you?" the woman said.

This time she was speaking to the driver. And suddenly as he stood there at the door, grimacing with comic irony at her, his whole head and face and neck and shoulders became bathed in crimson light, as though he had become the victim of a colossal blush. Startled, he lifted up his face and looked up at the shack from the outside. The bright electric sign with the naked letters saying simply *The Station* was like a fire of scarlet and white. At intervals it winked and darkened, on and out, scarlet to darkness, *The Station* to nothing. The driver stood with uplifted face, all scarlet, in surprised admiration.

"Blimey, that's a winner. When'd you get that?"

"It's new this week."

"It's a treat. It makes no end of a difference. How's it you didn't have it on when we came in?"

"I keep forgetting it. I'm so used to sitting here in the dark I can't get used to it. It's a bit uncanny."

The driver went down the shack steps, into the night. The woman, busy with the eggs, and the boy, leaning against the counter, could see him standing back, still faintly crimson, in admiration of the eternal winking light. And for a minute, as he stood there, the station was completely silent, the August darkness like velvet, the sultry night air oppressing all sound except the soft melancholy murmur of the simmering kettle. Then the woman called:

"You'd better get your plums. The eggs won't be two minutes."

The driver answered something, only barely audible, and after the sound of his feet crunching the gravel the silence closed in again.

It was like a stoke-room in the shack. The smells of coffee and eggs and oil were fused into a single breath of sickening heat. Like the driver, the boy stood in his shirt-sleeves. He stood still, very self-conscious, watching the woman breaking the eggs and stirring the coffee and finally mixing in a glass bowl the salad for himself. He did not know what to do or say. Her thin white dress was like the silky husk of a seed-pod, just bursting open. Her ripe breasts swelled under it like two sun-swollen seeds. And he could not take his eyes away from them. He was electrified. His blood quivered with the current of excitement. And all the time, even though she was busy with the eggs on the stove, and the mixing of the salad, very often not looking at him, she was aware of it. Looking up sometimes from the stove or the salad she would look past him, with an air of arrested dreaminess, her dark eyes lovely and sulky. The deliberation of it maddened him.

He remembered things the driver had said as they came along the road. The words flashed in his mind as though lit up by the electricity of his veins. "She's a peach, Albie. But I'll tell you what. One bloody wink out o' place and you're skedaddled. She won't have it. She's nice to the chaps because it's business, that's all. See what I mean, Albie? She'll look at you fit to melt your bleedin' heart out, but it don't mean damn all. She wants to make that station a success, that's all. That's why she runs the night shack. Her husband runs the day show and she's second house, kind of. It's her own idea. See?"

And suddenly his thoughts broke off. The lights in his brain, as it were, went out. His mind was blank. She was looking at him. He stood transfixed, his veins no longer electric but relapsed, his blood weak.

"Like it on the lorry?" she said.

"Yes." He hardly spoke.

She had finished making the salad and she pushed the bowl across the counter towards him before speaking again.

"You're not very old for the job, are you?"

"I'm eighteen."

"Get on with old Spike?"

"Yes."

"Isn't it lonely at first? They all say it's lonely when they first begin."

"I don't mind it."

"What's your girl say to it?"

It was as though the electric sign had been suddenly turned on him as it had been turned on the driver. He stood helpless, his face scarlet.

"I ain't got a girl."

"What? Not a nice boy like you?" She was smiling, half in mockery. "I know you must have."

"No."

"Does she love you much?" She looked at him in mock seriousness, her eyes lowered.

"I ain't got one."

"Honest?" She pushed the bottles of oil and vinegar across the counter towards him. "I'll ask Spike when he comes in."

"No, don't say anything to Spike," he begged. "Don't say nothing. He's always kidding me about her, anyway."

"You said you hadn't got a girl."

"Well—"

She took two plates from the rack behind the counter and then knives and forks from the drawer under the counter and then laid them out.

"Does she hate it when you're on nights?" she said.

"Yes."

"What's she like—dark or fair?"

"Dark."

"Like me?"

He could not answer. He only gazed straight at her in mute embarrassment and nodded. Every word she uttered fired him with passionate unrest. The current in his blood was renewed again. He felt himself tightened up. And she could see it all.

"You'd better call Spike," she said. "The eggs are ready."

He moved towards the door. Then he turned and stopped. "Don't say nothing," he said.

"All right."

He stood at the door, his face scarlet under the winking sign, and called out for Spike, singing the word, "Spi-ike!" And he could hear the sound echoing over the empty land in the darkness. There was a smell of corn in the air, stronger and sweeter even than the smell of the heat and cooking in the shack. It came in sweet waves from across the invisible fields in the warm night air.

"I know how you feel," she said.

He turned sharply. "How?"

"Come and eat this salad and cool down a bit."

He came from the door to the counter in obedience, pulling out a stool and sitting on it.

"Oil and vinegar?" she said. "The coffee will be ready by the time Spike comes."

"How do I feel? What do you mean?"

"You know."

"Yes, but how do you know?"

"I've felt like it myself."

She stood with her arms folded and resting on the counter edge, and leaning slightly forward, so that he could see her breasts beneath the open dress. She looked at him with a kind of pity, with tenderness, but half-amused. He saw the breasts rise and fall with the same slow and almost sulky passion as she looked at him. He stared from her breasts to her face, and she stared back, her eyes never moving. And they stood like that, not moving or speaking, but only as it were burning each other up, until suddenly Spike came in.

The woman stood up at once. Spike's cupped hands were full of plums.

"They're green," the woman said.

"By God, if I didn't think they was tart."

"Didn't you find the right tree? On the left?"

"I couldn't see a blamed thing."

"Eat your eggs. I'll get a torch and we'll go down and get some ripe ones before you go."

"Eggs look good an' all," Spike said.

The men ate in silence, the woman busy with bread and coffee. The boy put vinegar on his salad, but not oil, and once, noticing it, she unstoppered the oil bottle and pushed it across to him. It was her only sign towards him. The old manner of pity and intimacy had vanished. She was the proprietress; they were the drivers come in to eat. She stood almost aloof, busy with odd things at the far end of the counter. And the boy sat in fresh bewilderment, at a loss, and in wonder about her.

They each drank two cups of coffee and when the cups were finally empty she said:

"If you're ready we can go down and get the plums. But I don't want to hurry you."

"I'm fit," Spike said. "And my God the eggs were a treat. You missed a treat Albie, not having eggs."

"The salad was all right."

"I'll get the torch," the woman said. "You go out that door and I'll meet you round the back."

She went out of the shack by a door behind the counter, and the boy followed Spike through the front door, under the electric sign. Outside, behind the shack, the sweet smell of ripened corn and night air seemed stronger than ever. At the side of the shack and a little behind it, the bungalow stood out darker than the darkness. And after a minute the torch appeared from the bungalow and began to travel towards the men. The boy could see it shining white along the cinder path and on the woman's feet as she came along.

"You walk down the path," she said. "I'll show the light."

Spike began to walk down the path, the boy following him, and then the woman. The shadows strode like giants over the garden and were lost beyond the yellow snake fence in the dark land. The garden was short, and in a moment they all three stood under the plum tree, the woman shining the torch up into the branches, the tree turned to an immense net of green and silver.

"I'll shine, Spike," she said. "You pick them. If they're soft and they lift off they're ripe."

"This is better," Spike said. His mouth was already full of plums. "I struck one match to every blamed plum when I came down."

The woman stood a little away from the tree, shining the torch steadily, making a great ring of white light across which little moths began to flutter like casual leaves. The boy stood still, not attempting to move, as though he were uninvited.

"What about you?" she said.

And again he could feel the old softness of sympathy and pity and insinuation in her voice, and again his blood leapt up.

"I'm about full up," he said.

"Take some for the journey."

He stood still, electrified.

"Take some to eat on the way. Look here, come round the other side. They're riper."

She moved round the tree, shining the torch always away from her. He followed her in silence, and then in silence they stood against the plum branches, in the darkness behind the light. He saw her stretch up her arm into the silver leaves, and then lower it again.

"Where's your hand?" she was whispering. "Here. It's a beauty." The soft ripe plum was between their hands. Suddenly she pressed it hard against his hands, and the ripe skin broke and the juice trickled over his fingers. "Eat it, put it in your mouth," she said. He put the plum into his mouth obediently, and the sweet juice trickled down over his lips and chin as it had already trickled over his hands.

"Was that nice?" she said softly.

"Lovely."

"Sweet as your girl?"

It seemed suddenly as if his blood turned to water. She was touching him. She took his hand and laid it softly against her hip. It was firm and strong and soft. It had about it a kind of comforting maturity. He could feel all the sulky strength and passion of her whole body in it. Then all at once she covered his hand with her own, stroking it up and down with her fingers, until he stood helpless, intoxicated by the smell of corn and plums and the night warmth and her very light, constant stroking of his hand.

"Shine the light," Spike called. "I can't see for looking."

"I'm shining," she said. "Albie wants to see too."

"Getting many, Albie?"

"He's filling his pockets."

She began to gather plums off the tree with her free hand as she spoke, keeping her other hand still on his, pressing it against her by an almost mechanical process of caressing. He reached up and tore off the plums too, not troubling if they were ripe, filling one pocket while she filled the other, the secrecy and passion of her movements half demoralizing him, and going on without interruption until Spike called:

"Albie! Plums or no plums, we shall have to get on th' old bus again."

The boy could hardly speak. And suddenly as the woman took her hand away at last he felt as if the life in him had been cut off, the tension withdrawn, leaving his veins like dead wires.

He stumbled up the path behind Spike and the woman and the light. Spike was gabbling:

"Sweetest plums I ever tasted. When we come back I'll take a couple of pounds and the missus'll pie 'em."

"When will you be back?"

"The night after to-morrow."

"There'll be plenty," she said.

She said nothing to the boy, and he said nothing either.

"Let's pay you," Spike said.

"A shilling for you, and ninepence for the salad," she said.

"Salad's cheaper," Spike said. "I'll remember that. What about the plums?"

"The plums are thrown in."

They paid her. Then she stood on the shack steps while they crunched across the pull-in and climbed up into the cab, the bright red sign flashing above her.

"That sign's a treat," Spike called. "You could see it miles off."

"I'm glad you like it," she called. "Good night."

"Good night!"

Spike started up, and almost before the boy could realise it the lorry was swinging out into the road, and the station was beginning to recede. He sat for some moments without moving. Then the lorry began to make speed and the smell of corn and plums and the summer land began to be driven out by the smells of the cab, the petrol and oil and the heat of the engine running. But suddenly he turned and looked back.

"The light's out," he said.

Spike put his head out of the cab and glanced back. The sign was still flashing but the shack itself was in darkness.

"She's sitting in the dark," he said. "She always does. She says it saves her eyes and the light and she likes it better."

"Why?"

"Better ask her." Spike put a plum in his mouth. "I don't know."

"What's her husband doing, letting her run the place at night, and sit there in the dark?"

"It's her own idea. It's a paying game an' all, you bet your life it is."

The boy took a plum from his pocket and bit it slowly, licking the sweet juice from his lips as it ran down. He was still trembling.

And glancing back again he could see nothing of the station but the red sign flashing everlastingly out and on, scarlet to darkness, *The Station* to nothing at all.

Château Bougainvillaea*

The headland was like a dry purple island scorched by the flat heat of afternoon, cut off from the mainland by a sand-coloured tributary of road which went down past the estaminet and then, half a mile beyond, to the one-line, one-eyed railway station. Down below, on a small plateau between upper headland and sea, peasants were mowing white rectangles of corn. The tide was fully out, leaving many bare black rocks and then a great sun-phosphorescent pavement of sand, with the white teeth of small breakers slowly nibbling in. Far out, the Atlantic was waveless, a shade darker than the sky, which was the fierce blue seen on unbelievable posters. Farther out still, making a faint mist, sun and sea had completely washed out the line of sky.

From time to time a puff of white steam, followed by a peeped whistle, struck comically at the dead silence inland. It was the small one-line train, half-tram, making one way or the other its hourly journey between town-terminus and coast. By means of it the engaged couple measured out the afternoon.

"There goes the little train," he would say.

"Yes," she would say, "there goes the little train."

Each time she resolved not to say this stupid thing and then, dulled with sleepiness and the heat of earth and sky and the heather in which they lay, she forgot herself and said it, automatically. Her faint annoyance with herself at these times had gradually begun to make itself felt, as the expression of some much deeper discontent.

"Je parle français un tout petit peu, m'sieu." In a voice, which seemed somehow like velvet rubbed the wrong way, the man was talking. "I was all right as far as that. Then I said, 'Mais, dites-moi, m'sieu, pourquoi are all the knives put left-handed dans ce restaurant?' By God it must have been awfully funny. And then he said—"

"He said because, m'sieu, the people who use them are all left-handed."

* A bougainvillaea is a tropical plant that has its flowers almost hidden by small leaves

"And that's really what he said? It wasn't a mistake? All the people in that place were left-handed?"

"Apparently," she said, "they were all left-handed."

"It's the funniest thing I ever heard," he said. "I can't believe it."

Yes, she thought, perhaps it was a funny thing. Many left-handed people staying at one restaurant. A family, perhaps. But then there were many left-handed people in the world, and perhaps, for all you knew, their left was really right, and it was we, the right, who were wrong.

She took her mind back to the restaurant down in the town. There was another restaurant there, set in a sort of alley-way under two fig-trees, where artisans filled most of the tables between noon and two o'clock, and where a fat white-smocked woman served all the dishes and still found time to try her three words of English on the engaged couple. From here they could see the lace-crowned Breton women clacking in the shade of the street trees and the small one-eyed train starting or ending its journey between the sea and the terminus that was simply the middle of the street. They liked this restaurant, but that day, wanting a change, they had climbed the steps into the upper town, to the level of the viaduct, and had found this small family restaurant where, at one table, all the knives were laid left-handed. For some reason she now sought to define, this left-handedness did not seem funny to her. Arthur had also eaten too many olives, picking them up with his fingers and gnawing them as she herself, as a child, would have gnawed an uncooked prune, and this did not seem very funny either. Somewhere between olives and left-handedness lay the source of her curious discontent. Perhaps she was left-handed herself? Left-handed people were, she had read somewhere, light-brained. Perhaps Arthur was left-handed?

She turned over in the heather, small brown-eyed face to the sun. "Don't you do anything left-handed?"

"Good gracious, no." He turned over too and lay face upwards, dark with sun, his mouth small-lipped under the stiff moustache she had not wanted him to grow. "You don't either?"

For the first time in her life she considered it. How many people, she thought, ever considered it? Thinking, she seemed to roll down a great slope, semi-swooning in the heat, before coming up again. Surprisingly, she had thought of several things.

"Now I come to think of it, I comb my hair left-handed. I always pick flowers left-handed. And I wear my watch on my left wrist."

He lifted steady, mocking eyes. "You sure you don't kiss left-handed?"

"That's not very funny!" she flashed.

It seemed to her that the moment of temper flashed up sky high, like a rocket, and fell far out to sea, soundless, dead by then, in the heat of the unruffled afternoon. She at once regretted it. For five days now they had lived on the Breton coast, and they now had five days more. Every morning, for five days, he had questioned her: "All right? Happy?" and every morning she had responded with automatic affirmations, believing it at first, then aware of doubt, then bewildered. Happiness, she wanted to say, was not something you could fetch out every morning after breakfast, like a clean handkerchief, or more still like a rabbit conjured out of the hat of everyday circumstances.

The hot, crushed-down sense of security she had felt all afternoon began suddenly to evaporate, burnt away from her by the first explosion of discontent and then by small restless flames of inward anger. She felt the growing sense of insecurity physically, feeling that at any moment she might slip off the solid headland into the sea. She suddenly felt a tremendous urge, impelled for some reason by fear, to walk as far back inland as she could go. The thought of the Atlantic far below, passive and yet magnetic, filled her with a sudden cold breath of vertigo.

"Let's walk," she said.

"Oh! no, it's too hot."

She turned her face into the dark sun-brittled heather. She caught the ticking of small insects, like infinitesimal watches. Far off, inland, the little train cut off, with its comic shriek, another section of afternoon.

In England he was a draper's assistant: chief assistant, sure to become manager. In imagination she saw the shop, sun-blinds down, August remnant sale now on, the dead little town now so foreign and far off and yet so intensely real to her, shown up by the disenchantment of distance. They had been engaged six months. She had been very thrilled about it at first, showing the ring all round, standing on a small pinnacle of joy, ready to leap into the tremendous spaces of marriage. Now she had suddenly the feeling that she was about to be sewn up in a blanket.

"Isn't there a castle," she said, "somewhere up the road past the estaminet?"

"Big house. Not castle."

"I thought I saw a notice," she said, "to the château."

"Big house," he said. "Did you see that film, 'The Big House'? All about men in prison."

What about women in prison? she wanted to say. In England she was a school-teacher, and there had been times when she felt that the pale green walls of the class-room had imprisoned her and that marriage, as it always did, would mean escape. Now left-handedness and olives and blankets and the stabbing heat of the Atlantic afternoon had succeeded, together, in inducing some queer stupor of semi-crazy melancholy that was far worse than this. Perhaps it was the wine, the sour red stuff of the *vin compris** notice down at the left-handed café? Perhaps, after all, it was only some large dose of self-pity induced by sun and the emptiness of the day?

She got to her feet. "Come on, m'sieu. We're going to the castle." She made a great effort to wrench herself up to the normal plane. "Castle, my beautiful. Two francs. All the way up to the castle, two francs." She held out her hand to pull him to his feet.

"I'll come," he said, "if we can stop at the estaminet and have a drink."

"We'll stop when we come down," she said.

"Now."

"When we come down."

"Now. I'm so thirsty. It was the olives."

Not speaking, she held out her hand. Instinctively, he put out his left.

"You see," she said, "you don't know what's what or which's which or anything. You don't know when you're left-handed or right."

He laughed. She felt suddenly like laughing too, and they began to walk down the hill. The fierce heat seemed itself to force them down the slope, and she felt driven by it past the blistered white tables of the estaminet with the fowls asleep underneath them, and then up the hill on the far side, into the sparse shade of small wind-levelled oaks and, at one place, a group of fruitless fig trees. It was some place like this, she thought, just about as hot and arid, where the Gadarene swine had stampeded down. What made her think of that? Her mind had some urge towards inconsequence, some inexplicable desire towards irresponsibility that she could not restrain or control, and she was glad to see the château at last, shining with sea-blue jalousies through a break

* wine included free of charge with a meal

in the mass of metallic summer-hard leaves of acacia and bay that surrounded it. She felt it to be something concrete, a barrier against which all the crazy irresponsibilities of the mind could hurl themselves and split.

At the corner, a hundred yards before the entrance gates, a notice, of which one end had been cracked off by a passing lorry, pointed upwards like a tilted telescope. They read the word "château", the rest of the name gone.

"You see," she said, "château."

"What château?"

"Just château."

"You think we'll have to pay to go in?"

"I'll pay," she said.

She walked on in silence, far away from him. The little insistences on money had become, in five days, like the action of many iron files on the soft tissues of her mind: first small and fine, then larger, then still larger, now large and coarse, brutal as stone. He kept a small note-book and in it, with painful system, entered up the expenditure of every centime.

At the entrance gates stood a lodge, very much dilapidated, the paintwork of the walls grey and sea-eroded like the sides of a derelict battleship. A small notice was nailed to the fence by the gate, and the girl stopped to read it.

"What does it say?" he said. "Do we pay to go in?"

"Just says it's an eighteenth-century château," she said. "Admission a franc. Shall we go in?"

"A franc?"

"One franc," she said. "Each."

"You go," he said. "I don't know that I'm keen. I'll stop outside."

She did not answer, but went to the gate and pulled the porter's bell. From the lodge door a woman without a blouse on put her head out, there was a smell of onions, and the woman turned on the machine of her French like a high pressure steam-pipe, scrawny neck dilating.

The girl pushed open the gate and paid the woman the two francs admission fee, holding a brief conversation with her. The high pressure pipe finally cut itself off and withdrew, and the girl came back to the gates and said: "She's supposed to show us round but she's just washing. She says nobody else ever comes up at this hour of the afternoon, and we must show ourselves round."

They walked up the gravel road between sea-stunted trees

towards the château. In the sun, against the blue sky above the Atlantic, the stone and slate of it was burning.

"Well," she said, "what do you think of it?"

"Looks a bit like the bank at home," he said. "The one opposite our shop."

Château and sky and trees spun in the sunlight, whirling down to a momentary black vortex in which the girl found herself powerless to utter a word. She walked blindly on in silence. It was not until they stood under the château walls, and she looked up to see a great grape vine mapped out all across the south side, that she recovered herself and could speak.

"It's just like the châteaux you see on wine-bottles," she said. "I like it."

"It doesn't look much to me," he said. "Where do we get in?"

"Let's look round the outside first."

As they walked round the walls on the sun-bleached grass she could not speak or gather her impressions, but was struck only by the barren solitude of it all, the arid, typically French surroundings, with an air of fly-blownness and sun-weariness. To her amazement the place had no grandeur, and there were no flowers.

"There ought to be at least a bougainvillaea," she said.

"What's a bougainvillaea?"

Questioned, she found she did not know. She felt only that there ought to be a bougainvillaea. The word stood in her mind for the exotic, the south, white afternoons, the sea as seen from the top of just such châteaux as this. How this came to be she could not explain. The conscious part of herself stretched out arms and reached back, into time, and linked itself with some former incarnation of her present self, Louise Bowen, school-teacher, certificated, Standard V girls, engaged to Arthur Keller, chief assistant Moore's Drapery, sure to become manager, pin-stripe trousers, remnants madam, the voice like ruffled velvet, seventy-three pounds fifteen standing to credit at the post office, and in reaching back so far she felt suddenly that she could cry for the lost self, for the enviable incarnation so extraordinarily real and yet impossible, and for the yet not impossible existence, far back, in eternal bougainvillaea afternoons.

"Let's go inside," she said.

"How they make it pay," he said, "God only knows."

"It has long since," she said mysteriously, "paid for itself."

They found the main door and went in, stepping into the under-sea coldness of a large entrance hall. Now think that out, now think that out, now think that out. Her mind bubbling with bitterness, she looked up the great staircase, and all of a sudden the foreignness of her conscious self as against the familiarity of the self that had been was asserted again, but now with the sharp contrast of shadow and light. She put her hand on the staircase, the iron cool and familiar, and then began to walk up it, slowly but lightly, her hand drawn up easily, as though from some invisible iron pulley, far above her. She kept her eyes on the ceiling, feeling, without effort of thought, that she did not like and never had liked its mournful collection of cherubim painted in the gold wheel about the chandelier. For the first time that day, as she mounted the staircase and then went on beyond into the upstairs corridor, and into the panelled music-room with its air of having been imported as a complete back-cloth from some pink-and-gold theatre of the 'seventies, her body moved with its natural quietness, accustomed, infinitely light, and with a sense of the purest happiness. All this she could not explain and, as they went from music-room to other rooms, ceased to attempt to explain. Her bitterness evaporated in the confined coolness just as her security, outside on the hot headland, had evaporated in the blaze of afternoon. Now she seemed incontestably sure of herself, content in what she knew, without fuss, was an unrepeatable moment of time.

She did not like the music-room but, as she expected, Arthur did. This pre-awareness of hers saved her from fresh bitterness. As part of her contentment, making it complete, she thought of him with momentary tenderness, quietly regretting what she had said and done, ready now to make up for it.

"Shall we go up higher," she said, "or down to the ground-floor again?"

"Let's do the climb first," he said.

To her, it did not matter, and climbing a second staircase they came, eventually, to a small turret room, unfurnished, with two jalousied windows looking across to the two worlds of France and the Atlantic.

She stood at the window overlooking the sea and looked out, as from a lighthouse, down on to the intense expanse of sea-light. Her mind had the profound placidity of the sea itself, a beautiful vacancy, milkily restful.

"Funny," Arthur said. "No ships. The Atlantic, and not a ship in sight."

"You wouldn't expect to see ships," she said, and knew that

she was right.

Looking down from the other window they saw the headland, the brown-lilac expanse of heather, the minute peasants scribbled on the yellow rectangle of corn, the estaminet, the one-eyed station. And suddenly also, there was the white pop of steam inland, and the small comic shriek, now more than ever toy-like, pricking the dead silence of afternoon.

"Look," he said, "there's the little train."

"Yes," she said, "there's the little train."

Her mind had the pure loftiness of the tower itself, above all irritation. She felt, as not before in her life, that she was herself. The knowledge of this re-incarnation was something she could not communicate, and half afraid that time or a word would break it up, she suggested suddenly that they should go down.

Arthur remained at the window a moment longer, admiring points of distance. "You'd never think," he said, "you could see so far."

"Yes you would," she called back.

Now think that out, now think that out, now think that out. Her mind, as she went downstairs, sprang contrarily upwards, on a scale of otherwise inexpressible delight. Arthur engaged her in conversation as they went downstairs, she on one flight, he on one above, calling down: "It may be all right, but the rates must be colossal. Besides, you'd burn a ton of coal a day in winter, trying to keep warm. A six-roomed house is bad enough, but think of this," but nothing could break, suppress or even touch her mood.

Downstairs she went straight into the great reception hall, and stood dumb. At that moment she suddenly felt that she had come as far as she must. Time had brought her to this split second of itself simply in order to pin her down. She stood like an insect transfixed.

Arthur came in: "What are you looking at?"

"The yellow cloth. Don't do anything. Just look at it. It's wonderful."

At the end of the room, thrown over a chair, a large length of brocade, the colour of a half-ripe lemon, was like spilled honey against the grey French-coldness of walls and furniture. Instantaneously the girl saw it with eyes of familiarity, feeling it somehow to be the expression of herself, mood, past and future. She stood occupied with the entrancement of the moment, her eyes excluding the room, the day, Arthur and everything, her self drowned out of existence by the pure wash of watered fabric.

Suddenly Arthur moved into the room, and ten seconds later had the brocade in his hands. She saw him hold it up, measure it without knowing he measured it, feel its weight, thickness, value. She saw him suddenly as the eternal shopkeeper measuring out the eternal remnants of time: the small tape-measure of his mind like a white worm in the precious expanse of her own existence.

"If you bought it to-day," Arthur called, "it would cost you every penny of thirty-five bob a yard."

"Let's go," she said.

Half a minute later she turned and walked out of the door, Arthur following, and then past the wind-stunted trees and on down the road, past the estaminet. It was now herself who walked, Louise Bowen, Standard V girls, certificated, deduct so much for superannuation scheme, tired as after a long day in the crowded chalk-smelling class-room. As they passed the estaminet, the place looked more fly-blown and deserted than ever, and they decided to go on to the station, and get a drink there while waiting for the train. As they passed the fig trees her mind tried to grasp again at the thought of the Gadarene swine, her mood blasted into the same barrenness as the tree in the parable.

"Well, you can have your château," Arthur said. "But I've got my mind on one of those houses Sparkes is putting up on Park Avenue. Sixteen and fourpence a week, no deposit, over twenty years. That's in front of any château."

She saw the houses as he spoke, red and white, white and red, millions of them, one like another, sixteen and fourpence a week, no deposit, stretching out to the ends of the earth. She saw herself in them, the constant and never-changing material of her life cut up by a pair of draper's scissors, the days ticketed, the years fretted by the counting up of farthings and all the endlessly incalculable moods of boredom.

"Two coffees please."

At the little station café they sat at one of the outside tables and waited for the train.

"Well, we've been to the château and never found out its name," he said.

"It ought to be Château Bougainvillaea."

"That's silly," he said. "You don't even know what a bougainvillaea is."

She sat stirring the grey coffee. She could feel the sun burning the white iron table and her hands. She looked up at the château, seeing the windows of the turret above the trees.

"Now we can see the château," she said, "as we should have seen ourselves if we'd been sitting down here when—"

It was beyond her, and she broke off.

"What?" he said.

"I didn't mean that," she said.

"What did you mean?"

"I don't know."

"Well, in future," he said, "mind you say what you mean."

The future? She sat silent. Inland the approaching train made its comic little whistle, cutting off another section of the afternoon.

And hearing it, she knew suddenly that the future was already a thing of the past.

Time to Kill

He inquired at the station if they knew anyone named Edwards, but at first they did not know. Then a second porter came and stood thoughtfully looking up the empty single track, where the bright spring evening sun flashed on the metals and on the slanting sallow trees that broke with grey and silver the bare monotony of the cutting beyond the coal-yards.

"Y'see there's so many folks named Edwards."

"Yes, I know that."

"Same all round. At Hardwick it's nothing but Baxters. Over at Stanford they're all Drages or Bowens. Here it's all Edwardses."

Hanson began to wish he hadn't come.

"But wait a minute," he said. "You might know them if I tell you who the woman was before she was married. Her name was Claridge."

"Ah well," the porter said. "Well. Now I know who you mean. Now I know. You mean Clem Edwards. Got a milk-round. Comes round in a three-wheeler. That's who you mean."

"Where do they live?" Hanson said. "I haven't got much time."

"Well, without you go across fields it's a dinkin' long way round. Place called Ash Trees. It's no naughty walk if you go round by road."

"Which way do I go by field?"

The porter began to tell him the field way, pointing an arm over the tracks. Hanson turned to look and felt the north-east wind slice his face from across the low flat land, cutting away the thin warmth of the sun. When the porter had finished Hanson said, "Does that give me time to get back for the 7.47?"

"Just about," the porter said. "Only it's 7.53 now. Been altered."

"Thanks," Hanson said. "Thank you very much."

He walked away up the platform and over the iron footbridge and took the gravel path that went beyond the coal-yards and the last few houses of the town. The March sunlight was sharp and low on the level fields, making the young wind-pressed shoots of corn gleam like wire. In the naked ash trees that broke the lines of the hedges thrushes were singing high up against the sun, wild and clear in the bright wind. When he looked ahead Hanson could see the path quite clearly marked out, clay-brown in the young wheat, brighter green in the pasture.

He walked about a mile and a half before coming within sight of the house. A little distance off he stopped and looked at it. It was a small farm, a square flat-windowed house of light-red brick with a roof of blue slate that somebody had once left like a forgotten box on the flat land. He could see no ash trees, but above and beyond the outhouses and the wire fences a group of high black poplars were swinging heavily to and fro in the wind.

Coming into the farmyard he saw a man standing under a cart-shed, watching him. He held a spanner in his hand. He was small, with the high sharp cheek-bones of the district, rounded shoulders, and steady hostile eyes.

"Want somebody?"

"Yes," Hanson said. "Can I see Mrs Edwards?"

"You can go and try."

He stood weighing the spanner in his hand, hostile, intent, slightly puzzled.

"If it's got anything to do wi' insurance we don't want none."

"That's all right," Hanson said. "It's not that."

He walked on across the yard towards the house, uneasy, aware of the man still watching him. About the dry earth hens' feathers were being bounced by the wind among the many dark claret poplar catkins that had fallen from the trees.

Round the corner of the house, out of sight of the figure watching him, he knocked at the back door and waited. The voices of children crying in a room upstairs broke for a moment and then began again and in the short interval of silence he heard the beat of footsteps.

The face of the young woman who opened the door was not quite what he had expected. She stood shocked too, her dark bleak eyes beaten dead by the moment of astonishment. She stood looking at him with brief, inert silence, and then suddenly she came to herself and began to pull her stained torn pinafore over her head, ruffling her black short hair and then smoothing it, almost beating it down with her small narrow hands.

"Arthur," she said. "Arthur, whatever made you come up here?"

"I had some time to kill at the junction," he said. "I thought I'd just have time to come up on the branch. Just to see you."

She did not speak.

"You didn't answer my Christmas card," he said. "You didn't send one."

"No."

"I wondered if you were all right."

"I'm all right," she said. Unconsciously, in perplexity, she had screwed up the pinafore like a bundle of rag. "You'd better come in, hadn't you?"

She stood back from the door, which had dropped on its hinges and would not open any further. He went into the kitchen. A cold sour odour of milk, a stale breath of boiled onions, met him. Milk pans, waiting to be scoured, stood about the brick floor of the kitchen and the small dairy place leading off from it. Beyond, in the living-room, tea was partly laid on a deal table. Thick slices of white bread were waiting to be toasted on the hearth, where socks and napkins were drying on a line below the mantelshelf. More clothes were hanging diagonally across the lamp-darkened ceiling, by the staircase door. The wind rattled the window on the east side.

She asked him to sit down. She had dropped her pinafore in the kitchen and now stood with empty hands. If there was some slight hostility in the way she kept standing it was unconscious and he did not notice it. He looked hastily round the room, taking in the details, and saw through the windows the edges of the great poplars beating against the sky. A moment later he looked back at her and suddenly saw her, uneasy, untidy, taken unawares, as the remnant of the girl he had decided not to marry, for some trivial reason, six years before.

A child began crying upstairs before either of them could speak.

"Is it two children you've got?" he said, knowing it quite well.

"Two," she said.

The child cried loudly. Outside, the cries seemed to be reproduced in the short hollow sounds of a spanner beating on metal.

"There's nothing wrong, is there?" he said. The crying of the child had on him an effect of nervous distraction.

"It's earache," she said. "I'd better go up. Take your coat off." She looked at him with unhappy, disturbed eyes. "You'll have a cup of tea when I come down again?"

"Only if it's ready," he said. "Don't make it specially."

"It's our tea-time, now," she said, in a dead voice.

When she had gone upstairs he sat staring at the teatable without having taken off his coat. He tried to remember what things had been like six or seven years before, but the details were at first dead and would not revive in the oppressive ugly little room. Only the girl herself at once came back, involuntarily recalled in sudden, time-sharpened images. In those days they had both lived in the town. She was a school-teacher and belonged to one of those large, boisterous, clannish families who always stick and die together. There were five sisters and two brothers, all dark and rather self-willed, the girls very pretty, with small, proud faces. Several times a year the Claridges managed to find an excuse for a party, a coming-of-age, a wedding, New Year, in the big draughty local drill-hall. It was at one of these parties that Hanson, attending as the local reporter, had met Kitty Claridge. He remembered what a bright, impulsive, argumentative creature she had been: how she had argued with him all that evening, with militant smiles of triumph, on the merits of some writer whose name he had long ago forgotten, how every dance had been an exhausting, fascinating affair of beauty and conflict. After that they could never see enough of each other. On summer evenings, when there was little doing on the local paper, they would hire a boat and go on the river and float downstream between the willow trees to villages beyond the town, and in time the peace of the evening would be broken by the question of his going away and working on a larger paper. It gradually became apparent that she had no ambition to live anywhere but in the small, branch-line town, with the one tired newspaper, the flat countryside parched to concrete by the spring seawinds, and the little river with the waving willow trees; it seemed that all she wanted was to remain, even after marriage, part of the large, proud, boisterous family, as if there were no other life and she would get all the emotion and excitement and beauty she needed in their way and not his.

The end of it was that they had broken up on some such point as this, quite trivial in itself, but really part of the larger question of his also marrying the family, which at heart he disliked intensely. He remembered that the Claridges were very affronted at the affair, and never spoke to his own family again. Shortly afterwards he got another job and gladly moved out of the circle of small-town family hatred. But with Kitty it was different. They had kept up a correspondence which after a time had dwindled down to a Christmas card: but he knew all the same that the correspondence of the mind, with its half-captured passages of warm, regretful thought, had gone on.

She had been married four or five years now. He did not know how it had come about. At the back of his mind lay the uneasy thought, dropped there by something he had heard, that the family no longer had anything to do with her. For some reason the boisterous, proud loyalty had been broken.

He was once more beginning to wonder about the oppressive little room, the isolated farm with the seawinds striking at the poplars, and the man with the spanner outside, when she herself came downstairs again.

He was unaware of it until that moment, but the crying of the child had already ceased. For one moment the window ceased rattling, and he stood up, looking at her in the sudden silence. He wanted to say something to her: about the child, the weather, to tell her that she was not to make tea for him specially. But for some time he did not say anything, and she came over to the fireplace and began mechanically to remove the drying clothes, folding them and pressing them into a small heap with her hands.

"Don't move them for me," he said.

"No?"

In this one word it seemed to him that he heard the indirect echo of antagonism, but when he looked up at her, quite sharply, there was nothing on her face but the same look of bleak surprise. She was rather thin and he saw that she found it difficult to keep her eyes quite still. They were weak and dark with nervous pain.

After the clothes were folded she went away for a moment, into the kitchen, coming back with empty hands. She came to the fire for the kettle, to make tea, her dark head bent down. Abruptly the window rattled like a machine-gun.

"I had an idea your husband was a mechanic," he said. "How did you come up here?"

"His chest was weak."

She set the metal tea-pot in the hearth, afterwards turning away to the table. He looked after her and suddenly saw her come momentarily to life, setting the things on the table straight, moving cups, smoothing the cloth, her pride rising.

"The doctor ordered it. There was this little milkround, so we took it—until something better turns up. We're not stopping here." She turned round and spoke for a moment with defensive pride, holding up her head. "It's only something temporary. We shan't stop another winter."

Behind the pride he could detect the fear of it all in her voice; she seemed to know this and all of a sudden said something in a hurried whisper and then went out. He heard the outer door grating against the bricks as she tugged it open and afterwards, above the wind, he thought he heard her calling.

After two or three minutes she came back. Her hair was ragged from the wind, and in her hands she was clasping a bunch of coloured primroses, washed-blue and pink and red, tangled with scraps of leaf and grass, that she had hastily snatched up from somewhere. She put them into a cup of water which she set in the centre of the table, her face turned away from him as she did so.

And for a minute it was painful for him to look at her. He saw in the bland, soft glowing flowers the inexpressible recollection of other things. He again wanted to say something to her, but it was no use. He hated suddenly the flat drabness of the little room thrown into relief by the small glowing centrepiece of flowers. He was driven to hatred of the drying clothes under the ceiling, the rattling window, the sour smell of milk, the slight whimpering of the child which had again begun overhead.

He was saved from expressing or hiding what he felt by the noise of someone entering the kitchen, and a minute later the man with the spanner came into the living-room. He changed the spanner from one oil-greased hand to another as the woman spoke. "This is my husband—Mr Hanson," she said.

"You're the paper bloke," the man said.

"That's me."

"You want tell 'em to write some sense in some o' the papers."

"Yes?"

"Yeh, you do an' all!"

He wiped his oily palms on the flanks of his trousers and sat down at the table.

"Will you sit here?" she said to Hanson, and he sat down too. He heard the husband give a short laugh as he cut himself a lump of cheese, leaving on the wedge the greenish imprint of a finger.

"Flower show early, ain't it?" He pointed the cheese at the cup of primroses, ironically. "Well, well. Very nice. Very nice."

As she poured out tea the woman gave no sign. Upstairs the short whimpered cries of the child became fused into a single unbroken cry, and the father lifted his head.

"What's up wi' Jean?"

"Earache again."

"Then why the bleedin' hell don't you fetch her down?" He

ceased gnawing at the cheese with small chimbling bites like those of a rat. "Sittin' here jawin' and lettin' the kid bawl."

"I'll fetch her," she said.

"You neen't bother!" he said. "I'll fetch her meself. I'll fetch her."

He went with a show of temper out of the room, and she stood for a moment in silence, looking painfully down at her hands, not able to speak.

"I think I'll go," Hanson said.

"I—"

Her words would not come, and she made instead a brief, stupefied gesture towards the cups and the food. Before he could reply he could hear footsteps on the stairs, and then for a second her voice came to life. "Don't take too much notice. He's not strong. It's because he's not really well. He can't hold his temper. It's just when strangers come."

Hanson could not speak.

"It's nothing. I get used to it, I get used to it," she said.

A second later the man came in with the child, a girl of three, in his arms. At the sight of a stranger the child turned away her puffed tear-damp face. The man brought her to the table, holding her on his knee, talking to her in a new, wheedling, tender voice, pouring out tea for her in a saucer and then sopping into it lumps of broken cake. "Make old ear better, won't it? Dad make old ear better?"

In the few minutes before Hanson got up to go the father continued to hold the child apart, in a kind of alliance with himself against the mother and even, Hanson thought, against him. During all this time the child did not speak. In the silences the window broke into the renewed chattering of a machine-gun, and sometimes the echo of the sea itself could be heard in the mournful beating of the poplars.

"If I'm to get that train," Hanson said, "I ought to go."

He got up from the table, saying good-bye to the child, who did not answer. Without holding out his hand, he said good afternoon to the father, who grunted in answer something about getting the newspapers to write the truth about things. They were at the root, he said, of everything, damn near everything. One way or another you could trace it all to the newspapers.

Hanson said a final good afternoon and went into the kitchen and so outside, the woman going with him. In the strong March wind her hair was flung tortuously about her cold face. For a moment she stood gazing at the earth and then said, "I'll walk as far as the gate with you, and they walked together across the wind-dried yard with its storm-driven litter of feathers and straw and golden-claret catkins. All the time it appeared to him as if she were about to stop and say something. She wanted perhaps to express regret for things: or she wanted to get off her mind some oppressive, tortured explanation.

Whatever she wanted to say was never spoken. She halted by the gate in the wire fence and said good-bye, holding out her hand. The wind had beaten her hair unmercifully, giving her face a wild, bloodless look. He searched it in vain for a sign of pride or vivacity, but the eyes that were lifted up to him were quite dark and cold, and strangely repressed, as if they had got into the habit of not looking far.

After walking away at last he turned and looked back. She was walking back to the house, pressing her body against the wind and at the same time gazing down at the earth. He halted a moment in the hope that she would turn round, but nothing happened and he went on.

When he turned again she had disappeared altogether and nothing moved against the dead little house except the high sunless poplars beaten by the sea-wind.

The Loved One

Alice Woodman had a soft loving face and brown almond eyes that seemed to be always on the verge of smiling at something. At twenty-two she married a man who manufactured mustard.

A few weeks after they were married she began to go about the district with her husband, in a small 10 h.p. van marked Pypper's Prepared Mustard, trying to establish this commodity on the market. Her husband, a man of inexhaustible and changeable enthusiasm, was convinced that one-half of the world was dying to eat a really decent mustard and that the other half was dying because it did not eat mustard at all. It was quite true that former manufacturers of mustard had made fortunes out of what was left on the plate. But here was a mustard you did not leave on the plate. It was a prepared mustard, in the French manner, and it was wonderful. It kept indefinitely in the little brown stone jars of which the 10 h.p. van was always full. At forty James Pypper had been a vacuum cleaner salesman, an agent for fire-extinguishers, a traveller in boiled sweets, a door-to-door salesman of cures and preventives for rheumatism, a partner in a firm of patent corset manufacturers. He spoke of the vacuum cleaners and the fire-extinguishers, the boiled sweets, the rheumatism and the corsets, much as he spoke of the French mustard. Every household in the kingdom was in danger of fire. Everyone ate sweets. There were more deaths every year from rheumatism than from any other disease. Every woman wore corsets. Alice, who was slim and delicate, did not wear corsets; she had given up eating sweets and did not suffer from rheumatism. She had a warm, contemplative, loving face but she did not eat mustard.

As time went on, however, she began to be affected by the tireless enthusiasm of James Pypper for the mustard he was trying to sell to country grocers, village stores and even to public houses and wayside tea-shacks. For the first few weeks, whenever they came to a shop or some other place where the mustard might possibly be sold, Alice would sit in the car outside and wait for James Pypper to come out again. As she sat there she would look at the shop and sometimes she would see James Pypper talking with earnest rapidity to the shopman, waving his arms and striking the little brown sample pot of mustard on the counter: a man preaching a mustard sermon. This went on for several weeks; and then Alice, who at first had been shy of doing such a thing, began to go into shops herself and try to induce people to take sample orders. To her surprise and to James Pypper's surprise she was very successful. She did not preach about the mustard, she did not wave her hands and she did not strike the pot on the counter. She would look straight at the shopkeeper with her lovable, candid eyes and say in a simple way that the mustard was beautiful. Almost immediately it was as though the shopkeeper became confused between the beauty of the mustard and the quiet, lovable beauty of the girl who was speaking. He would give an order, "Well, can't be no harm in trying a dozen. See if they've moved next time you come," and he would watch her out of the shop, hoping that next time would not be long.

In this way Alice got many orders for James Pypper's brand of prepared mustard. James Pypper, however, did not notice it. When Alice returned from shops which had taken an order he would say "Knew he would. Couldn't help it. You see, I told you." Her going and coming and her success were simple proof of his enthusiastic creed that people needed mustard. It could never occur to him that they were proof that Alice was a lovable creature; he was concerned with saleable products only.

As they drove about the countryside Alice had a way of looking, in spring time, over the heads of the flowering chestnut trees, the cream clouds of may, the olive mountains of oak; or in summer over the long swinging distances of corn and the uniform green of distant trees. As she looked she appeared to be smiling. This supposed smile, completely unconscious, had first attracted James Pypper. He had seen Alice smiling like this at a dance, had taken it automatically to mean that she was enchanted by James Pypper, about to embark on a great enterprise. Now he was often irritated by it. "What on earth are you smiling at?"

"I don't think I was smiling at anything."

"Think? Don't you know? Don't you know whether you smile or not?"

"Yes. But perhaps I wasn't thinking."

At times Alice would wonder whether James Pypper really did or really ever had loved her; then it became obvious that there were more important things on his mind than Alice's love, her almond eyes and her smile. It became obvious that the mustard was failing. It became obvious, by September, that the world did not eat mustard at all.

Up to this time Alice and James Pypper had lived in the middle of the town; theirs was a big, ill-proportioned house of ugly white brick with grey iron railings round it. The mustard was made in a little two-storied factory, formerly a warehouse, farther down the street. James Pypper had begun by employing three men and a boy, then one man and two boys, and then, as the mustard began to fail, a boy and an old man. He was just about to ask Alice if she too would leave the house and come to help retrieve the fortunes of the factory when something happened. James Pypper was in a grocer's shop one day when a man walked in with two huge baskets of white and brown eggs. James Pypper looked at them casually, then with a sudden jump of interest, and then realised all at once that he was seeing eggs for the first time in his life. He asked the man how many eggs there could be in a basket. "About ten score each basket," the man said. James Pypper wanted to know how many days' laying that represented and the man said: "That's two days' lay. Eggs are falling off a bit." James Pypper went out of the shop impelled by a terrific idea: the stunning cataclysmic, revolutionary idea of the egg.

As he rushed home to tell Alice of this, his mind worked out like an arithmetical machine the whole scheme of egg production, egg distribution, egg profit. He realised that he had got hold of something truly stupendous. He couldn't think why he, and indeed anyone else, had never thought of it before. He was seized with a primitive fever of simple wonder for one of the basic forces of the universe: the egg.

As he told it to Alice it was like a daydream worked out by figures. The mustard was forgotten now, but the story of the egg was literally the story of the mustard over again.

"Don't you see? Every man, woman and child in the country must eat an average of one egg per day. You wouldn't call that an extravagant estimate, would you? Eggs for breakfast, eggs in puddings, eggs for tea, omelettes, custards, cakes, thousands of things. One egg per day per person," James Pypper said, striking one hand into another. "That's forty million eggs a day. In round figures that's fifteen thousand million eggs a year. Just think of it. The average price of an egg is twopence. That means that roughly £125,000,000 are spent on eggs annually in this country. Think of it. It's colossal! It's almost pitiful."

Alice sat staring into the distance, seeming to smile.

"You're not listening?" James Pypper said.

"Yes, I am listening. I am."

"You're not only not listening. You're laughing about it too."

"Oh, no!"

"It's not a laughing matter!" James Pypper said. "It's colossal! There's a fortune in it. All big fortunes have been made out of something very simple, like this. We must get started on it. The thing's so infernally simple. We must."

Nearly a week later James Pypper had closed down the mustard business. He rushed home to Alice one day to say that he had rented a house and four acress of land out in the country. That afternoon he and Alice drove out in the 10 h.p. van to see the house and land.

When she saw the house Alice was too appalled to say anything. It stood on high exposed ground like a slice cut out of a working-class street. It seemed as if it had been cut out of a strange impoverished town, dumped down and that the occupants had hastily fled because of the raw hideousness of the place, because they were miles from anybody or anywhere, because of some bleak, sour quality of loneliness in the surrounding land. Then Alice saw another reason why they had fled. Out of the distance came the sound of a train. It came shrieking and piping up a deep cutting fifty yeards from the house, its long line of white smoke rising, hanging for a few moments and then vanishing in the clear sunny autumn air.

A few minutes later, while James Pypper was enthusiastically pacing up and down on the neglected path of grass adjoining the house, Alice walked the short distance along the road to the railway cutting. She was surprised to find it very deep. At the track the road made a dead end. There was no bridge, but steps went down the cutting, and over the single set of metals there was a wooden foot-crossing.

Alice climbed the stile in the hedge and went down the wooden steps towards the permanent way. Along the railway banks yellow flags of ragwort, torn about by early autumn winds, waved between bright pink patches of late willow herb. Now that the train had passed the air was at rest, with settled echoes. Alice walked down the steps, stood still at the bottom of them, and gazed up and down the line with her habitual expression of unconsciously smiling repose. The lines, chromium bright in the sun, stretched away dead straight on either side. The train that had passed had come down a long steep gradient and farther up the slope deep woods closed in on both sides of the track. Beyond this wooded gully, at the crest of the gradient, stood a white signal-box. As Alice stood looking at it the track became so quiet that small companies of rabbits began to come and feed on the grass and wood pigeons began to moan softly in the woods, the low sounds coming down the lines like softly telegraphed messages.

Alice stood looking up the line for almost five minutes, before James Pypper's voice, calling her name from the vicinity of the house, aroused her. All this time her brown almond eyes had been fixed on the signal box, with remote and disquieted thoughtfulness, as though she were thinking deeply about something or even not thinking at all.

II

For some time, on into the beginning of the next year, things went fairly well with James Pypper's simple scheme for making a fortune out of the egg. Neat rows of expensive mobile chicken-houses covered the field by the house, and sometimes the broken ruminative talk of two or three hundred brown and white hens was the only sound Alice heard, except the sound of the trains, on the dark quiet winter afternoons. Sometimes, when James Pypper left early to go to one market or another with the crates of eggs that now replaced the pots of mustard in the 10 h.p. van, it was the only sound she heard all day. After a time it seemed that she did not hear the trains. At first they had shaken and disturbed her, shaking crockery in the house, shaking the windows so that she did not sleep at nights. They had shaken and broken the days by their shrieking and clamour into harsh sections that made her so nervous that she felt sometimes that the north-bound trains, expressing down the gradient, were coming straight into the house. Then gradually she grew used to them, gradually forgot them.

On some days the only living soul she saw was the boy who cleaned the chicken-houses and collected the eggs and made himself generally useful. Working out in the raw open air of the bare hillside she became strong and healthy, her breasts and arms filling out, her face warmly fresh. But her brown almond eyes still retained their disquieting habit of smiling at inconceivably remote distances or simply at nothing at all, and soon, twice or three times a week, they were smiling or seeming to smile at the men who drove up the road and turned into the gateway with lorry loads of chicken feed or peat-litter or simply with the vans delivering meat and groceries. By the simple and unconscious habit of appearing to smile she seemed to confer on each of them a special sort of affection. She had another habit by which she curled her left arm completely over her head, so that she could play softly with the lobe of her right ear. Standing like this, against the door-post, the shape of one breast and one arm beautifully exposed, she had an air of serene and disturbing invitation. In a gentle sort of way she was very fascinating and soon the men were driving up the dead-end road on the pretext of having forgotten an order or on no pretext whatsoever. Sometimes on cold mornings, as she gave them cups of hot tea and lumps of bread and cheese, treating them all equally at various times, they would remind her of things she might have forgotten—"Any corn, Mrs Pypper, any sausages, any coke this time?"—and she would say, perhaps, "No, not this time, perhaps next time", and like the men behind the grocers' counters they would hope that next time would not be long. And as signs of spring began to show themselves in the longer days and the stronger light over the claret-coloured buds of the birch trees that fringed the woods on the railway line, there would be greetings like "Beautiful morning, Mrs Pypper, lovely day", and again it would seem as if the beauty of the day became confused in the men's minds with the charming lovable beauty of the girl leaning on the door-post, playing with her ear and smiling at the fresh spring sky.

But occasionally, in the afternoons, she was not there to answer the door. As spring came on she began to find more and more pleasure in walking along the banks of the railway. Beyond the hedge a path ran along the crest of the bank and she gradually got into the habit of walking there for an hour or so on fine spring afternoons.

By this time, on the sheltered part of the bank, under the woods, primroses were making soft yellow rosettes in the wintry grass, and wands of silvery wine pussy-willow were pushing out from the mass of darker leafless trees. Except for the trains and an occasional plate-layer walking below her by the line and the dainty patter of pheasants' feet on the dry leaves under the birch trees in the woods there would be scarcely a sound or movement during the whole of her walk up the track and back again. It was not only out of this secluded sort of quietness and the primroses and the sight of the young birch trees that she got a happiness that she did not ever experience with James Pypper, but out of the mere sight and nearness of the endless lines of steel running below her. In the shining metals, running away into the distances, her vague smile into space seemed to find its foundation. It seemed to be able to follow the lines to some point of permanence and reality.

One afternoon she walked as far as the signal-box. She had primroses in her hand and as she sat down opposite the box she kept touching her face with the flowers, disturbing velvety breaths of scent.

She sat and looked at the signal-box. She could see the signalman working inside it, pulling levers. She heard the ringing of the telegraphs, strange urgent sounds in the silence of the track, and she could see a tall red geranium flowering in one of the windows.

For a long time she sat there fascinated. She could see for miles up and down the empty metals, and presently she realised that the signal-box was on the highest point of the gradient and that, by watching, she could see the signals give their responses to the levers.

In about five minutes she heard the sound of a train coming uphill from the north. Though it was an express it came fairly slowly, forcing its way up the gradient laboriously. As it came nearer she felt a curious rising emotion, an advance of a moment of dramatic power. With the approach of the great double-engined train she began to tremble, and she realised that the moment would come when the train passed the signal-box. The intensity of her feeling was sharpened because the train came slowly. It had the effect of drawing out her emotion like a thread of bright hot glass.

In the middle of feeling all this she saw that the signalman had opened the window of his box and was leaning out, watching the approaching train. She had just time to note that he was a lean dark young man in his shirt sleeves before the train rose to the high point of the gradient and passed the box. At this moment the hot glass thread of her emotions seemed to solidify, become brittle and splinter violently. She was aware of being suddenly relieved and happy: the sort of feeling that might have followed the aversion of a catastrophe. She discovered that she was smiling, really smiling this time, and was waving her hand. To add to her delight the signalman was waving his hand too.

When the train had finally gone by there was an interval of about half a minute before the signalman went back into his box. In this moment he looked up at her. She was still smiling and it seemed for a second as if he smiled too.

She remained there for another hour, watching the trains and between the trains watching the shadowy figure of the signalman at work in the box below. Each train produced in her the same effect of drawn-out emotion, as of hot glass drawing out, hardening and smashing explosively into relief and happiness. She knew that the signalman must have been aware of her sitting there, yet he did not appear at the window again.

The next day she walked up the track at the same time and sat down in the same place and remained for about the same length of time. She saw the same train come laboriously up the gradient again, and experienced the same deep emotion, terrifying in its peculiar and too-fine ecstasy. Once again she had primroses in her hand, and once again she waved her hand and smiled at the man in the signal-box and it seemed again as if he smiled too.

The next day she was there again. And that day she had no doubt that the signalman was very aware of her presence. He came several times to the window, and once to the door of the signal-box. He looked up at her and she smiled. It was now a real smile, its true perspective fixed, its direction and object fully conscious. She felt that nothing could have been more soothing and beautiful than this fully realised moment of her smile and its return from a man she did not know and perhaps could never speak to.

After this she began to go up to the signal-box almost every afternoon. She complained to James Pypper, when he asked why she left the chickens, that the oil from the incubators gave her a headache and that the walk would do her good. James Pypper did not protest. Spring was coming on and there were a million eggs too many in the world and he was preoccupied by all the problems that an egg can raise.

Spring also began to strengthen and become very beautiful along the railway track. There were violets now, white snowdrop-like buds in the grass and patches of dark purple and pale mauve lace all along the slanting yellow banks of primroses. The birches were showing a little leaf and the sallows had bright golden beards that trembled with bees in the sun.

There was something else, besides the trains, the excitement and the beauty of spring breaking on the woodsides, that appeared to Alice very wonderful. It was the awakening and stilling and reawakening of many voices in the woods by the passing of the trains. If she could not speak to the man in the signal-box—and she did not see how it could ever be possible—this clamour of voices and echoes could be a kind of common speech between them: the speech of the trains which now controlled so much of both their lives, though their lives had no other contact.

Then one day something new happened. Alice sat on in the sunshine above the bright glistening metals until six o'clock. Just before six o'clock she saw another man coming down the opposite bank. She saw him enter the signal-box and realised that it was time for the change of shift.

She waited to see what would happen. In about a minute she saw the first man, the dark lean young man, come out of the box. She saw that he was carrying the red geranium: perhaps to take home for a window, perhaps to re-pot it, perhaps, she thought, to give it to her. And suddenly she wanted him to give it to her. She wanted him to come across the track and say something and give her the geranium. She wanted him to take the first step that would lead to friendship, perhaps affection, perhaps intimacy.

And having come down the steps of the signal-box the signalman paused on the edge of the track as if the same thought were in his mind. He must have been puzzled by her. He must have reasoned out for himself that it was not because of the spring or the thrill of trains or the voices in the woods that she came there smiling, but solely because of himself. He stood there for about half a minute, holding the bright red geranium, trying, it seemed, to make up his mind to come across the lines to her. Then, perhaps because he was self-consciously aware of being watched by the other man in the box, he decided against it. He turned and walked up the diagonal path of the bank.

By the time he had reached the top of the bank Alice had got to her feet and was walking along too. They walked a little way in the same direction, as it were side by side, although separated by the tracks. This short walk produced in her a deep sense of intimacy, so deep that a train roared down the gradient and passed them before she had time to realise it had come and gone.

A moment later the signalman stopped and climbed a fence on the edge of the wood. For a moment Alice stopped too. Then he waved his hand. She waved her hand back to him and kept waving it as she slowly walked away.

This same thing began to happen every evening. Gradually

she knew that she was more intimate with the signalman, to whom she never spoke and from whom she was continually separated by the tracks of a railway, than she had been or could ever be with James Pypper, now struggling with increasing desperation with all the maddening problems of the egg.

She had become not only intimate, but she had an increasingly deep conviction that she was in love. But it was not so much that she was in love as that she herself was the loved one. The structure of both the love she was giving and the love she was being given was built on things that had nothing to do with love: on the passing of trains, the strange ringing of telegraphs in the silence of the spring afternoons, the fall and rise of signals. The emotion of the passing trains was now identified with her feelings for the signalman, waving his hand each night before going home through the wood. She began to feel that her life was stretched out to the limitless extent of the metals; that it was so tenuous and delicate that it might suddenly snap, like bright hair-thin glass.

Finally she could bear it no longer. One evening the sky was duller than usual and there was a heavy unkind wind blowing loudly down the empty track. She was cold and she felt that she could not go home without speaking to the signalman at last.

She waved her hand as usual as he reached the woodside, and then she called him.

"Come over a minute!"

The wind took her words and broke them up, so that they could not travel. He raised his hand, as though to say that he could not hear.

"Come over a minute!"

She was smiling. There was something in the smile that was like a concentration of all the remote, tenderly captivating smiles she had ever given. It went across the track with an intimate and secret swiftness that held the man momentarily spellbound.

Then he started to run down the bank. The way he ran, not heeding anything, made it seem as if this was the moment he too had been waiting for. He ran with arms out, to steady himself, as if ready to embrace her. He was running without thinking and suddenly she knew that he could not stop himself.

She did not exactly hear the approaching train. She felt all of a sudden the intense dramatic emotion that the approach of a train always gave her. The train was coming very fast down the gradient. She looked with great horror across the track and she saw that in a moment the man and the train would meet.

A moment later her life lay all along the metals, an illimitable thread of glass smashed by the train that had passed. The echoes were smashing the dark woods to pieces and she could not see anything except on the lines below a splash of scarlet that might have been a red geranium.

Some weeks later James Pypper found that he could not master the problem of making a fortune out of the egg. He sold the chickens and the chicken-houses as suddenly as he had bought them, and he and Alice moved away from the house that was like a harsh slice cut from a street in a town.

Summer was coming on and James Pypper now had a wonderful idea. It was the idea of making a pile of quick money out of a dance-hall, in which he had bought part interest at a seaside resort. During the summer months it was bound to be a good thing, James Pypper said, a very good thing, a wonderful thing, because at some time or other everybody felt like dancing.

Alice, who had not liked mustard and had become indifferent towards the many problems of the egg, went with him. But she had lost her way of smiling, and she did not feel like dancing now.

The Ox

The Thurlows lived on a small hill. As though it were not high enough, the house was raised up, as on invisible stilts, with a wooden flight of steps to the front door. Exposed and isolated, the wind striking at it from all quarters, it seemed to have no part with the surrounding landscape. Empty ploughed lands, in winter-time, stretched away on all sides in wet steel curves.

At half-past seven every morning Mrs Thurlow pushed her great rusty bicycle down the hill; at six every evening she pushed it back. Loaded, always, with grey bundles of washing, oilcans, sacks, cabbages, bundles of old newspaper, boughs of wind-blown wood, and bags of chicken food, the bicycle could never be ridden. It was a vehicle of necessity. Her relationship to it was that of a beast to a cart. Slopping along beside it, flat heavy feet pounding painfully along under mudstained skirts, her face and body ugly with lumpy angles of bone, she was like a beast of burden.

Coming out of the house, raised up even above the level of the small hill, she stepped into a country of wide horizons. This fact meant nothing to her. The world into which she moved was very small: from six to nine she cleaned for the two retired sisters, nine to twelve for the retired photographer, twelve-thirty to three for the poultry farm, four to six for the middle-aged bachelor. She did not think of going beyond the four lines which made up the square of her life. She thought of other people going beyond them, but this was different. Staring down at a succession of wet floors, working always for other people, against time, she had somehow got into the habit of not thinking about herself.

She thought much, in the same stolid pounding way as she pushed the bicycle, of other people: in particular of Thurlow, more particularly of her two sons. She had married late; the boys were nine and thirteen. She saw them realising refined ambitions, making their way as assistants in shops, as clerks in offices, even as butlers. Heavily built, with faces having her own angular boniness, they moved with eyes on the ground. She had saved money for them. For fifteen years she had hoarded the scrubbing-and-washing money, keeping it in a bran bag under a mattress in the back bedroom. They did not know of it; she felt that no one, not even Thurlow, knew of it.

Thurlow had a silver plate in his head. In his own eyes it set him apart from other men. "I got a plate in me head. Solid silver. Enough silver to make a dozen spoons and a bit over. Solid. Beat that!" Wounded on the Marne, and now walking about with the silver plate in his head, Thurlow was a martyr. "I didn't ought to stoop. I didn't ought to do nothing. By rights. By rights I didn't ought to lift a finger." He was a hedge cutter. "Lucky I'm tall, else that job wouldn't be no good to me." He had had days and good days, even days of genuine pain. "Me plate's hurting me! It's me plate. By God, it'll drive me so's I don't know what I'm doing! It's me plate again." And he would stand wild and vacant, rubbing his hands through his thin black hair, clawing his scalp as though to wrench out the plate and the pain.

Once a week, on Saturdays or Sundays, he came home a little tipsy, in a good mood, laughing to himself, riding his bicycle up the hill like some comic rider in a circus: "Eh? Too much be damned. I can ride me bike, can't I? S' long as I can ride me bike I'm all right." In the pubs he had only one theme, "I got a plate in me head. Solid silver," recited in a voice challenging the world to prove it otherwise.

All the time Mrs Thurlow saved money. It was her creed. Sometimes people went away and there was no cleaning. She then made up the gap in her life by other work: picking potatoes, planting potatoes, dibbing cabbages, spudding roots, pea picking, more washing. In the fields she pinned up her skirt so that it stuck out behind her like a thick stiff tail, making her look like some bony ox. She did washing from five to six in the morning, and again from seven to nine in the evening. Taking in more washing, she tried to wash more quickly, against time. Somehow she succeeded, so that from nine to ten she had time for ironing. She worked by candlelight. Her movements were largely instinctive. She had washed and ironed for so long, in the same way, at the same time and place, that she could have worked in darkness.

There were some things, even, which could be done in darkness; and so at ten, with Thurlow and the sons in bed, she blew out the candle, broke up the fire, and sat folding the clothes or cleaning boots, and thinking. Her thoughts, like her work, went always along the same lines, towards the future, out into the resplendent avenues of ambitions, always for the two sons. There was division in herself, the one part stolid and uncomplaining in perpetual labour, the other fretful and almost desperate in an anxiety to establish a world beyond her own. She had saved fifty-four pounds. She would make it a hundred. How it was to be done she could not think. The boys were growing, the cost of keeping them was growing. She trusted in some obscure providential power as tireless and indomitable as herself.

At eleven she went to bed, going up the wooden stairs in darkness, in her stockinged feet. She undressed in darkness, her clothes falling away to be replaced by a heavy grey nightgown that made her body seem still large and more ponderous. She fell asleep almost at once, but throughout the night her mind, propelled by some inherent anxiety, seemed to work on. She dreamed she was pushing the bicycle down the hill, and then that she was pushing it up again; she dreamed she was scrubbing floors; she felt the hot stab of the iron on her spittled finger and then the frozen bite of icy swedes as she picked them off unthawed earth on bitter mornings. She counted her money, her mind going back over the years throughout which she had saved it, and then counted it again, in fear, to make sure, as though in terror that it might be gone in the morning.

II

She had one relaxation. On Sunday afternoons she sat in the kitchen alone, and read the newspapers. They were not the newspapers of the day, but of all the previous week and perhaps of the week before that. She had collected them from the houses where she scrubbed, bearing them home on the bicycle. Through them and by them she broke the boundaries of her world. She made excursions into the lives of other people: tragic lovers, cabinet ministers, Atlantic flyers, suicides, society beauties, murderers, kings. It was all very wonderful. But emotionally, as she read, her face showed no impression. It remained ox-like in its impassivity. It looked in some way indomitably strong, as though little things like beauties and suicides, murderers and kings, could have no possible effect on her. About three o'clock as she sat reading, Thurlow would come in, lumber upstairs, and sleep until about half-past four.

One Sunday he did not come in at three o'clock. It was after four when she heard the bicycle tinkle against the woodshed outside. She raised her head from the newspaper and listened for him to come in. Nothing happened. Then after about five minutes Thurlow came in, went upstairs, remained for some minutes, and then came down again. She heard him go out into the yard. There was a stir among the chickens as he lumbered about the woodshed.

Mrs Thurlow got up and went outside, and there, at the door of the woodshed, Thurlow was just hiding something under his coat. She thought it seemed like his billhook. She was not sure. Something made her say:

"Your saw don't need sharpening again a'ready, does it?"

"That it does," he said. "That's just what it does. Joe Woods is going to sharp it." Thurlow looked upset and slightly wild, as he did when the plate in his head was hurting him. His eyes were a little drink-fired, dangerous. "I gonna take it down now, so's I can git it back tonight."

All the time she could see the saw itself hanging in the darkness of the woodshed behind him. She was certain then that he was lying, almost certain that it was the billhook he had under his coat.

She did not say anything else. Thurlow got on his bicycle and rode off, down the hill, his coat bunched up, the bicycle slightly crazy as he drove with one tipsy hand.

Something, as soon as he had gone, made her rush upstairs. She went into the back bedroom and flung the clothes off the mattress of the small iron bed that was never slept in. The money: it was all right. It was quite all right. She sat down heavily on the bed. And after a moment's anxiety her colour returned again—the solid, immensurably passive calm with which she scrubbed, read the newspapers, and pushed the bicycle.

In the evening, the boys at church, she worked again. She darned socks, the cuffs of jackets, cleaned boots, sorted the washing for the following day. The boys must look well, respectable. Under the new scheme they went, now, to a secondary school in the town. She was proud of this, the first real stepping-stone to the higher things of the future. Outside, the night was windy, and she heard the now brief, now very prolonged moan of wind over the dark winter-ploughed land. She worked by candlelight. When the boys came in she lighted the lamp. In their hearts, having now some standard by which to judge her, they despised her a little. They hated the cheapness of the candle-light. When they had eaten and gone lumbering up to bed, like two colts, she blew out the lamp and worked by candlelight again. Thurlow had not come in.

He came in a little before ten. She was startled, not hearing the bicycle.

"You want something t' eat?"

"No," he said. He went straight into the scullery. She heard him washing his hands, swilling the sink, washing, swilling again.

"You want the light?" she called.

"No!"

He came into the kitchen. She saw his still-wet hands in the candlelight. He gave her one look and went upstairs without speaking. For some time she pondered on the memory of this look, not understanding it. She saw in it the wildness of the afternoon, as though the plate were hurting him, but now it had in addition fear, and, above fear, defiance.

She got the candle and went to the door. The wind tore the candle flame down to a minute blue bubble which broke, and she went across the yard, to the woodshed, in darkness. In the woodshed she put a match to the candle again, held the candle up at eye level, and looked at the walls. The saw hung on its nail, but there was no billhook. She made a circle with the candle, looking for the bicycle with dumb eyes. It was not there. She went into the house again. Candleless, very faintly perturbed, she went up to bed. She wanted to say something to Thurlow, but he was dead still, as though asleep, and she lay down herself, hearing nothing but the sound of Thurlow's breathing and, outside, the sound of the wind blowing across the bare land.

Asleep, she dreamed, as nearly always, about the bicycle, but this time it was Thurlow's bicycle and there was something strange about it. It had no handles, but only Thurlow's billhook where the handles should have been. She grasped the billhook, and in her dream she felt the pain of the blood rushing out of her hands, and she was terrified and woke up.

Immediately she put out her hands, to touch Thurlow. The bed was empty. That scared her. She got out of bed. "Thurlow! Bill! Thurlow! Thurlow!"

The wind had dropped, and it was quiet everywhere. She went downstairs. There, in the kitchen, she lighted the candle again and looked round. She tried the back door; it was unlocked and she opened it and looked out, feeling the small ground wind icy on her bare feet.

"Thurlow!" she said. "Bill! Thurlow!"

She could hear nothing, and after about a minute she went back upstairs. She looked in at the boys' bedroom. The boys were asleep, and the vast candle shadow of herself stood behind her and listened, as it were, while she listened. She went into her own bedroom: nothing. Thurlow was not there—nothing. Then she went into the back bedroom.

The mattress lay on the floor. And she knew, even before she began to look for it, that the money was gone. She knew that Thurlow had taken it.

Since there was nothing else she could do, she went back to bed, not to sleep, but to lie there, oppressed but never in despondency, thinking. The money had gone, Thurlow had gone, but it would be all right. Just before five she got up, fired the copper, and began the washing. At seven she hung it out in long grey lines in the wintry grey light, holding the pegs like a bit in her teeth. A little after seven the boys came down to wash in the scullery.

"Here, here! Mum! There's blood all over the sink!"

"Your dad killed a rabbit," she said. "That's all."

She lumbered out into the garden, to cut cabbages. She cut three large cabbages, put them in a sack, and, as though nothing had happened, began to prepare the bicycle for the day. She tied the cabbages on the carrier, two oilcans on the handlebars, and then on the crossbar a small bundle of washing, clean, which she had finished on Saturday. That was all: nothing much for a Monday.

At half-past seven the boys went across the fields, by footpath, to catch the bus for school. She locked the house, and then, huge, imperturbable, planting down great feet in the mud, she pushed the bicycle down the hill. She had not gone a hundred yards before, out of the hedge, two policemen stepped into the road to meet her.

"We was wondering if Mr Thurlow was in?"

"No," she said, "he ain't in."

"You ain't seen him?"

"No, I ain't seen him."

"Since when?"

"Since last night."

"You mind," they said, "if we look round your place?"

"No," she said, "you go on up. I got to git down to Miss Hanley's." She began to push the bicycle forward, to go.

"No," they said. "You must come back with us."

So she turned the bicycle round and pushed it back up the hill again. "You could leave your bike," one of the policemen said. "No," she said, "I'd better bring it. You can never tell nowadays what folk are going to be up to."

Up at the house she stood impassively by while the two policemen searched the woodshed, the garden, and finally the house itself. Her expression did not change as they looked at the blood in the sink. "He washed his hands there last night," she said.

"Don't touch it," the policeman said. "Don't touch it." And then suspiciously, almost in implied accusation: "You ain't touched nothing—not since last night?"

"I got something else to do," she said.

"We'd like you to come along with us, Mrs Thurlow," they said, "and answer a few questions."

"All right." She went outside and took hold of her bicycle.

"You can leave your bicycle."

"No," she said. "I'll take it. It's no naughty way, up here, from that village."

"We got a car down the road. You don't want a bike."

"I better take it," she said.

She wheeled the bicycle down the hill. When one policeman had gone in the car she walked on with the other. Ponderous, flat-footed, unhurried, she looked as though she could have gone on pushing the bicycle in the same direction, at the same pace, for ever.

They kept her four hours at the station. She told them about the billhook, the blood, the way Thurlow had come home and gone again, her waking in the night, Thurlow not being there, the money not being there.

"The money. How much was there?"

"Fifty-four pounds, sixteen and fourpence. And twenty-eight of that in sovereigns."

In return they told her something else.

"You know that Thurlow was in the Black Horse from eleven to two yesterday?"

"Yes, I dare say that's where he'd be. That's where he always is, Sundays."

"He was in the Black Horse, and for about two hours he was arguing with a man stopping down here from London. Arguing about that plate in his head. The man said he knew the plate was aluminium and Thurlow said he knew it was silver. Thurlow got very threatening. Did you know that?"

"No. But that's just like him."

"This man hasn't been seen since, and Thurlow hasn't been seen since. Except by you last night."

"Do you want me any more?" she said. "I ought to have been at Miss Hanley's hours ago."

"You realise this is very important, very serious?"

"I know. But how am I going to get Miss Hanley in, and Mrs Acott, and then the poultry farm and then Mr George?"

"We'll telephone Miss Hanley and tell her you can't go."

"The money," she said. "That's what I can't understand. The money."

III

It was the money which brought her, without showing it, to the edge of distress. She thought of it all day. She thought of it as hard cash, coin, gold and silver, hard-earned and hard-saved. But it was also something much more. It symbolized the future, another life, two lives. It was the future itself. If, as seemed possible, something terrible had happened and a life had been destroyed, it did not seem to her more terrible than the fact that the money had gone and that the future had been destroyed.

As she scrubbed the floors at the poultry farm in the late afternoon, the police telephoned for her again. "We can send the car for her," they said.

"I got my bike," she said. "I'll walk."

With the oilcans filled, and cabbages and clean washing now replaced by newspapers and dirty washing, she went back to the police station. She wheeled her bicycle into the lobby and they then told her how, that afternoon, the body of the man from London had been found, in a spinney, killed by blows from some sharp instrument like an axe. "We have issued a warrant for Thurlow's arrest," they said.

"You never found the money?" she said.

"No," they said. "No doubt that'll come all right when we find Thurlow."

That evening, when she got home, she fully expected Thurlow to be there, as usual, splitting kindling wood with the billhook, in the outhouse, by candlelight. The same refusal to believe that life could change made her go upstairs to look for the money.

The absence of both Thurlow and the money moved her to no sign of emotion. But she was moved to a decision.

She got out her bicycle and walked four miles, into the next village, to see her brother. Though she did not ride the bicycle, it seemed to her as essential as ever that she should take it with her. Grasping its handles, she felt a sense of security and fortitude. The notion of walking without it, helplessly, in the darkness, was unthinkable.

Her brother was a master carpenter, a chapel-going man of straight-grained thinking and purpose, who had no patience with slovenliness. He lived with his wife and his mother in a white-painted electrically-lighted housed whose floors were covered with scrubbed coco-matting. His mother was a small woman with shrill eyes and ironed-out mouth who could not hear well.

Mrs Thurlow knocked on the door of the house as though these people, her mother and brother, were strangers to her. Her brother came to the door and she said:

"It's Lil. I come to see if you'd seen anything o' Thurlow?"

"No, we ain't seen him. Summat up?"

"Who is it?" the old woman called.

"It's Lil," the brother said, in a louder voice. "She says have we seen anything o' Thurlow?"

"No, an' don't want!"

Mrs Thurlow went in. For fifteen years her family had openly disapproved of Thurlow. She sat down on the edge of the chair nearest the door. Her large lace-up boots made large black mud prints on the virgin coco-matting. She saw her sister-in-law look first at her boots and then at her hat. She had worn the same boots and the same hat for longer than she herself could remember. But her sister-in-law remembered.

She sat untroubled, her eyes sullen, as though not fully conscious in the bright electric light. The light showed up the mud on her skirt, her straggling grey hair under the shapeless hat, the edges of her black coat weather-faded to a purplish grey.

"So you ain't heard nothing about Thurlow?" she said.

"No," her brother said. "Be funny if we had, wouldn't it? He ain't set foot in this house since dad died." He looked at her hard. "Why? What's up?"

She raised her eyes to him. Then she lowered them again. It was almost a minute before she spoke.

"Ain't you heard?" she said. "They reckon he's done a

murder."

"What's she say?" the old lady said. "I never heard her."

Mrs Thurlow looked dully at her boots, at the surrounding expanse of coco-matting. For some reason the fissured pattern of the coco-matting, so clean and regular, fascinated her. She said: "He took all the money. He took it all and they can't find him."

"Eh? What's she say? What's she mumbling about?"

The brother, his face white, went over to the old woman. He said into her ear: "One of the boys is won a scholarship. She come over to tell us."

"Want summat to do, I should think, don't she? Traipsing over here to tell us that."

The man sat down at the table. He was very white, his hands shaking. His wife sat with the same dumb, shaking expression of shock. Mrs Thurlow raised her eyes from the floor. It was as though she had placed on them the onus of some terrible responsibility.

"For God's sake," the man said, "when did it happen?"

All Mrs Thurlow could think of was the money. "Over fifty pounds. I got it hid under the mattress. I don't know how he could have found out about it. I don't know. I can't think. It's all I got. I got it for the boys." She paused, pursing her lips together, squeezing back emotion. "It's about the boys I come."

"The boys?" The brother looked up, scared afresh. "He ain't —they—"

"I didn't know whether you'd have them here," she said. "Till it's blowed over. Till they find Thurlow. Till things are straightened out."

"Then they ain't found him?"

"No. He's done a bunk. They say as soon as they find him I shall git the money."

"Yes," the brother said. "We'll have them here."

She stayed a little longer, telling the story dully, flatly, to the two scared pairs of eyes across the table and to the old shrill eyes, enraged because they could not understand, regarding her from the fireplace. An hour after she had arrived, she got up to go. Her brother said: "Let me run you back in the car. I got a car now. Had it three or four months. I'll run you back."

"No, I got my bike," she said.

She pushed the bicycle home in the darkness. At home, in the kitchen, the two boys were making a rabbit hutch. She saw that they had something of her brother's zeal for handling wood. She saw that their going to him would be a good thing. He was a man who had got on in the world: she judged him by the car, the white-painted house, the electric light, the spotless coco-matting. She saw the boys, with deep but inexpressible pride, going to the same height, beyond it.

"Dad ain't been home," they said.

She told them there had been a little trouble. "They think your dad took some money." She explained how it would be better for them, and for her, if they went to stay with her brother. "Git to bed now and I'll get your things packed."

"You mean we gotta go and live there?"

"For a bit," she said.

They were excited. "We could plane the wood for the rabbit hutch!" they said. "Make a proper job of it."

IV

That night, and again on the following morning, she looked under the mattress for the money. In the morning the boys departed. She was slightly depressed, slightly relieved by their excitement. When they had gone she bundled the day's washing together and tied it on the bicycle. She noticed, then, that the back tyre had a slow puncture, that it was already almost flat. This worried her. She pumped up the tyre and felt a little more confident.

Then, as she prepared to push the bicycle down the hill, she saw the police car coming along the road at the bottom. Two policemen hurried up the track to meet her.

"We got Thurlow," they said. "We'd like you to come to the station."

"Is he got the money?" she said.

"There hasn't been time," they said, "to go into that."

As on the previous morning she pushed her bicycle to the village, walking with one policeman while the other drove on in the car. Of Thurlow she said very little. Now and then she stopped and stooped to pinch the back tyre of the bicycle. "Like I thought. I got a slow puncture," she would say. "Yes, it's gone down since I blowed it up. I s'll have to leave it at the bike shop as we go by."

Once she asked the policeman if he thought that Thurlow had the money. He said, "I'm afraid he's done something more serious than taking money."

She pondered over this statement with dull astonishment. More serious? She knew that nothing could be more serious. To her the money was like a huge and irreplaceable section of her life. It was part of herself, bone and flesh, blood and sweat. Nothing could replace it. Nothing, she knew with absolute finality, could mean so much.

In the village she left the bicycle at the cycle shop. Walking on without it, she lumbered dully from side to side, huge and unsteady, as though lost. From the cycle-shop window the repairer squinted after her, excited. Other people looked from other windows as she lumbered past, always a pace or two behind the policeman, her ill-shaped feet painfully set down. At the entrance to the police station there was a small crowd. She went heavily into the station. Policemen were standing about in a room. An inspector, many papers in his hand, spoke to her. She listened heavily. She looked about for a sign of Thurlow. The inspector said, with kindness, "Your husband is not here." She felt a sense of having been cheated. "They are detaining him at Metford. We are going over there now."

"You know anything about the money?" she said.

Five minutes later she drove away, with the inspector and two other policemen, in a large black car. Travelling fast, she felt herself hurled, as it were, beyond herself. Mind and body seemed separated, her thoughts nullified. As the car entered the town, slowing down, she looked out of the side windows, saw posters: "Metford Murder Arrest." People, seeing policemen in the car, gaped. "Murder Sensation Man Detained."

Her mind registered impressions gravely and confusedly. People and posters were swept away from her and she was conscious of their being replaced by other people, the police station, corridors in the station, walls of brown glazed brick, fresh faces, a room, desks covered with many papers, eyes looking at her, box files in white rows appearing also to look at her, voices talking to her, an arm touching her, a voice asking her to sit down.

"I have to tell you, Mrs Thurlow, that we have detained your husband on a charge of murder."

"He say anything about the money?"

"He has made a statement. In a few minutes he will be charged and then probably remanded for further inquiries. You are at liberty to see him for a few moments if you would like to do so."

In a few moments she was standing in a cell, looking at Thurlow. He looked at her as though he did not know what had happened. His eyes were lumps of impressionless glass. He stood with long arms loose at his sides. For some reason he looked strange, foreign, not himself. It was more than a minute before she realised why this was. Then she saw that he was wearing a new suit. It was a grey suit, thick, ready-made, and the sleeves were too short for him. They hung several inches above his thick protruberant wrist bones, giving his hands a look of inert defeat.

"You got the money, ain't you?" she said. "You got it?"

He looked at her. "Money?"

"The money you took. The money under the mattress."

He stared at her. Money? He looked at her with a faint expression of appeal. Money. He continued to stare at her with complete blankness. Money?

"You remember," she said. "The money under the mattress."

"Eh?"

"The money. That money. Don't you remember?"

After some moments she went out of the cell. She carried out with her the sense of Thurlow's defeat as she saw it expressed in the inert hands, the dead, stupefied face, and his vacant inability to remember anything. She heard the court proceedings without interest or emotion. She was oppressed by a sense of increasing bewilderment, a feeling that she was lost. She was stormed by impressions she did not understand. "I do not propose to put in a statement at this juncture. I ask for a remand until the sixteenth." "Remand granted. Clear the court."

This effect of being stormed by impressions continued outside the court, as she drove away again in the car. People. Many faces. Cameras. More faces. Posters. The old sensation of mind severed from body, of thoughts nullified. In the village, when the car stopped, there were more impressions: more voices, more people, a feeling of suppressed excitement. "We will run you home," the policemen said.

"No," she said. "I got my cleaning to do. I got to pick up my bicycle."

She fetched the bicycle and wheeled it slowly through the village. People looked at her, seemed surprised to see her in broad daylight, made gestures as though they wished to speak, and then went on. Grasping the handles of the bicycle, she felt a return of security, almost of comfort. The familiar smooth handlebars hard against her hands had the living response of other hands They brought back her sense of reality: Miss Hanley, the cleaning, the poultry farm, the time she had lost, the boys, the money, the fact that something terrible had happened, the monumental fact of Thurlow's face, inert and dead, with its lost sense of remembrance.

Oppressed by a sense of duty, she did her cleaning as though nothing had happened. People were very kind to her. Miss Hanley made tea, the retired photographer would have run her home in his car. She was met everywhere by tender, remote words of comfort.

She pushed home her bicycle in the darkness. At Miss Hanley's, at the poultry farm, at the various places where she worked, the thought of the money had been partially set aside. Now, alone again, she felt the force of its importance more strongly, with the beginnings of bitterness. In the empty house she worked for several hours by candlelight, washing, folding, ironing, About the house the vague noises of wind periodically resolved themselves into what she believed for a moment were the voices of the two boys. She thought of the boys with calm unhappiness, and the thought of them brought back with renewed force the thought of the money. This thought hung over her with the huge preponderance of her own shadow projected on the ceiling above her.

On the following Sunday afternoon she sat in the empty kitchen, as usual, and read the stale newspapers. But now they recorded, not the unreal lives of other people, but the life of Thurlow and herself. She saw Thurlow's photograph. She read the same story told in different words in different papers. In all the stories there was an absence of all mention of the only thing that mattered. There was no single word about the money.

During the next few weeks much happened, but she did not lose the belief that the money was coming back to her. Nothing could touch the hard central core of her optimism. She saw the slow evolution of circumstances about Thurlow as things of subsidiary importance, the loss of the life he had taken and the loss of his own life as things which, terrible in themselves, seemed less terrible than the loss of ideals built up by her sweat and blood.

She knew, gradually, that Thurlow was doomed, that it was all over. She did not know what to do. Her terror seemed remote, muffled, in some way incoherent. She pushed the bicycle back and forth each day in the same ponderous manner as ever, her heavy feet slopping dully beside it.

When she saw Thurlow for the last time his face had not changed, one way or the other, from its fixed expression of defeat.

Defeat was cemented into it with imperishable finality. She asked him about the money for the last time.

"Eh?"

"The money. You took it. What you do with it? That money. Under the mattress." For the first time she showed some sign of desperation. "Please, what you done with it? That money. My money?"

"Eh?" And she knew that he could not remember.

V

A day later it was all over. Two days later she pushed the bicycle the four miles to the next village, to see her brother. It was springtime, time for the boys to come back to her. Pushing the bicycle in the twilight, she felt she was pushing forward into the future. She had some dim idea, heavily dulled by the sense of Thurlow's death, that the loss of the money was not now so great. Money is money; death is death; the living are the living. The living were the future. The thought of the boys' return filled her with hopes for the future, unelated hopes, but quite real, strong enough to surmount the loss of both Thurlow and money.

At her brother's they had nothing to say. They sat, the brother, the mother, and the sister-in-law, and looked at her with eyes over which, as it were, the blinds had been drawn.

"The boys here?" she said.

"They're in the workshop," her brother said. "They're making a bit of a wheelbarrow."

"They all right?"

"Yes." He wetted his lips. His clean-planned mind had been scarred by events as though by a mishandled tool. "They don't know nothing. We kept it from 'em. They ain't been to school and they ain't seen no papers. They think he's in jail for stealing money."

She looked at him, dully. "Stealing money? That's what he did do. That money I told you about. That money I had under the mattress."

"Well," he said slowly, "it's done now."

"What did he do with it?" she said. "What d'ye reckon he done with it?"

He looked at her quickly, unable suddenly to restrain his anger.

"Done with it? What d'ye suppose he done with it? Spent it. Threw it away. Boozed it. What else? You know what he was like. You knew! You had your eyes open. You knew what—"

"Will, Will," his wife said.

He was silent. The old lady said: "Eh? What's that? What's the matter now?"

The brother said, in a loud voice, "Nothing." Then more softly: "She don't know everything."

"I came to take the boys back," Mrs Thurlow said.

He was silent again. He wetted his lips. He struck a match on the warm fire-hob. It spurted into a sudden explosion, igniting of its own volition. He seemed startled. He put the match to his pipe, let it go out.

He looked at Mrs Thurlow, the dead match in his hands. "The boys ain't coming back no more," he said.

"Eh?" she said. She was stunned. "They ain't what?"

"They don't want to come back," he said.

She did not understand. She could not speak. Very slowly he said:

"It's natural they don't want to come back. I know it's hard. But it's natural. They're getting on well here. They want to stop here. They're good boys. I could take 'em into the business."

She heard him go on without hearing the individual words. He broke off, his face relieved—like a man who has liquidated some awful obligation.

"They're my boys," she said. "They got a right to say what they shall do and what they shan't do."

She spoke heavily, without bitterness.

"I know that," he said. "That's right. They got a right to speak. You want to hear what they got to say?"

"Yes, I want to," she said.

Her sister-in-law went out into the yard at the back of the house. Soon voices drew nearer out of the darkness and the two boys came in.

"Hullo," she said.

"Hello, Mum," they said.

"Your Mum's come," the carpenter said, "to see if you want to go back with her."

The two boys stood silent, awkward, eyes glancing past her.

"You want to go?" the carpenter said. "Or do you want to stay here?"

"Here," the elder boy said. "We want to stop here."

"You're sure o' that?"

"Yes," the other said.

Mrs Thurlow stood silent. She could think of nothing to say in protest or argument or persuasion. Nothing she could say would, she felt, give expression to the inner part of herself, the crushed core of optimism and faith.

She stood at the door, looking back at the boys. "You made up your minds, then?" she said. They did not speak.

"I'll run you home," her brother said.

"No," she said. "I got my bike."

She went out of the house and began to push the bicycle slowly home in the darkness. She walked with head down, lumbering painfully, as though direction did not matter. Whereas, coming, she had seemed to be pushing forward into the future, she now felt as if she were pushing forward into nowhere.

After a mile or so she heard a faint hissing from the back tyre. She stopped, pressing the tyre with her hand. "It's slow," she thought; "it'll last me." She pushed forward. A little later it seemed to her that the hissing got worse. She stopped again, and again felt the tyre with her hand. It was softer now, almost flat.

She unscrewed the pump and put a little air in the tyre and went on. "I better stop at the shop," she thought, "and have it done."

In the village the cycle-shop was already in darkness. She pushed past it. As she came to the hill leading up to the house she lifted her head a little. It seemed to her suddenly that the house, outlined darkly above the dark hill, was a long way off. She had for one moment an impression that she would never reach it.

She struggled up the hill. The mud of the track seemed to suck at her great boots and hold her down. The wheels of the bicycle seemed as if they would not turn, and she could hear the noise of the air dying once again in the tyre.

The Good Corn

For twenty-five years Joe Mortimer and his wife had lived in a valley, getting a living from raising hens and geese, a few cows and calves, the fruit from half a dozen cherry trees and an acre or two of corn.

Their small red brick house, surrounded by coops of wire and low wooden sheds for chickens, stood close to a railway line, and occasionally passengers could look out and see, walking about the small grass paddock or across the bare autumn stubbles, a woman with wispy fair hair and long brown arms. Sometimes she was lovingly leading a calf by a halter; sometimes she seemed to be earnestly talking to flocks of geese and hens. At times a man was with her: a tall gaunt-framed man with close-cut hair and spare knotty muscle and water-blue eyes that slowly lifted themselves and gazed absently on the windows of passing trains. In summer there were always many children on the trains, eagerly pressing faces to the glass as they travelled down to the sea, and whenever the Mortimers caught sight of them there was a sudden brightness on their faces, a great eagerness, almost an illumination, as they smiled and waved their hands.

Every Tuesday and again on Saturday the Mortimers drove in a small black truck to market. They took with them cases of eggs, half a dozen unplucked brown chickens, a few chips of cherries in their season and odd things like bunches of turnips *and* onions, a brace of pigeons, a hare, and daffodils carefully tied in dozens.

In the evenings, when they came home again, they counted out their money on the kitchen table. They laid it out in little piles of silver and copper and notes, counting it several times to make sure how much they had.

Then when the counting was finished Joe Mortimer would divide the money exactly in half. Solemnly, from the very beginning of their marriage, he would put one half into a tin cash box and then push the other across to his wife, who took it from him with long, uneager hands.

"You know what that's for," he would say, "put that away."

At first they were quite sure about children. It seemed as natural to think of children coming as to think of eggs in the hen-runs and calves for cows and flowers on cherry trees. It was merely a question of time before children came. Mrs Mortimer thought of children laughing and running among flocks of hens, scattering grain, tossing it among the snapping, quarrelling brown feathers. In early spring in cold wet weather, she sometimes nursed the first yellow chicks in warm flannel, in baskets, under the kitchen stove. That was the sort of thing children always loved, she thought.

It was in summer, when the corn was ready, that Mortimer thought of them most. In imagination he saw boys riding in harvest carts or chasing rabbits among shocks of wheat and barley. He saw himself cutting them ash-plants from hedgerows or teaching them to thresh wheat in the palms of their hands. He saw them bouncing on piles of fresh light straw on threshing days.

Then gradually, as time went by and there were no children, he became resigned to it in a puzzled, absent sort of way. It did not embitter him. If there were no children there were no children, he thought. That was nature; that was how it was. You could not alter that. It turned out like that with some people. There was nothing you could do about it but hope and make the best of it.

But his wife could not see it like that. It was not simply that she wanted children; it was not merely a question of pride. It was a woman's duty to have children; it was all of a woman's life to give birth. Not to bear children, when her pride was deep, was something more to a woman than misfortune. It was a failure in her living. It was like a hen that did not lay eggs or a cow that was sterile or a tree that never came into blossom. There was no point in the existence of them.

As time went on she drew more and more into herself. With something more than injured pride she drew deep down into an isolation where she thought of nothing but the failure that came from sterility. The reproach of failure never left her; she could not grow used to the pain of it. It was like a gnawing physical disability, an ugly mark she wanted to hide.

All the time, waiting for children, the two of them worked very hard. They saved money. Chickens and eggs went to market every week; cherries brought good money in summer; there was always enough corn for the hens and enough hay for the cows and calves and plenty over.

Whenever a new calf came she cried a little. The mournful tender glassiness of a cow's big eyes after birth was something she could not bear. She liked to lift the soft wet heads of the new calves and hold them in her arms. She liked the smell of milk on their faces and the gluey suck of their mouths if she fed them from the bucket.

After they had been married twenty-five years she stood one morning in the small cow-shed at the back of the house and watched a calf die in her arms. It was a red heifer calf and she began to cry bitterly. The calf had been dropped in the meadow the previous afternoon, prematurely, while she and Mortimer were at market. A cold wet wind with hail in it was blowing from the west. The calf could not stand on its feet by the time she and Mortimer found it and there was a drift of wet hail along the side of its body.

She went on to grieve about the calf. The death of the calf became a personal thing. She found she could not sleep at night. She bit the edges of the pillow so that she could lay and cry without a sound. After a time there was a continuous pain in her chest: a great bony bolt that shot across her throat and made it difficult to swallow.

At the same time she began to despise herself.

"Don't come near me. I'm no good to you. You should have found someone else, not me. What have I done for you? What good have I ever been?"

"Don't say that. Don't talk like that," Mortimer said. "You're not well. You're not yourself. I'm going to get the doctor to look at you."

The doctor spent a long time with her in the bedroom, alone, sitting on the edge of the bed, asking questions. She stared at him most of the time with pallid, boring eyes. After a time he went downstairs and gave Mortimer a pipe of tobacco and walked about the yard, among the crying geese, and talked to him.

"All she can talk about is how she's been no good to me," Joe said. "How I'm not to go near her. How she hates herself. How she's been a failure all the time."

The doctor did not answer; the geese cried and squawked among the barns.

"Neither one of us is sleeping well," Joe said. "I can't put up with it. I can't stand it much longer."

"Was there something that began it?"

"The calf. We lost a calf about three weeks ago. She blamed

herself for that."

"Never thought of going away from here?" the doctor said.

"Away?"

"How long have you lived here?"

"Five and twenty years. Nearly six and twenty."

"I believe you might do well to move," the doctor said.

"Move? Where to? What for?"

"It might be that everything here has the same association. This is where she wanted her children and this is where she never had them. She might be happier if you moved away from here."

"She misses children. She'd have been all right with children," Joe said.

"Think it over," the doctor said. "She needs a rest too. Get her to take it a little easier. Get a girl to help in the kitchen and with the hens. It'll be company for her. Perhaps she won't think of herself so much."

"All right. It upsets me to see her break her heart like that."

"I wish I were a farmer. If I were a farmer you know what I'd like to do?" the doctor siad. "Grow nothing but corn. That's the life. Give up practically everything but corn. With the cows and stock and birds it's all day and every day. But with corn you go away and you come back and your corn's still there. It's a wonderful thing, corn. That's what I'd like to do. There's something marvellous about corn."

The following spring they moved to a farm some distance up the hill. All their married lives they had lived on flat land, with no view except the hedges of their own fields and a shining stretch of railway line. Now they found themselves with land that ran away on a gentle slope, with a view below it of an entire broad valley across which trains ran like smoking toys.

The girl who answered their advertisement for help was short and dark, with rather sleepy brown eyes, a thick bright complexion and rosy-knuckled hands. She called at the house with her mother, who did most of what talking there was.

"She's been a bit off colour. But she's better now. She wants to work in the fresh air for a bit. You want to work in the fresh air, don't you, Elsie?"

"Yes," Elsie said.

"She's very quiet, but she'll get used to you," her mother said. "She don't say much, but she'll get used to you. She's not particular either. You're not particular, are you, Elsie?"

"No," Elsie said.

"She's a good girl. She won't give no trouble," her mother said.

"How old is she?" Mortimer said.

"Eighteen," her mother said. "Eighteen and in her nineteen. She'll be nineteen next birthday, won't you, Elsie?"

"Yes," Elsie said.

The girl settled into the house and moved about it with unobtrusive quietness. As she stood at the kitchen sink, staring down across the farm-yard, at the greening hedgerows of hawthorn and the rising fields of corn, she let her big-knuckled fingers wander dreamily over the wet surface of the dishes as if she were a blind person trying to trace a pattern. Her brown eyes travelled over the fields as if she were searching for something she had lost there.

Something about this lost and dreamy attitude gradually began to puzzle Mrs Mortimer. She saw in the staring brown eyes an expression that reminded her of the glazed eyes of a calf.

"You won't get lonely up here, will you?" she said. "I don't want you to get lonely."

"No," the girl said.

"You tell me if you get anyways lonely, won't you?"

"Yes."

"I want you to feel happy here," Mrs Mortimer said. "I want you to feel as if you was one of our own."

As the summer went on the presence of the girl seemed occasionally to comfort Mrs Mortimer. Sometimes she was a little more content; she did not despise herself so much. During daytime at least she could look out on new fields, over new distances, and almost persuade herself that what she saw was a different sky. But at night, in darkness, the gnaw of self-reproaches remained. She could not prevent the old cry from breaking out:

"Don't come near me. Not yet. Soon perhaps—but not yet. Not until I feel better about things. I will one day, but not yet."

Once or twice she even cried: "You could get someone else. I wouldn't mind. I honestly wouldn't mind. It's hard for you I know it is. I wouldn't mind."

Sometimes Mortimer, distracted too, got up and walked about the yard in summer darkness, smoking hard, staring at the summer stars.

All summer, in the afternoons, after she had worked in the house all morning, the girl helped about the yard and the fields. By July the corn was level as a mat of thick blue-green pile between hedgerows of wild rose and blackberry flower. In the garden in front of the house bushes of currant were bright with berries that glistened like scarlet pearls from under old lace curtains.

The thick fingers of the girl were stained red with the juice of currants as she gathered them. Her fingermarks were bright smears across the heavy front of her cotton pinafore.

As the two women knelt among the bushes, in alley-ways of ripe fruit, lifting the bleached creamy curtains in the July sun, Mrs Mortimer said:

"I'm glad of another pair of hands. I don't know what I should have done without another pair of hands. Your mother will miss you back home I reckon."

"She's got six more to help," the girl said. "She don't need me all that much."

"Six? Not children?"

"When I was home there was seven. Eight before the baby went."

"Before the baby went? Whose baby? What happened to the baby?"

"It was mine. I gave it away," the girl said. "I didn't know what to do with it no sense, so I gave it away. My sister adopted it. They all said it was best like that. I gave it to my married sister."

"Gave it away?" Mrs Mortimer sat on the earth, between the bushes, feeling sick. "Gave it away? A baby? You gave it away?"

"Yes," Elsie said. "It's no bother to me now."

Towards the end of the month the first corn began to ripen. The sheen of olive on the wheat began to turn pale yellow, then to the colour of fresh-baked crust on bread.

As he looked at it Mortimer remembered what the doctor had said. "You go away and you come back and your corn's still there. It's a wonderful thing, corn. There's something marvellous about corn."

Now as he looked at it he could not help feeling proud of the corn. It helped him too as he thought of his wife. It hurt him to hear her cry that he must keep away from her, that the pride in her was still tortured, the love in her not smoothed out. The corn helped to soothe him a little. The wind that ran darkly across it on cloudy days had a beautiful twist as if long snakes were slipping among the ears.

In the evenings, after supper, while the two women washed the dishes, he was often alone with the corn. And one evening as he stood watching it he did something he had always liked to do. He broke off an ear and began to thresh it in his hands, breaking the husk from the grain with the pressure of the balls of his thumbs.

While he was still doing this the girl came down the hillside from the house with a message that a man had called to deliver a sailcloth. Mortimer blew on the grain that lay in his cupped hands, scattering a dancing cloud of chaff like summer flies.

"I'll be up in a minute," he said. "Here—tell me what you think of that."

"The wheat?" she said.

She picked a few grains of wheat from the palm of his hand. She did not toss them into her mouth but put them in one by one, with the tips of her fingers, biting them with the front of her teeth. Her teeth were surprisingly level and white and he could see the whiteness of the new grains on her tongue as she bit them.

"They're milky," she said.

"Still want a few more days, I think," he said.

As they walked back up the field she plucked an ear of wheat as high as the girl herself, rustled in her fingers. When she bent down to blow on the husks a small gust of wind suddenly turned and blew the chaff up into her face. She laughed rather loudly, showing her teeth again, and he said:

"Here, you want to do it like this. You want to bring your thumbs over so that you can blow down there and make a chimney."

"How?" she said.

A moment later he was holding her hands. He stood slightly behind her and held her hands and showed her how to cup them so that the chaff could blow out through the chimney made by her fingers.

"Now blow," he said.

"I can't blow for laughing."

Her mouth spluttered and a new gust of laughter blew into her hands and a dancing cloud of chaff leapt up in a spurt from her fingers. She laughed again and he felt her body shaking. A few husks of wheat blew into her mouth and a few more stuck to the moist edges of her lips as she laughed.

She pulled out her handkerchief to wipe her lips, still laughing, and suddenly he found himself trying to help her and then in a clumsy way trying to kiss her face and mouth at the same time.

"Elsie," he said. "Here, Elsie——"

She laughed again and said, "We don't want to fool here. Somebody will see us if we start fooling here. Mrs Mortimer will see us. Not here."

"You were always so quiet," he said.

"It isn't always the loud ones who say most, is it?" she said. She began to shake herself. "Now I've got chaff down my neck. Look at me."

She laughed again and shook herself, twisting her body in a way that suddenly reminded him of the twist of dark air running among the ripening corn. He tried to kiss her again and she said:

"Not here I keep telling you. Some time if you like but not here. Not in broad daylight. I don't like people watching me."

"All right——"

"Some other time. It's so public here," she said. "There'll be another time."

By the end of August the corn was cut and carted. The stubbles were empty except for the girl and Mrs Mortimer, gleaning on fine afternoons, and a few brown hens scratching among the straw. "I could never quite give up the hens," Mrs Mortimer said. "It would be an awful wrench to give them up. I didn't mind the cherries and I didn't even mind the calves so much. But the hens are company. I can talk to the hens."

About the house, in the yard, bright yellow stacks stood ready for threshing, and there was a fresh clean smell of straw on the air. During summer the face of the girl had reddened with sun and air and as autumn came on it seemed to broaden and flatten, the thick skin ripe and healthy in texture.

"Soon be winter coming on, Elsie," Mrs Mortimer said. "You think you'll stay up here with us for the winter?"

"Well, I expect I shall if nothing happens," Elsie said.

"Happens? If what happens?"

"Well, you never know what may happen," Elsie said, "do you?"

"I want you to stay if you can," Mrs Mortimer said. "They get a lot of snow up here some winters, but perhaps we'll be lucky. Stay if you can. I got now so as I think of you as one of our own."

In a growing fondness for the girl Mrs Mortimer occasionally remembered and reflected on the incident of the baby. It was very strange and inexplicable to her, the incident of the baby. It filled her with mystery and wonder. It was a mystery beyond comprehension that a girl could conceive and bear a child and then, having delivered it, give it away. She felt she would never be able to grasp the reasons for that. "You'd think it would be like tearing your own heart out to do a thing like that," she thought.

Towards the end of November the first snow fell, covering the hillsides down to within a hundred feet of the valley. The house stood almost on the dividing line of snow, like a boat at the edge of a tide, between fields that were still fresh green with winter corn and others smooth with the first thin white fall.

"I got something to tell you," the girl said to Mrs Mortimer. "I don't think I'll be staying here much longer."

"Not staying?"

"No."

"Why not?"

"I don't think I will, that's all."

"Is it the snow? You don't like the snow, do you? That's what it is, the snow."

"It's not the snow so much."

"Is it us then?" Mrs Mortimer said. "Don't you like us no more?"

"I like you. It isn't that," the girl said.

"What is it then, Elsie? Don't say you'll go. What is it?"

"It's the baby," Elsie said.

"The baby?" Mrs Mortimer felt a pain of tears in her eyes. "I somehow thought one day you'd want it back. I'm glad."

"Not that baby," the girl said. "Not that one. I'm going to have another."

Mrs Mortimer felt a strange sense of disturbance. She was shaken once again by disbelief and pain. She could not speak and the girl said:

"In the Spring. April I think it'll be."

"How did you come to do that?" Mrs Mortimer said. "Up here? With us——?"

"I know somebody," the girl said. "I got to know somebody. That's all."

"I don't understand," Mrs Mortimer said. She spoke quietly, almost to herself. She thought, with the old pain, of her years of sterility. She remembered how, in distraction, she had so much despised herself, how she had turned, out of pride, into isolation, away from Joe. "I don't understand," she said.

At night she turned restlessly in her bed. Splinters of moonlight between the edges of the curtains cut across her eyes and kept them stiffly open.

"Can't you sleep again?" Joe said.

"It's the girl," she said. "Elsie. I can't get her out of my mind."

"What's wrong with Elsie?"

"She's having another baby," she said. "In the Spring."

"Oh! no!" he said. "Oh! no. No. You don't mean that? No."

"It seems she got to know somebody. Somehow," she said. She felt across her eyes the hard stab of moonlight. She turned and put her hand out and touched Joe on the shoulder. "Joe," she said. "That doesn't seem right, does it? It doesn't seem fair."

Joe did not answer.

"It doesn't seem fair. It's not right. It seems cruel," she said.

The following night she could not sleep again. She heard a westerly wind from across the valley beating light squalls of rain on the windows of the bedroom. The air was mild in a sudden change and she lay with her arms outside the coverlet, listening to the rain washing away the snow.

Suddenly Joe took hold of her hands and began crying into them.

"I didn't know what I was doing. She kept asking me. It was her who kept asking me."

She could not speak and he turned his face to the pillow.

"I didn't think you wanted me. You used to say so. I got so as I thought you didn't want me any more. You used to say——"

"I want you," she said. "Don't be afraid of that."

"Did she say anything?" he said. "Did she say it was me?"

"No. She didn't say."

"Did you think it was me?"

"I'd begun to think," she said. "I thought I could tell by the way you couldn't look at her."

She heard him draw his breath in dry snatches, unable to find words. Suddenly she was sorry for him, with no anger or reproach or bitterness, and she stretched out her long bare arms.

"Come here to me," she said. "Come close to me. I'm sorry. It was me. It was my fault."

"Never," he said. "Never. I won't have that——"

"Listen to me," she said. "Listen to what I say."

As she spoke she was aware of a feeling of being uplifted, of a depressive weight being taken from her.

"Listen, Joe, if I ask her perhaps she'll give it to us. You remember? She gave the other away."

"No," he said. "You couldn't do that——"

"I could," she said. She began smiling to herself in the darkness. "Tomorrow I'll ask her. We could do it properly—so that it was ours."

"If you forgive me," Joe said. "Only if you do that——"

"I forgive you," she said.

She went through the rest of the winter as if she were carrying the baby herself. "You mustn't do that, Elsie. Don't lift that," she would say: "Take a lie down for an hour. Rest yourself—it'll do you the world of good to rest." She looked forward to Spring with a strange acute sensation of being poised on a wire, frightened that she would fall before she got there.

When the baby was born she wrapped it in a warm blanket and succoured it like the early chickens she had once wrapped in flannel, in a basket, under the stove.

"And I can have him?" she said. "You haven't changed your mind? You won't change your mind, will you?"

"No," the girl said. "You can have him. I don't want the bother. You can look after him."

"We'll love him," she said. "We'll look after him."

On a day in late April she took the baby and carried him down through the yard, in the sunshine, to where the fields began. Hedgerows were breaking everywhere into bright new leaf. Primroses lay in thick pale drifts under the shelter of them and under clumps of ash and hornbeam. In every turn of wind there was a whitening of anemones, with cowslips trembling gold about the pasture.

She lifted the baby up, in the sunshine, against the blue spring sky, and laughed and shook him gently, showing him the world of leaf and flower and corn.

"Look at all the flowers!" she said. "Look at the corn! The corn looks good, doesn't it? It's going to be good this year, isn't it? Look at it all!—isn't the corn beautiful?"

High above her, on the hill, there was a sound of endless lark song and in the fields the young curved lines of corn were wonderfully fresh and trembling in the sun.

Mr Penfold

Mr Penfold, a travelling draper and haberdasher, easy terms arranged, a painfully shy, retreating man with almost invisible eyelashes, who looked as if he would have been much happier walking backwards, struggled out into the countryside every other Thursday on a massive basket-work tricycle, and called on Mrs Armitage, a war-widow, and her daughter Katie. Mr Penfold, who was in his early forties, was a single man.

Mr Penfold had been calling on Mrs Armitage and her daughter ever since the war: so long that he had become like one of the family. To the Armitages, who lived at the bottom of a hill, in a red-brick house surrounded by large clumps of lilac under which there was a great trembling spread of snowdrops in early spring, Mr Penfold had become an institution. "Well, it's Mr Penfold's day," they said, every other Thursday; then, as the clock drew on to five in the afternoon, "It's nearly Mr Penfold's time"; and then, at last, as they heard the huge wicker-work carrier of the tricycle squeak and clump over the grass verge outside the house, "That'll be Mr Penfold". Then they waited for Mr Penfold's knock: a gentle retreating kind of knock, as if Mr Penfold had made it and run away. Finally, when with great timidity and decency Mr Penfold stepped over the threshold they would say, "Well, it's Mr Penfold!" as if he were a stranger turned up from a far country.

On this same afternoon once a fortnight there was always a cup of tea for Mr Penfold in the Armitages' comfortable living-room, and with it whatever the Armitages had: a boiled egg, tinned salmon, cake, fresh lettuce in summer. In return, after tea was over and the table cleared, Mr Penfold would carefully and almost religiously lay out his lines, stockings, knickers, handkerchiefs, ribbons, elastic, buttons, woollen combinations. And there would suddenly hang in the air a smell which, after so many years, had become to symbolise Mr Penfold: the dry, discreet odour of new drapery, a smell that had become to stand for the grave and timid discretion of a man who appeared to be for ever on the verge of folding himself up and putting himself away. It seemed sometimes as if this discretion might flower into something else. It seemed to Mrs Armitage, who was lonely and who had nothing to look forward to except the careful saving of her meagre pension and the growing up and perhaps finally the loss of Katie, that it might flower into something beyond friendship. For many years it seemed as if this might happen, but every Thursday she watched Mr Penfold go through the same painful, too-discreet process of folding himself up and putting himself away for another fortnight. She watched him manoeuvre the tricycle away from the house, and felt a strange conflict of anger and despair, and became resigned at last to the fact that Mr Penfold would never change, was perhaps incapable of change, except under the impetus of a revolution.

Though she did not notice it, this revolution was going on under her eyes, and once every fortnight under the eyes of Mr Penfold, though for many years he did not notice it either. There was a revolution going on in the young girl, Katie. When Mr Penfold first began to call on Mrs Armitage there was a baby in the house, and sometimes he would take the child on his knee. He had a small gold watch which struck the hours like a little bell, and the child would listen to it for a long time, with dark eyes that had alternate moods of sulkiness and vivacity. As she sat on Mr Penfold's knee he would stroke his hand backwards and forwards with grave pleasure across her hair, which was the colour of sun-bleached straw and which, Mrs Armitage said, would grow darker as she grew older. But for some reason, and to Mr Penfold's secret happiness, the hair never grew darker, but remained the one constant and beautiful element in the changing and growing girl.

For some years there were no changes in the girl that could startle Mr Penfold. He would see sometimes that the child had grown from one fortnight to another; there periodically came a time when she needed the next size in underclothes. When he expressed any feeling about the way the girl was growing and changing it was always one of surprise: surprise that time could go so quickly. "She'll be telling us what to do before we know where we are," he would say.

Then one summer, during the whole month of August, Katie went away to stay with an aunt, and it was six weeks before Mr Penfold saw her again. During this time there were changes, but to Mr Penfold unnoticed changes, in the behaviour of Mrs Armitage. One afternoon she said that the plums were ripe in the garden. Would he like to see them? He said yes, and in his simple way, that had no connection with and did not understand subtleties, he went into the garden with her. The plums were dark and thick on the high tree, the skins warm in the rich August sunshine. He took off his coat and climbed the long high ladder and found himself in a deep sun-trembling world of fruit and leaves, his basket hooked on a branch, his two hands free for the great bunches of plums that hung everywhere like blue grapes on the brittle branches. After a time he heard Mrs Armitage's voice and looked down and saw her coming up the ladder. It was very warm and she had loosened the neck of her dress. She was a neat, firm little woman with dark brown crinkled hair and a still young figure, and he had only to glance down in order to see the hollow of her breasts opening darkly in her loosened dress. She came up the ladder smiling, with slightly parted lips, but he did not seem to see either her breasts or her smile, and it did not occur to him that he had only to reach down and she would fall into his life more easily than the plums were falling into his hands.

He remained in the plum tree with her for more than two hours that afternoon, and at no time did he come near to understanding what had brought and kept him there. When he breathed the sweet, almost autumnal fragrance of ripe plums and saw the sunlight breaking through and quivering between the leaf-shadows on his hands and he said how lovely it was in the country, he did not grasp the meaning of her answer, that it was lovely but that you only understood how lovely it was until you lived there always. And when finally they left the tree and he carried the plums indoors for her and she gave him two glasses of her cool home-made wine to drink and begged him to stay and have a little supper, he was still as remote from the meaning of it all as ever. It was still as if he could never reverse the fixed process of habit and nature, and for once unfold and give himself, instead of folding himself up and putting himself away.

She was more angry than despairing when he went away that evening, but he did not know that either. He could not begin to know it, incapable as he was of understanding an inner meaning, kept as he had been by great shyness from any entry into a single great experience. He understood simple, visible things like a yard of velvet, a tree of plums, snowdrops in bloom, a pair of combinations. He understood that Mrs Armitage had been buying things from him every fortnight more or less for fifteen years and that she paid him by a system of rather parsimonious instalments which in his shyness he called "this week's", but he did not understand that she was lonely and unsatisfied.

A fortnight later he called again as usual, knocking in his timid way and waiting for an answer. But when the door opened he got for a moment the impression that it had been answered by a stranger.

This impression, which went stabbing through his mind like a needle, was gone almost at once, and he saw that the stranger was Katie. He saw with astonishment a clear, unmistakable thing before his eyes. In her absence Katie had grown up. She was some inches taller, but he saw more than that. She stood very erect, her young, newly-formed breasts pushing against her frock, and it seemed to him that she looked at him with eyes that had in them a kind of sulky hostility. The one thing about her that had not changed was her hair: it had the same shining blondness, but now against the dark self-conscious eyes it seemed doubly beautiful and striking.

He was so affected by this transition in the girl that as he came into the house he felt as if something were waiting to explode behind his shyness. He wanted to talk about it, to remark to Mrs Armitage how suddenly and unmistakably Katie had grown up. But he could not say anything and gradually his great sense of astonishment was repressed and folded away, to become in turn part of his shyness, to become as time went on something that he could not speak about or reveal.

But that afternoon he found himself forced to face the change in the girl in other ways. It was time, Mrs Armitage said, that Katie wore some sort of support. She believed in support early; there was nothing like it, she always held, for starting a good figure.

"Besides, she's going to leave school, and start to work."

"Work?" Mr Penfold said. "Why, what work, where?"

"She's going to work down in Denton," she said, "in Chapman's office. She starts next week. Yes, she's starting to work."

"Well," Mr Penfold said. "It doesn't seem five minutes since she was a baby."

As he said this, Mr Penfold looked up at the girl, who was standing in the room, her back against a high dresser, her arms folded behind her. He smiled, half expecting her to smile back, but he saw on her face only the new-born, adolescent resentment, not yet hostility, to what he suddenly felt was a foolish remark. Her direct, sulky stare brought all his own self-consciousness rushing to the surface, and he felt strangely, miserably foolish.

He turned hurriedly to the things on the table, and was immediately faced with a new problem. It was very rare that he carried such lines as belts or brassières and in fact corsetry was rather out of his line, and he knew that he had nothing suitable for the girl.

"But I could run the tape round her and bring some over special to-morrow."

"Well, that would do as well," Mrs Armitage said. "Katie, let Mr Penfold run the tape over you."

Mr Penfold produced the tape-measure from his pocket and unrolled it in his hands, but before he could do anything the girl sprung away from the dresser and went swiftly out of the room.

"Well!" Mrs Armitage said. "Well! And that's how she's been ever since she got back. Too big to be spoken to, too big to do anything. And now throwing her weight about. Well!"

"It's all right," Mr Penfold said. "Leave her alone. Shall I bring some sizes over to-morrow and she can try them on?"

"I don't know," Mrs Armitage said. "I'm sure I don't know. Perhaps we'd better go down to Lee and Porters and go up into the ladies' department and get it there."

"All right," Mr Penfold said.

"Seems they grow up to be ladies while your back's turned."

The girl did not come into the room again, and later Mr Penfold took away with him the startling impression of her sudden transition and the still more startling impression of her exit from the room. Whenever he thought of the two things he was filled with a sense of her beauty and rebellion. He was aware of the presence in her of moods and attributes which he had never foreseen in the child who had once sat on his knee, listening to his watch as it chimed the hours like a little bell.

When he called at the house again, a fortnight later, Katie was not there. Mrs Armitage looked at the clock on the mantelpiece and said, "She'll be here very shortly. She gets home about half-past five. Sometimes six."

"Does she like it?"

"You better ask her!" Mrs Armitage said. "I can't get a word out of her whether she likes it or not. She's got that proud she won't tell you anything."

Mr Penfold did not know what to say. Proud? It was a strange thing to be angry about. He sat down at the table as usual and Mrs Armitage gave him a cup of tea. And then, about half an hour later, he heard the door open and shut and the footsteps of the girl going upstairs.

"That's her," Mrs Armitage said. "One time o' day you couldn't horsewhip her into washing her hands before she sat down to table. Now she finicks about with them for hours."

Once again Mr Penfold did not say anything. He lingered over his tea with even more diffidence than usual, partly because the egg that Mrs Armitage had set before him seemed suddenly distasteful, partly because he wanted to remain in the room until the girl herself came down. In this mood of uncertainty, in which there was also a strange feeling of suspense, he let his tea grow cold, drinking it without quite knowing what he was doing.

The cup was actually at his lips when the girl came in, proud and silent and very soft-moving, so that she slipped into her chair, opposite him, as soundlessly as a soft blonde cat. He bade her good-evening, the tea still cold on his lips, and she answered him in a low voice. He saw at once that she had grown still more and that the transition from childhood to adolescence, just begun when he had seen her last, was now complete. Every movement and lack of movement now was mutinous with the self-conscious sense of her own beauty, so that he felt his own sense of surprise grow and change into a kind of absent-minded wonder, the cold tea-cup still in his hands and still foolishly suspended midway between his lips and the table, until he abruptly realised it and set it down with a clatter against the spoon.

A moment later he got up from the table and made some excuse about going. He knew that he could not sit there at the table with the girl any longer without something happening: something momentous or foolish or even, to his way of thinking, something terrible. He went out into the warm early September evening with a feeling very like fear uppermost in his heart. He did not know what he had to be afraid about; he was not even sure that what he felt was fear. But like fear the emotion propelled him forward, deeply disquieted, uncertain. That evening it still seemed like summer, with delicate fingers of honeysuckle outspread in the hedges, and the sun flat and warm and golden on the bright renewed September grass. The papers were saying that it was the finest September for many years, but now all at once he realized that he felt its beauty keenly not just because it was splendid weather but because it was emotionally linked with the beauty of the girl. He saw in the straw-gold colour of the honeysuckle the exact shade of her hair reproduced with fearful and lovely fidelity. The honeysuckle floated dreamily by him as he cycled past and in the same way he felt his dreamy thoughts about her run past him and gather in the distance, too numerous and diffident and troubled to catch.

From this moment he went on thinking of her, as it were, from a distance. He called at the house every other Thursday, not as if nothing had happened but in the hope that as time went on something would happen. Sometimes he saw the girl, but always with her mother; sometimes she was late from the office. More often than not he never spoke to her. She continued to remain mutinous and cool, her lips richly defiant, her young breasts rapidly growing ripe, to be carried soon with a new and conscious air of voluptuousness. In her presence he felt shyer than ever: shy, painfully inexperienced and sometimes foolish, the girl old and mature and fixed in beautiful contempt above him.

It was not until three years later that he suddenly found himself alone with her one evening. He had been held up by a puncture three miles away late in the afternoon and had mended it himself on the roadside. It was almost seven o'clock when he got to the house. He knocked shyly on the door as usual, and waited, and it was the girl herself who came in answer.

"Oh! it's Mr Penfold," she said. "Come in."

He went into the house. It was November and the milk-globed lamp was alight on the table. The light shone upward into the girl's blonde face and on her bright blue jumper and on her bare smooth arms and hands. But it was not only the beauty of her body, in the milky lamplight, that struck him. There was something else. There was a change in her voice and manner.

A moment later he knew the reason. "Is your mother in?" he said.

"No," the girl said. "She thought you couldn't be coming. She waited till six and now she's gone down to the village."

Her voice was amazingly friendly and free of all the old mutinous reserve. He had no time to understand it before in a warm, eager way she asked him if he would like some tea. He excused himself by saying it was too late but she said no, a place had been left for him and all she had to do was boil the kettle.

His astonishment at this change in her manner was tremendous. He felt as if he were speaking to her for the first time. He sat and warmed himself by the fire while waiting for the tea and then, as she began to pour it out, the curve of her bare arm clean as marble in the lamplight, he saw that she had brought two cups.

Yes, she said, she would have a cup with him, and if he didn't mind she was a bit cold and she would have it sitting on the rug. Before he knew what to say she curled herself up between a chair and the fender, her legs shining with the silvery-pink of ripe oat-straw in the firelight, her breasts drawn up under the close blue wool whenever she turned to look up at him. Then the reason for her prolonged strained attitude began gradually to be clear to him. He did not know what began it, but they began to talk about money. He was saying that the business was there if only the money was behind it. But he was finding money very tight. It had been tight all that year. "Not that I'm grumbling. I've saved and taken care of what I have had," he said, "only it's difficult to go on putting it by if you don't have it coming in."

When she spoke there was a flash of the old rebellion in her voice. "Yes, and it would puzzle you still more to save if you never had any to save," she said.

For a moment he did not grasp her meaning. Then it all began to come out, as if she had waited for a long time for a moment like this. She began to talk in a rapid, emotional voice, telling him her troubles. She had been at work for three years now and she was still being carried about by her mother. She worked with other girls who had freedom, took some part of their wages as a right, and had fun in the evenings. She had no money and no fun. All of her money went back to her mother, to be doled back in sixpences when she asked for it, to be sparingly saved in a penny-bank and, once saved, never touched again. All that the girl asked was a little freedom, some fun, a dance or two, an evening out once in a while. "That's all I want," she said passionately. "That's all I want. I want fun. That's all. And all the time she wants to keep me locked in a glass case."

Mr Penfold listened without knowing what to say, the tea once again growing cold in his hands. The girl would be about nineteen now and it grieved him deeply to see her reaching out for something, for happiness and fun, and not getting it.

He looked down at her a moment later and saw that she was crying. He found himself almost glad of her tears, which now saved him from the painful necessity of talking. He let her cry for a few moments and then put his hands lightly on her shoulders. It was the first time he had touched her. She did not move but, as though unaware of him, cried quietly and immovably into her hands. He wanted to move his own hands and grasp her tightly and in that way express the sympathy and affection he felt for her, but for what seemed a long time he could not overcome his shyness. At last he did overcome it and very gently moved his hands across her shoulders and partially embraced her.

They were sitting like this when Mrs Armitage suddenly burst into the room, almost as if she had been standing outside in the kitchen, listening. Mr Penfold hastily sat back in his chair and said that Katie was getting him some tea.

"Funny way of getting tea," Mrs Armitage said.

He went away shortly afterwards, without speaking again to the girl and without another word being said about her or about what Mrs Armitage had seen.

But when he called, a fortnight later, he knew that something had happened. That day he purposely changed his route, not arriving till six o'clock, but the girl was not there and it seemed to him that the atmosphere of the house was strange. He felt that the hostility that had so long been the girl's had for some reason suddenly been transferred to her mother. The table was not laid for tea and Mrs Armitage's hat and gloves and Mr Penfold's weekly payment book were on the table. No, she didn't want anything. No, there was nothing at all, and she was sorry but she had to go out in a hurry now.

"Where's Katie?" he said.

She looked at him with frank hostility and he knew that she was blaming him for something.

"Katie?" she said. "Katie's started to live in lodgings in Denton. She's been worrying about it long enough and now she's got her way."

"Oh," he said. He did not know what to say. It came to him that it was a very strange, sudden decision. There must be a reason for such an abrupt change of attitude. Suddenly he looked at Mrs Armitage. Her dark eyes were fixed on him with clear rebellious resentment and he knew then that the reason was himself. He knew that, prompted by some bitter, narrow sense of jealousy, she had taken the girl away from him.

"Will there be anything next time?" he said. It was all he could think to say. He had never said it in fifteen years.

"No!" she said. "I don't think there will."

"I'll call, just in case."

"Just as you like!" she said. She stood with her hat and gloves, waiting for him to go.

Two weeks later, for the first time in fifteen years, he did not call. He pushed the heavy tricycle about the lanes with a deep and pointless sense of frustration. He found himself taking the complication of events like a skein of tangled wool and trying to roll them into a simple ball. For what he wanted now was very simple. He wanted the love and beauty of the girl for himself. He wanted to open a little shop in the town and give up the tricycle. At the back of the shop there would be, he imagined, a room where they could eat, and over the shop a room where they could sit and look down at people passing in the street below. As he lived now he did not eat very well: hasty cold meals in the country, bits of bread and cheese washed down by cocoa in the evenings. But in the shop there would be contentment and comfort and the smell of steak and onions.

Finally he could bear it no longer. He decided to go back and call once again on Mrs Armitage. Conquering his shyness, he would somehow tell her what it was all about. For once he would unfold himself, and say how he wanted the girl, how he could go on no longer without her.

The following week, almost six weeks after his last call, he again knocked with his habitual timidity on the door, and then waited. It was a grey January afternoon, not quite dark, the land settled deep in winter, and he saw that the snowdrops were not yet out in the grass. It was Mrs Armitage who answered his knock, and she said:

"Oh! it's Mr Penfold."

She held open the door and he went into the house. As he entered the room he almost stopped. It seemed to him, just as it had once before, that a strange girl was sitting by the fire. It was Katie. She was wearing the same bright blue jumper as before and her hair, still as pale as honeysuckle, was brushed in the same way, yet she looked like an inexpressibly strange person, farther away from him than ever. As he came in she stood up, smiling a little. In a moment he knew that the smile, sudden and a little forced and without a trace of hostility, was the signal that something was the matter, and before he could speak to her she went out of the room.

He was surprised by that action but not really troubled. Perhaps it would be easier without her. "Has Katie come back?" he said. "I mean for good."

"I don't know what you mean, good," Mrs Armitage said. "She's come back."

"Is anything the matter?" he said.

"Matter?" she said. She walked away from him and stood looking bitterly into the fire. "She's going to be married."

He stood immovable; he felt deeply and inexpressibly sick at heart.

"She's got to be married," she said, "that's all. You might as well know first as last."

He stood there for some moments before realising fully what she had said. Then he knew that there was nothing he could do or say, and he went out of the house. It was dark outside, and he lit the lamp of his tricycle. As he rode away he recalled that in the papers that morning there had been a forecast of rain, and now he could feel it spitting on his face and hands out of the strong heavy western wind.

He rode on for some distance before the gradient of the road made him dismount. He could not think clearly, but was conscious only of the strange, once rebellious and now resigned beauty of the girl filling and troubling his heart. He did not feel any bitterness, but only that behind his lifelong shyness something terrible was at last preparing to explode and shatter him. It was as if he had no longer anything to which he could look forward. He walked heavily, oblivious of the rain. The winter was dead all about him and back in the Armitages' house the snowdrops had not yet come in the grass. "Oh! my God," he said to himself, "Oh! my God, my God."

The Maker of Coffins

Every Sunday evening in summertime she sat at the front window and watched until he came up the hill. Her hands on the horsehair rests of the chair were like pieces of stone-grey paper painted with thin lines of water-colour, palest blue, the skin transparent and the fingers crabbed over the little palms. She always wore a straw hat that had once evidently been purple, the shadows of the trimmings, dark grey, on the mildew grey of the faded, remaining straw.

She sat surrounded by a mass of greenery in brass and china pots, set about on bamboo stands. The curtains in the big bay window were like blankets of red chenille bearing fruitings of soft bobbles down the sides. The old-fashioned gas-brackets over the mantelshelf bore opaque globes of pink and under them were ornaments of twisted yellow glass from which sprouted dead stalks of feathery brown reed and bunches of paper spills. She made the spills for Luther, with her own hands, every Saturday.

Whenever he came round the corner of the long steep hill she always thought that he looked, in his black suit and carrying the black fiddle case, so much like a doctor. Even from that distance the big rough-angled body dwarfed the fiddle case so that it did not look much larger than a doctor's bag. She had in mind particularly Dr Farquharson's bag because it was the bag she had known best. It had brought her the twelve children, beginning with Luther.

The illusion of bag and doctor remained with her through his journey up the hill. He walked with a slight groping roll, big feet splayed out as if he wanted to grip the hill with his toes. She knew he did not roll like that because he was drunk but only because his feet were bad. His feet had always been bad. They had been bad ever since the time he was a child and had grown so fast that she could never afford to buy shoes to catch up with him. In those days he had had to suffer a lot of things in that way because he was the first and times were desperate. She felt keenly that she had never been able to do her best for him. The others had been luckier.

When he came into the room at last it was always with a series of bungling noisy clashes as he tried to find a resting-place for the fiddle case somewhere among the many little tables, the piano, the bookcase and the chairs. He could never find room for the damn fiddle, he thought. The bookcase and the piano were both locked up, polished as glass, and she kept the keys on a chain. He groped among the chairs with bull-like stupor but she never at any time took a great deal of notice of it. He had always been clumsy on his feet. He had been a day or two short of nineteen months before he had started walking at all. She always remembered that, of being so afraid that he would never walk: an awful thing, to have a child so fragile that it never walked.

If she was aware of feeling that the enormous body still enshrined the fragile child she did not reveal it. She turned on him with little grunts of peevish affection that had no effect on him at all.

"It'll be dark before you get up here one of these days."

"Had a rush job on. Wonder I got finished at all."

When he had at last disposed of the fiddle he liked to sit by the piano, in the dark patch caused by one end, so that she could not see his face.

"Who was it?" she said. "Thought you said trade was so bad."

"So it is. Man in Canal Street. Burying tomorrow."

"What man?"

"A man named Johnson."

"Who's he? What name?"

"Johnson. Call him Polly Johnson. Kin to Liz Johnson—"

"Nobody I know."

The lines of her face would crease themselves in deeper ruts of disapprobation. Her mouth would go on muttering without sound for some moments longer while he settled himself by the piano with hot discomfort and perhaps a belch or two.

"You can take your coat off."

She liked him better with his coat off. It reminded her of the Sundays when all of them were at home, at dinner, all the boys with clean white aprons on, so that the gravy from the Yorkshire pudding did not drop on their chapel suits.

The absence of the coat revealed a man of gross, crusty width, with watery blue eyes starting beerily from a face fired by summer to lines of smouldering bruisy red. His collar-stud pressed brassily on his thick throat and his shirt-sleeves were rolled up above arms massive and blackly haired.

His voice had a yeasty thickness:

"All of 'em gone chapel?"

"Rose and Clarice and Will have gone. Lawrence and Nell went this morning."

Lawrence and Will were good boys: steady boys, fellows with enough ambition to get good jobs and enough sense to hang on to them when they got them. They were solid, pin-stripe men. She had never had any bother with Will and Lawrence; they never troubled her. They did not approve of Luther, but then, They did not understand him.

"Ain't bin out nowhere this week, I reckon? Too hot for you."

"Went up to Rose's Thursday," she said.

"Git the bus?"

"Bus! What d'ya think my legs are for?"

"You wanta git the bus," he said. "One o' these days you'll be doing that traipse up there once too much and you'll be dropping down."

"If I do you'll be there measuring me out 'fore I'm cold," she said swiftly, "I'll warrant that."

"Ah, don't sit there horse-facing so much. You horse-face too much by half."

"Don't you tell me I horse-face," she said.

He did not answer. It pained him when she horse-faced at him. He dreaded the day when he would be measuring her out, he thought. His only compensating thought about that was that he would make her something very nice; something really high-class and lovely; something fitting and worthy of the old lady.

She sat there for some time looking like a bone carving, and at last he broke the silence by saying:

"Anything to eat? I could do with a mite o' something."

"I'll be bound you never got your dinner again, did you?"

"Never had time. Bin at it since daylight."

"Funny how you get so many jobs a-Sundays," she said and her nose rose, pointed as a bird's.

Then because he sat there without moving for a second or two longer she said:

"Well: you know where the pantry is. You don't expect me to put it in your mouth for you, do you?"

Daylight was fading a little when he came lumbering back into the room with hunks of jam tart and cheese and bread and cold new potatoes and a slice of cold Yorkshire pudding on a plate. He sat with the plate on his knees. He knew that he had to be careful of the crumbs; he knew she would horse-face if he dropped the crumbs. But the taste of the new potatoes and the cold Yorkshire pudding were the taste of all the summer Sunday evenings of his boyhood and he crammed them in with blind-eyed pleasure, bolting them down, licking thick red lips and wishing to God she had a pint in the house to wash them down.

She muttered at last:

"Anybody'd think you'd never had a mite in your life. Don't she ever get you nothing a-Sundays?"

"Never care whether I get much a-Sundays," he said.

"It don't look like it," she said.

That was the worst of his mother, he thought. She couldn't hit it off with Edna. He had given up trying to make her now. It was like trying to turn a mule.

"You can get yourself a spill when you want one," she said.

Edna was a bit easy-going, he knew, but on the whole he didn't complain. She had let herself go a bit, perhaps, after the last baby. She was a bit sloppy round the middle. Her face was nothing much to write home about but then he wasn't a picture either. The chief thing was she didn't nag him; he really didn't get drunk very much and if he was late at *The Unicorn* on a Sunday she and the children ate the dinner without him and he pacified her with a pint of Guinness afterwards.

By the time he had finished eating it was almost dark and he got up and did the thing he always did, without fail, every Sunday. He lit one of the gas-lamps above the mantelshelf and then, holding his big red face under the light, adjusted the burner until it gave a pure white glow. Then he filled his pipe and lit one of her paper spills from the gas-mantle and put it to his pipe. The flame was sucked down by his red powerful mouth into the pipe bowl until at last he blew out strong blue clouds of smoke that almost smothered him.

As she sat in the window she let the smoke come over to her with her head slightly uplifted, as if it were a cool breeze blowing through the warm airless room in which no window had been open all day. There were three moments she really waited for all evening, and this was the second of them. The first was when she saw him turn, so like a doctor with the fiddle case, at the bottom of the hill. The second was the moment of the gas-lamp, the pure white glow on his face, the great sucked-down flame and the smoke puttering across the room in blue string clouds. It was the smoke above all that she associated with that clumsy massiveness of his and after she smelled it she was aware of the slow dying of cantankerousness inside herself, a softening of all the edges of the day.

When the pipe was really going she knew what he was going to do next. She began unconsciously to finger the keys of the piano and the bookcase that hung on the chain round her neck. That was the third moment: the moment when he reached for the fiddle case and undid it and opened it and took out the bow.

He had begun to play the fiddle when he was seven years old. That had been her ambition for him: a fiddler, a violinist, a great player of the violin in the household. Mr Godbold, who had been a fiddler himself in a great orchestra in Leicester or Birmingham or some other big city up in that part of the world, gave him lessons in his front room, twice a week, after school, at two shillings a time.

"He has fine hands," Mr Godbold said. "He will make a fine player. He is slow but in the end he will make a fine player."

The walls of Mr Godbold's front room were hung with many pictures of Mr Godbold playing the violin as a soloist or in orchestras or at social evenings and smoking concerts. She thought Mr Goldbold, in pieces like *The Spring Song* and excerpts from *Maritana* and *Il Trovatore*, played like an angel, and she thought it would be wonderful if Luther could rise as far as that. The first winter he persevered through many exercises and the second winter he came to his first piece, *Robin Adair*. Most children who learned the piano or the violin went to a Miss Scholes, in the High Street, where they learned *The Bluebells of Scotland* as their first piece and Miss Scholes gave them sixpence for doing so. Mr Godbold did not believe in bribing his pupils; they worked hard on exercises that were the real foundation of music and then went straight on to pieces like *Robin Adair*.

Luther stuck at *Robin Adair*. He played it through for a whole winter and then his hands began to grow. By the time he was twelve he was a big awkward gargoyle of a boy in whose hands the violin looked effete and fragile. She thought by that time he could play beautifully: perhaps not quite as beautifully as Mr Godbold. Perhaps it only seemed to her almost as beautiful because he was so very young.

"You want the key?" she said. She took it off the chain and held it out to him.

The sound of the fifths as he spaced them out on the piano was, she thought, a most wonderful thing. It was different from anything else that was ever heard on the piano: those queer. sharp steps of notes climbing up and starting a trembling on the air. That was the true violin sound: that wonderful prelude of quivering that drew out finally into the glassy, soaring singing of strings.

She had never been very happy about his being a carpenter and at first she opposed it. It was probably that, she thought, that had made his hands so large and clumsy. She was certain the hands of a carpenter could not also be the hands of a violinist; the one could only ruin the other. But his father had said a man had his living to earn and what was wrong with a man being a carpenter? "There was One who was a carpenter and there was no shame in that," he said.

"Play the' old un?" Luther said, but she said nothing because she knew he never began with any other.

The time he took to play through *Robin Adair* always seemed to go by, perhaps because she shut her eyes, very quickly. It flew away on the song's own delicacy. He liked to play too with the pipe in his mouth, so that it seemed as if every scrape of the bow gave out its own rank cloud of smoke that finally choked the room with gas-green fog.

After *Robin Adair* he played several other pieces he knew: *The Jolly Miller* and *Oh! Dear, What Can the Matter Be?* She thought he played better as he got older; but that, after all, was only natural. That was only as it should be. He was a man of over fifty now. He had been playing the same pieces, on the same violin, for forty years.

"Gittin' dark," Luther would say, after the third piece. "Better be gittin' steady on home."

He sat with the fiddle case on his knee and the pipe and the violin in his right hand, waiting to pack up. There would be just time, he thought, to nip into *The Unicorn* and have a couple of beers, perhaps even three or four beers, before they closed at half-past ten. Old Shady Parker would be there and Bill Flawn and Tom Jaques and Flannel Clarke and they would stand each other a round or two. That would rouse him up nicely and he would go home to Edna happy, belching through the dark summer streets, up and down the hills. Tomorrow he would begin to cut out another coffin. Trade was never what you called good in the summer but someone was always going, unexpected or not, and he mucked along somehow. Damn what the family said. That was good enough for him.

"Better put the key back afore you forgit," he would say and she would take the key from him and clip it back on the chain.

The poise of her hands, held for a second or two about her throat, was the signal that she gave him every Sunday.

"Want me to gie y' another?"

"Have you got time? Don't you hang about if you haven't got time."

"Plenty o' time." The big voice was crude and massive as the hands. "You jes" say and I'll play it. Want another? What's it goin' a-be?"

"Play me the old one," she would say.

The old one was *Robin Adair*. As he played it she stared beyound the smoky gaslight into spaces empty of shape. She sat ageless and tranquil as if already embalmed among the greenery of fern-pots, before a shroud of blanketing curtains, under a gas-blue summer sky. The harsh sound of the fiddle strings drew out thinner and thinner across the spaces into which she was staring until her eyes went cloudily after them and she was sightless as she listened.

"Ah! y' can't beat th' old uns," Luther said. "They take a bit o' beatin'."

She did not answer. She felt always that she could hear the sound of the strings long after they were silent. They were like the sound of pigeons' voices echoing each other far away in summer trees, and in the sound of them was all her love.

The Little Jeweller

Mr Elisha Peacock woke suddenly at four o'clock in the morning, in the dead of darkness, feeling very ill. For some moments immediately before waking he was aware of a strange sound of tinkling glass, of his whole body fighting a violent constriction in his chest. When he woke at last it was some time before he realised that the sound was that of the night wind shaking the coloured glass chandelier above his head, that the conflict in his body was in reality a wire of pain boring down into his heart.

It was then be realized he was very ill. In the moment of realization he suddenly heard too the striking of ten or a dozen clocks downstairs in the small jeweller's shop he had kept for thirty-five years. The sounds, not quite simultaneous, at first clear and then discordantly confused, rolled over and over his half-wakened mind in waves of metallic tumult. He managed at last to struggle up on one elbow. The pain, as if a hot gimlet were being turned slowly down into his chest, had now slightly lessened. The clocks had ceased. In the night silence he could hear no sound except the small renewed clash of the glass hangings above his head, and there was only one thought in his mind. It was the strange, painful thought that he, Elisha Peacock, after sixty-eight years of tranquil living, had reached the point where he must die in the night, alone, frightened like a child by the silence and the darkness, before anyone could reach him or he could get downstairs to the telephone.

With this thought in his mind he managed to get slowly out of bed and put his feet into his slippers. The pain in his heart had now ceased to have direction or motion, and lay there only like a dull embedded bullet. He felt that he wanted to press it away and so he'd both hands locked across his chest, staggering a little as he walked. He felt very weak as he walked downstairs, slowly, not troubling to put on the lights, feeling his way by the cold walls of the staircase, and he was troubled by a remote but fierce idea that he did not want to die. By the time he reached the passage which led from the stairs to the glass door of the shop this thought had replaced all others: had become not merely a wish but a determination. He at last put on the lights of the shop, where the telephone was, and then stood still: a small, grey, perplexed little figure, his pain-washed eyes blinking in the white reflected light that sprang at him from the cabinets and shelves of glass and silver with which the shop was full.

For one moment he looked at the telephone, thought better of it, and then went into the room behind the shop, switching on the light. By the fireplace, in which the fire was quite dead, there was a cupboard. He stood with his hand on the brass knob of it, intending to get himself a glass of brandy. But for a long time he could not move. The upward motion of his arm had brought on the pain in his heart again. Suddenly he shut his eyes and felt that he was falling.

It was some moments later that he came to himself, knowing that he must have fainted. He pulled himself up to the cupboard and found the bottle of brandy and a glass. He poured out a little brandy and drank it. It smoothed away the harsh edges of his weakness and pain and for a second or two he looked vaguely about him, slowly coming back to his senses before going back upstairs, still carrying the bottle and the glass, still half-stupefied, so that he forgot to switch off the lights.

From that moment until eight o'clock he lay in bed, thinking. The pain in his heart had ceased, there remained in its place a huge, accumulative fear. He felt that he had been down to the edge of life, had looked over into a vast space of unknown darkness, and had only just managed to come back. This fear was sometimes so strong that he held himself immobile, not daring to move. He lay looking at the grey winter morning light distribute itself reluctantly on the tiny pieces of rose and emerald glass of the chandelier, which still shook and tinkled in the moving air. After sixty-eight years something almost catastrophic had happened to him, and now fear of its recurrence drove his thoughts back into the past. He recalled his life in the shop. He was not married. Outside, in permanent gilt lettering, he had had put up a quarter of a century ago a large notice: "Peacock for Presents. Pence to Pounds," and on this simple motto he had built up a secure, comfortable business. He had tried during all that time not to harm anyone; he felt he could recall honestly that he had never cheated a single person out of a single penny. He was not afraid of the opinion of any man. He had tried to be decent, upright, considerate, and he felt that perhaps he had succeeded. No, he was not afraid of that.

It was only the conscious realisation of his fear of death that disturbed him. He knew suddenly, as he lay looking at the pieces of glass quivering above his head in the increasing light, that he had been afraid of it for years. The desire never to give pain to others had made him sensitive to the thought of any pain to himself. In one sense it had made him an ultra-careful man—he remembered how in the days of gas-lighting he would never go to bed without turning off the main for fear of being blown up or asphyxiated in the night—in another, quite careless. What had happened that morning had brought to his mind another result of his fear. Somehow he had shrunk from making a will.

But now he would rectify that. Yes, now he must see to it. When Edward came at eight o'clock he would explain what had happened; they would call in a solicitor. Edward would understand; you could talk to Edward. Edward was his assistant: a thoughtful, conscientious young man remarkable for resource and promptitude. He was not only a shop-assistant, but he came in every morning an hour earlier than opening time in order to cook breakfast. When he thought of Edward the little jeweller felt his mind instantly strengthened and tranquillised.

At eight o'clock the clocks downstairs began striking the hour and they had no sooner finished than he heard the sound of Edward unlocking and opening the back door. He lay still for a few moments, listening, and then called.

"Edward!" he called. "Edward!"

He was surprised at the weakness of his own voice. It dissolved against the walls of the room, unheard. He tried to raise himself slightly on his elbow, but it seemed as if his body were made of wax that dissolved too under its own slight motion. He could only lie back on the pillows, weakly repeating Edward's name.

A few moments later he heard the young man mounting the stairs; then his voice:

"Mr Peacock! Are you there, Mr Peacock? Was that you calling? Mr Peacock!"

"In here, Edward," was all he could say. "In here."

Edward came hurriedly into the bedroom, a bespectacled young man with brown, alarmed eyes.

"Oh! there you are, Mr Peacock. All the lights were on downstairs, Mr Peacock, and I couldn't make it out. Whatever's the matter?"

"Nasty turn, Edward," he said. "In the night. About four o'clock." He tried to smile. "An awful pain in my heart, Edward.

Nasty." He tried again to struggle up in bed.

"I wouldn't try to get up if I were you, Mr Peacock," Edward said.

"No good lying here, Edward."

"That's all very well, Mr Peacock," Edward said, "but if you're not well, I ought to ring up the doctor. Shall I?"

"I don't know, Edward. I don't know what to say. I've never been like this before, Edward. I don't know—"

He tried again to get up. For the second time his body melted like wax on the pillows. He shut his eyes for a moment, weak and tired, and when he opened them again Edward had gone out of the room, and he called after him:

"Edward! Edward!"

It was only after he had called six or seven times that he realised once more how weak his voice was, that it had no more strength than the gentle, insistent sound of the chandelier trembling above his head, that it was now very like the voice of a child, crying in trouble and getting no answer.

II

He lay in the bedroom all that day, irritated and tired, yet restless. Frequently he found himself troubled by the motions and the sound of the chandelier. It was a very strange thing that he had never noticed it before. Yet now it troubled him. Once or twice he settled back on the pillows, trying to sleep, but the tinkling of the little pieces of glass, stirring in the wind blowing in at the open window, made a tiny maddening curtain between himself and oblivion. At other times he lay thinking: about the shop, then Edward, about the chrysanthemums in his little green-house behind the shop, about the doctor. When the doctor had been and departed he turned over in his mind what he had said. He tried to read into his reticent words at first more and then less than they seemed to mean. "The heart has had a nasty bump, Mr Peacock, that's the trouble. A nasty little bump. It needs rest and quiet, that's all, Mr Peacock. If I were you I should get someone in to look after you." In time these words began to have on him the same effect of irritation as the sound of the chandelier. They told him nothing. Very clever to say the heart had had a nasty bump; wonderful to advise getting someone in. The trouble was that he had nobody: except a sister who lived at the far end of the town, married to a third-rate insurance-agent who rolled his own miserable ragged cigarettes for the sake of economy. He did not like either his sister or her husband; he did not think they liked him. It annoyed him that he should be forced even to think of them now.

He was glad when, about twelve o'clock, Edward came upstairs to say that his solicitor had arrived. Yet once again his feelings instantly took the form of fresh irritation.

"All right, all right, all right!" he said. "Show him up! What's the sense in tramping upstairs twenty times when once will do?"

"Yes, Mr Peacock, yes." Edward hurriedly left the room.

"Wasting shoe leather!"

He lay back on the pillows, ashamed. His heart was beating very rapidly. He had not intended to speak like that. Far from it. No. He did not know at all what was coming over him. A few minutes later his solicitor came in, a tall narrow-jawed man who enjoyed a little shooting two or three days a week and who now entered the room with great heartiness, smiling. Suddenly the little jeweller, who had lived for so many years without contention or malice, felt that he hated him. He felt illogically that the solicitor and the idea of the will were the causes and not the result of his pain. His mouth set itself coldly against the bed-sheet, his eyes levelly transfixed.

"Sorry to see you like this, Mr Peacock. Awfully sorry. Understand you wanted to see me?"

"No!" the little jeweller said. "No!"

"Well, Mr Peacock—"

"I don't want to see you! I don't want to see anybody!"

"All right, Mr Peacock, all right, all right. As you like, Mr Peacock. As you like. Perhaps I might come in again to-morrow?"

"No!" the little jeweller shouted. "No!"

For some moments after the solicitor had gone he was still speaking, repeating that angry monosyllable in a voice that was foreign to him. When he had finished he was again ashamed. He lay silent, his hands pressing his nightshirt against his heart. Closing his eyes, he tried to search for the causes of his strange behaviour. He then discovered that he was lonely. He felt suddenly a great need for companionship, for some objective event or circumstance that would make him forget his fear.

Lying there, he recalled the chrysanthemums in his little greenhouse behind the shop, and it seemed to him that he had found a solution. He felt a great hunger for the sight of the flowers. He called Edward, and then when Edward came upstairs he began to explain what he wanted: how Edward was to go downstairs to the greenhouse and cut the chrysanthemums. The young man stood listening reticently, with an expression of grave concern, asking at last how many chrysanthemums he was to bring? Something about the young man's earnest gravity suddenly seemed very funny to the little jeweller and he began laughing.

"Cut them all," he said. "Cut them all, Edward. Bring them up here so that I can look at them. All of them, Edward, all of them! Go on! Go on!"

"You don't mean it, Mr Peacock?"

"Bless me, mean it? Of course I mean it. Why should I say it if I didn't mean it?"

"What shall I do for vases, Mr Peacock?"

The little jeweller suddenly began laughing again, telling the young man that he was to get the vases out of the shop. The assistant looked very troubled but said, "Yes, Mr Peacock", and left the room. Ten minutes later he began to bring up the first of the flowers, great stalks of bronze and yellow and amber and pink, which he held at arm's length, like torches. He laid them first on the bed, where the little jeweller could reach out and touch them with the tips of his fingers, and then began to arrange them in bowls and vases brought up from the living-room and the shop. The little jeweller watched him with bright, alert eyes, the chandelier and the solicitor and the pain in his heart momentarily forgotten. It seemed to him now that the room was alight. For the first time that day he lay untroubled by fear. He let the lids of his eyes relax and from his prostrate position on the bed he watched the great curled chrysanthemums swim about the room like constellations that brightened and soothed his mind. He asked at last how many flowers there were. The young assistant said he did not know, and the little jeweller said, "Count them, Edward, there must be fifty or sixty."

"Yes, Mr Peacock," the young man said and began to move his hands, counting the flowers, turning his head at last to say, "Sixty, Mr Peacock. Exactly sixty. Funny how you guessed."

"Guessed?" The little jeweller began laughing in a strange way again. "No, Edward, no. I counted them! Counted them." He laughed at the young man's grave disturbed face. "Caught you that time, Edward, eh? Caught you?"

"Yes, Mr Peacock," Edward said.

"Caught you nicely, eh, Edward?" He continued for some moments to laugh with bright eyes. He ceased only to turn again to the young man and speak.

"Like having sixty moons shining in the room together," he said. "Eh, Edward, eh?"

III

Later that afternoon he fell asleep, awaking with fear in his heart about half-past three, momentarily disturbed by the November twilight and the sound of the chandelier. Earlier, before sleeping, he had been along to the bathroom. The catch of the bedroom door had not fastened properly, and the door now stood partially open. In this way he could hear voices. He lay listening intently for some moments, and then it came to him that they were the voices of his sister and her husband, talking to Edward at the foot of the stairs.

For some time he could not hear what they were saying. He caught only the tone of their voices. They seemed almost to be arguing. He heard Edward make a sudden exclamation, as if in protest. He heard the aggressively pitched note of his sister's voice, surprised, resentful, dominating Edward. He did not know why he concluded that his brother-in-law was there: except perhaps because he was completely silent.

Soon the voices came nearer. He heard the sound of feet on the stairs, and caught a sentence of his sister's: "Well, then I think we'll go up and see what just *is* the matter."

He lay gripping his hands under the sheet. He did not know why he should feel suddenly so antagonistic towards his sister, towards everyone. He had never liked his sister, but his attitude had been one of remote indifference. But now pain had ripped away the near edge of his nerves, and he was angry because his sister had somehow been able to discover that he was ill.

He had withdrawn himself almost entirely under the sheets by the time his sister, preceding Edward and her husband, came into the room: a small, juiceless, volatile woman, with crinkled skin, her hands grasping a large patent leather handbag.

"Well?" she said. "Well! What have you been doing to yourself?"

He muttered sounds of denial and protest that had on her the effect of a challenge.

"Well, of course, if you're going to be like that after we've traipsed all the way up from North End!"

"Like what?" he murmured. "Like what?"

"Jumping down folks' throats! Muttering!" she said "Muttering!"

He did not say anything. The slight exertion of protest had made him feel once again old and tired. In a moment the tranquillising effect of sleep and flowers had been lost. He turned with slight weariness in the bed.

At that moment he saw that his sister had seen the flowers. Her eyes were behaving like lights of warning in their wrinkled sockets. Her mouth, falling open, revealed a colourless dark gap between the plate of her false teeth and the roof of her mouth; but a single word of speech was enough to bring the plate into place again with a click of acid astonishment.

"Well!" she said. "I wonder what next, I wonder what next!"

The little jeweller clenched his hands even harder under the sheets. As he did so his brother-in-law spoke for the first time.

"Been bringing the greenhouse indoors, eh?" He spoke with false robustness, as if trying to be funny. His words became as it were knotted in his moustache, which his habit of smoking loose cheap cigarettes had turned a gingery yellow.

"And what if I have?" the little jeweller said. "What if I have? What exactly is it to do with you?"

"Mr Peacock," Edward said. "Mr Peacock. The doctor said you were on no account to get excited."

"Excited?" the woman said. "Excited. It looks as if that's the trouble. Over-excitement about something. Bringing a greenhouseful of flowers into the house."

"Can't I do what I like with them?" he said, trying to raise his voice. "They're my flowers! Without you interfering?"

"Mr Peacock," Edward began.

"Be quiet, Edward!" he said. "Get downstairs! Get down to the shop. What do you suppose customers will be doing? Get down to the shop!"

As the young assistant went reluctantly out of the room the little jeweller's sister began speaking again, in protest, but he suddenly cut her off with an attack of angry words, at the same time throwing up his hands and bringing them down on the sheets.

"And you get out, too! Both of you. Before I lose my temper.

How can I get rest if you come up here arguing? How can I? How can I?"

"All right!" his sister said. "All right! But it looks to me as if you want someone to look after you!"

"I don't want anything except a little peace and quiet!" he shouted. "Get out!"

Rather hurriedly his brother-in-law went out of the room, his sister following, her lips strangely set. Suddenly he shouted after them that they could leave the door open. He wanted a little fresh air in there, a little fresh air!

The door was left slightly open. Exhausted, astonished at himself, feeling slightly ashamed, he lay back on the pillows. It took him some moments to get his breath. Then in the silence he lay listening, hearing again the voices from downstairs.

It was only after three or four minutes, after his anger was really passed and had become in recollection something foreign and meaningless to him, that he got out of bed, put on his slippers, and went to his bedroom door. As he opened it, he took his grey woollen dressing-gown off the door-peg and slipped it over his shoulders. Then he went slowly along the landing. The voices had already become clearer, yet not distinct. It was already late in the afternoon and as he went cautiously down the first few steps of the stairs he could see the chinks of electric light splintering sharply the darkness between stairs and shop. Half-way down the stairs he sat down, looking very small, slightly perplexed with his head to one side, and very solitary. He could hear the voices quite clearly now.

They came from the living-room: mainly the voices of his sister, catechising, and of Edward, answering. His sister seemed to be immensely concerned about the flowers.

"Didn't it strike you as very funny," she said to Edward, "that he should ask you to cut *all* the flowers?"

"Well, it did rather. Yes."

"Fifty of them if there's one," she said.

"There's just sixty," Edward said. "Mr Peacock counted them. He said it was like having sixty moons shining together in the bedroom."

"What?" she said. *"What?"*

The little jeweller heard Edward repeat what he had said.

"Well!" she said. "Well! Well, that settles it, that settles it. I'm stopping here until things are straightened out a bit. First he acts funny with the solicitor, then with us. Then he talks about seeing moons shining in the room. I think it's a good job we found out about it when we did."

The little jeweller made his way slowly back upstairs while she was still speaking, catching now and then some more strident passage in what she was saying. In the bedroom the colour of the many flowers had died, but the room was full of a strong odour of chrysanthemums that hung pleasantly on the damp November air. Tired now, he lay down in bed. As he began to try to think, turning over in his mind what he had just heard, the chandelier stirred and began to drop down on him its small tinkling irritant bits of sound. It was this repetitive maddening sound, he thought suddenly, that throughout the day had goaded him into brief fits of anger. Why was it? He did not want to be angry. He felt recurrently ashamed of himself, miserable. Yet underneath the shame he was aware of a strange, dormant anxiety. It seemed to him that unless he took a terribly firm hold on himself he must sooner or later leap up in bed and seize the chandelier and smash it to pieces.

He was struggling with the perplexity brought about by this desire when his sister came upstairs and into the darkening room. Though he did not see it, she had taken off her hat and coat. It was in explanation of this that she addressed him in a challenging voice:

"Well, I've decided to stay for a night or two and look after you, Elisha, whether you like it or not. I've sent Fred home for the things. I hope you hear what I say?"

He did not answer. In a momentary flash of cunning he decided to lie still and silent, in a pretence of sleep.

IV

When he woke again it was late in the evening; the room was dark and still, and he was no longer tired. He did not know what time it was, but soon he caught from the street outside the broken echoes of passing voices and traffic and then, raising himself on his elbow, he looked out of the uncurtained window and saw lights in the street below. He felt briefly reassured, and then turned to look at the bedroom. He could see better now, and suddenly he realised that something strange had happened.

The flowers had gone. He sat up in bed and switched on the

light. An accidental breath of wind stirred the hanging glasses of the chandelier, and in this moment he felt all the violence of the day's anger renew itself with tremendous strength. It was beyond mere irritation now. It no longer sprang from within him. It was an external force which seemed to take hold of him bodily and jerk him out of bed.

For a few moments he stood in the centre of the room, in his nightshirt, staring before him. Yes: the flowers had gone. They had gone and he knew that only one person could have taken them away. His anger at these simple facts beat him into violent movement. He put out the light and began to dress. Anger directed his hands to things he did not consciously know were there: trousers, coat, a loose black beret which he often wore in the shop, his boots, which he did not lace up. It seemed to take hold of him and lead him downstairs: the same immense external anger aroused simply by the fact that his flowers had gone. Outside on the landing he almost stumbled over the vases of flowers lined up against the railings of the stairs, but his anger did not cease. It drove him from the stairs into the passage that ran between stairs and living-room, shining through the glass door of which he could see a light.

This light made him stop. Through the lighted glass door he could see his sister and her husband. They had taken possession. They were having supper at a table directly under the electric light. Beating straight down, the light threw their faces into shadow, depressing them. Bottles of stout stood on the table. He saw his sister, mouth full, reach out her hand and grasp the glass of stout and drink rapidly, her face excited by food and drink and some expounded intention he could not hear.

He turned away and went back along the passage. He unlocked the side door at the foot of the stairs and went out into the street. It seemed again as if anger had driven him there. The night air was not cold, and he was still not tired. He began to walk rapidly, knowing in a strange way that he was not fully responsible for his movements.

But soon, as he walked along the street, his anger underwent a change. It became an idea. It was the idea that his sister and her husband had installed themselves at the house for the sole purpose of taking away his money. He moved under the street lights with an oblivious swaying movement, looking at the ground. From the nucleus of his single idea sprang others. He began to walk more quickly, impelled by the idea of escape. He became aware of the idea that he was being persecuted. They had taken away his flowers, they had come to take away his money. In time, if he did not escape, they would take away him.

He struggled along to the next corner, and then he had another idea. Out of the darkness there came a taxi, driven slowly, going home perhaps after meeting the last important train at the station. He put up his hand and shouted. The taxi pulled up and he told the driver to go straight to Mr Archibald Foster's house, forty-five Edward Street.

"What street?" the driver said.

"Edward Street."

"Edward Street?" the driver said. "Never heard of it. Edward Street?"

The little jeweller stood slightly swaying by the side of the taxi, trying to think. Edward Street? No, that was not right. It couldn't be right. He was thinking of Edward. It occurred to him suddenly that he needed Edward. What street did Edward live in? Foster Street? Archibald Street? He ran his hand vaguely across his face. No, he thought, no, what was he thinking about? Archibald was the name of his solicitor, who lived in Foster Street. It was his solicitor he needed, Mr Archibald. He needed to make his will. Then he remembered that Mr Archibald was dead, that the firm was carried on by somebody of another name. Mr Foster? No: he recalled abruptly that Foster was his sister's married name. He stood swaying on his feet, his mind for the space of several seconds quite blank. Where did he want to go? What was he trying to remember?

The voice of the taxi-driver aroused him at last. "Thought of it yet?"

"No," the little jeweller said, "I haven't thought of it." He now suddenly felt weak and cold from standing. "Let me get in. You can drive on and I'll tell you when I remember. I shall remember it in a minute."

What was it? he thought. What was it? As he lay back on the cushions of the taxi he tried desperately to beat his mind into a coherent effort of memory. What in God's name was it? He shut his eyes, pressing his hands against his forehead. The taxi swung from side to side, turning a corner, swinging him as if he were suspended by a rope. He knew again that he was very ill. His mind had ceased in its reactions. The knowledge of his illness was part of the darkness, the street lights swinging giddily past, the strange droning noise of the taxi boring with infinite melancholy down into his brain. Once the driver turned and spoke to him, but he did not reply. He was seized by the idea that he was being forcibly carried away into the darkness of a strange place. He had long since ceased his effort of memory. He felt now that he was fighting to escape. He felt very frightened by the dark confinement of the taxi and suddenly began to shout like a child.

"Let me get out!" he shouted. "Let me get out!" He wiped his hand across his face and found his forehead cold with the sweat of great anguish. "Let me out! Stop it! Stop it! Stop it! Stop it!" he shouted. "Please stop it now!"

V

When he came to himself again he did not recognise his own skinny white hands lying on the dark grey blanket of the bed. In the same way, when he lifted one of his hands and drew it unsteadily across his face, he could not recall who he was. The strange details of the face, a growth of beard, the fleshless cheekbones, the deep-sunken eyes, might have been those of some other person. He knew that the bed, too, was strange. He fixed in his mind the reality of its black iron shape, the grey blanket, the grey light falling on it from a distant window. Then he realised that it was one of many others.

Where was he? His eyes cast themselves with slow weariness from side to side. They alighted and dwelt upon a double row of grey beds. In these beds, all exactly resembling his own, other men were lying, one or two asleep. He tried to understand his relationship to them. He looked at the walls of the room, the ceiling. The whitewash had begun in places to peel away. He considered again the grey winter light falling through the high narrow windows, trying to determine what time of day it was.

Gradually his mind began to clear. Wakefulness itself had broken a tiny hole of light in his troubled consciousness. It now began to widen, and as the distribution of light quickened he gripped his hands tightly on the blanket, remembering. Fixing his eyes on the ceiling he remembered the chandelier, his bedroom, the flowers, his sister. But between these things and the present moment he was aware of a great blank. Then slowly he realised that this blankness was the key to where he was.

He looked again at the faces of the men about him. Some were staring at the ceiling, some straight before them, out of the windows; a few were asleep. With an abrupt calmness of pity he saw them as the faces of men not responsible for themselves: the faces of the partially insane. For a moment or two this realisation did not trouble him. He saw calmly, with detachment, that it did not affect him. He himself was not one of those silent staring creatures; he had no part in their strange immobility. He understood and was sorry for them, his heart no longer calm but crying unspeakably with pity.

Suddenly it was as if he had stepped on a revolving trap. He seemed to take a step forward and was flung violently out of calmness into a pit of terror. He had a sensation of being hit on the head. He struggled to save himself, and all at once was completely calm again. This new calmness remained for a moment unbroken. Then it was shattered by his own voice, shouting at him in his own brain. "You are one of them!" it shouted at him. "You are one of them! You are! *You are!*"

As the voice died, he lay very still. A voice calling in his mind? In answer he felt fear slowly begin to creep back to him: not merely his former, shadowy fear of death, but the very cold, terrible fear of truth.

He lay for a long time trying to reason things out. He found memory very difficult, but finally he had an idea. As it came to him he looked slowly round the room. The figures of the men, staring and wooden, had not moved. Cautiously he moved his legs under the blanket, bending his knees. At either end of the room were double glass doors, beyond which he could see a corridor. He watched this corridor during some moments for a sign of life, but nothing happened. He was thinking with peculiar clearness now.

Suddenly he leapt out of bed, flung himself bodily at the swing doors at the nearer end of the room, and rushed down the corridor. He heard behind him an abrupt murmur of voices, which the closing of the swing doors cut off again. For a short space he was alone in the corridor, running along the grey stone floors in his bare feet. Then he heard other feet running behind him. They were feet with heavy boots on them. They ran fast, catching up with him. He turned to look, involuntarily holding up his hands. The feet with boots belonged to a man in a brown uniform. The man rushed at him and locked his arms behind his back. The little jeweller began to struggle. He felt himself possessed suddenly by a colossal strength. He began shouting. The attendant put one of his hands over his mouth, bruising his lips. The little jeweller swung one arm free and then the attendant began to hit him, striking him again on the face and the body. He continued to fight violently and the attendant continued to hit him, until at last he gave up the struggle.

"Come on," the attendant said. "Back you go. They all try this trick once, but you'll learn better. Come on. Back again."

It was almost two hours later when he opened his eyes to see figures, a doctor and a nurse, standing over him.

"Where am I?" he said. "Where is this?"

The doctor did not answer the question. "You're all right now?" he said. "Better?"

"I want to go home, please."

"In time."

"I want to know who brought me here? Please who brought me here? A lady?"

"Your sister."

"I want to see my doctor," he said. "My own doctor. You know him—Doctor—Doctor—" he tried to make a great effort of memory, "Doctor—"

"It's all right. I'm your doctor."

"I want Edward," he said. He suddenly felt an intense revulsion of feeling against his sister. "Why did she do this?" he said, raising his voice. "Why did she do it? She'd no right! I never did anyone any harm! I never did anything." He clenched his hands. "Damn her! Damn her!"

"Please," the doctor said.

"She wants my money!" he shouted. "Damn her!"

"Listen," the doctor said. "Quietly. Your sister is paying to keep you here. She is struggling to pay as best she can. Don't misjudge her. How can she have your money if it's safe in the bank?" The doctor spoke with heavy kindness, as if in reality the little jeweller had no money and was under an immense delusion. "Now how can she?"

"She gets it if I die!" he said. "There's no one else. She gets it if I die!"

"I know," the doctor said. "But you're not going to die." He held clean light fingers on the little jeweller's pulse. "You've been getting excited. You mustn't do that. If you want us to help you, you must help us. Couldn't you manage some sleep again?"

"I want to go home," the little jeweller said. "Please, I want to go home."

The doctor walked away, passing like a white ghost out of the swing doors. Seeing him go, the little jeweller lay back on his pillows, determined for one moment to be quite calm. The nurse remained about his bed, tucking in his blankets. He looked at her face, quite young, alive and soft, and it seemed to him suddenly the most human thing he had seen since waking in the grey, impersonal room.

"Nurse," he said. He held himself rigid under the blankets, more than ever determined to be quite calm.

"Yes," she said, "yes?"

"Nurse," he said, "Nurse." He was speaking with great earnestness, in a whisper, unaware that his eyes were glancing rapidly to and fro about the room, for fear of listeners. "Nurse, I've got money," he said. "Plenty of money. Two or three thousand. See? Plenty." He spoke in a whisper of desperation. "If you'll help me get away I'll see that you get something. A cheque for fifty pounds. More than that." He stared at her with terrible earnestness, almost wildly. "You can come to my shop and pick yourself a little jewellery. Anything. You see? You see?"

For a moment there was no response in her face except a remote smile. Then she spoke. "Jewellery. Well, that's nice," she said. "Jewellery?"

He wanted to speak again, but he could not. He looked instead at her eyes, which contained no hint of understanding. They were regarding him instead with a kind of impersonal pity.

He knew then what she was thinking. He lay back and closed his eyes in order to shut her out, and when he opened them again she was gone. On the walls and the blanket and on the scarred ceiling the grey light was growing greyer now with the dying of the afternoon.

When the nurse came back past the bed again she saw the little jeweller lying with closed eyes and the palms of his small, shrunken hands upturned across the bed. His lips were moving very slightly, but with her casual glance she did not notice them.

Nor could she hear what he was saying now. "Take me away. Take me away, please. O Lord! take me away."

Where the Cloud Breaks

Colonel Gracie, who had decided to boil himself two new-laid eggs for lunch, came into the kitchen from the garden and laid his panama hat on top of the stove, put the eggs into it and then, after some moments of blissful concentration, looked inside to see if they were cooking.

Presently he sensed that something was vaguely wrong about all this and began to search for a saucepan. Having found it, a small blue enamel one much blackened by fire, he gazed at it with intent inquiry for some moments, half made a gesture as if to put it on his head and then decided to drop the eggs into it, without benefit of water. In the course of doing this he twice dipped the sleeve of his white duck jacket into a dish of raspberry jam, originally put out on the kitchen table for breakfast. The jam dish was in fact a candlestick, in pewter, the candle part of which had broken away.

Soon the Colonel, in the process of making himself some toast, found himself wondering what day it was. He couldn't be sure. He had recently given up taking *The Times* and it was this that made things difficult. He knew the month was July, although the calendar hanging by the side of the stove actually said it was September, but that of course didn't help much about the day. He guessed it might be Tuesday; but you never really knew when you lived alone. Still, it helped sometimes to know whether it was Tuesday or Sunday, just in case he ran short of tobacco and walked all the way to the village shop only to find it closed.

Was it Tuesday? The days were normally fixed quite clearly in his mind by a system of coloration. Tuesday was a most distinct shade of raspberry rose. Thursday was brown and Sunday a pleasant yellow, that particularly bright gold you got in sunflowers. Today seemed, he thought, rather a dark green, much more like a Wednesday. It was most important to differentiate, because if it were really Wednesday it would be not the slightest use his walking down to the shop to get stamps after lunch, since Wednesday was early closing day.

There was nothing for it, he told himself, but to semaphore his friend Miss Wilkinson. With a piece of toast in his hand he set about finding his signalling flags, which he always kept in a cupboard under the stairs. As he stooped to unlatch the cupboard door a skein of onions left over from the previous winter dropped from a fragile string on the wall and fell on his neck without alarming him visibly.

One of the flags was bright yellow, the other an agreeable shade of chicory blue. Experience had shown that these two colours showed up far better than all others against the surrounding landscape of lush chestnut copse and woodland. They were clearly visible for a good half mile.

In the army, from which he was now long retired, signalling had been the Colonel's special pigeon. He had helped to train a considerable number of men with extreme proficiency. Miss Wilkinson, who was sixty, wasn't of course quite so apt a pupil as a soldier in his prime, but she had nevertheless been overjoyed to learn what was not altogether a difficult art. It had been the greatest fun for them both; it had whiled away an enormous number of lonely hours.

For the past five weeks Miss Wilkinson had been away, staying on the south coast with a sister, and the Colonel had missed her greatly. Not only had there been no one to whom he could signal his questions, doubts and thoughts; he had never really been quite sure, all that time, what day it was.

After now having had the remarkable presence of mind to put an inch or two of water into the egg saucepan the Colonel set out with the flags to walk to the bottom of the garden, which sloped fairly steeply to its southern boundary, a three foot hedge of hawthorn. Along the hedge thirty or forty gigantic heads of sunflower were in full flower, the huge faces staring like yellow guardians across the three sloping open meadows that lay between the Colonel and Miss Wilkinson, who lived in a small white weatherboard house down on the edge of a narrow stream. Sometimes after torrential winter rains the little stream rose with devastating rapidity, flooding Miss Wilkinson, so that the Colonel had to be there at the double, to bale her out.

In the centre of the hedge was a stile and the Colonel, who in his crumpled suit of white duck looked something like a cadaverous baker out of work, now stood up on it and blew three sharp blasts on a whistle. This was the signal to fetch Miss Wilkinson from the kitchen, the greenhouse, the potting shed, or wherever she happened to be. The system of whistle and flag suited both the Colonel and Miss Wilkson admirably, the Colonel because he hated the telephone so much and Miss Wilkinson because she couldn't afford to have the instrument installed. For the same reasons neither of them owned either television or radio, the Colonel having laid it down in expressly severe terms, almost as if in holy writ, that he would not only never have such antisocial devices in the house but that they were also, in a sense, degenerate: if not immoral.

Miss Wilkinson having appeared in her garden in a large pink sun hat and a loose summery blue dress with flowers all over it, the Colonel addressed her by smartly raising his yellow flag. Miss Wilkinson replied by promptly raising her blue one. This meant that they were receiving each other loud and clear.

The day in fact was so beautifully clear that the Colonel could actually not only see Miss Wilkinson in detail as she stood on the small wooden bridge that spanned the stream but he could also pick out slender spires of purple loosestrife among the many tall reeds that lined the banks like dark green swords. Both he and Miss Wilkinson, among their many other things in common, were crazy about flowers.

Having given himself another moment to get into correct position, the Colonel presently signalled to Miss Wilkinson that he was frightfully sorry to trouble her but would she very much mind telling him what day it was?

To his infinite astonishment Miss Wilkinson signalled back that it was Thursday and, as if determined to leave no doubt about it, added that it was also August the second.

August? the Colonel replied. He was much surprised. He thought it was July.

No, no, it was August, Miss Wilkinson told him. Thursday the second—the day he was coming to tea.

The Colonel had spent the morning since ten o'clock in a rush of perspiring industry, cleaning out the hens. The fact that he was going to tea with Miss Wilkinson had, like the precise date and month, somehow slipped his mind.

"You hadn't forgotten, had you?"

"Oh! no, no, I hadn't forgotten. Had an awfully long morning, that's all. Would you mind telling me what time it is now?"

In the clear summer air the Colonel could distinctly see the movement of Miss Wilkinson's arm as she raised it to look at her watch. He himself never wore a watch. Though altogether less pernicious than telephone, television and radio, a watch nevertheless belonged, in his estimation, to that category of inventions that one could well do without.

"Ten to four."

Good God, the Colonel thought, now struck by the sudden realisation that he hadn't had lunch yet.

"I was expecting you in about ten minutes. It's so lovely I thought we'd have tea outside. Under the willow tree."

Admirable idea, the Colonel thought, without signalling it. What, by the way, had he done with the eggs? Were they on the boil or not? He couldn't for the life of him remember.

"Do you wish any eggs?" he asked. "I have heaps."

"No, thank you all the same. I have some." It might have been a laugh or merely a bird-cry that the Colonel heard coming across the meadows. "Don't be too long. I have a surprise for you."

As he hurried back to the house the Colonel wondered, in a dreamy sort of way, what kind of surprise Miss Wilkinson could possibly have for him and as he wondered he felt a sort of whisper travel across his heart. It was the sort of tremor he often experienced when he was on the way to see her or when he looked at the nape of her neck or when she spoke to him in some specially direct or unexpected sort of way. He would like to have put this feeling into words of some kind—signalling was child's play by comparison—but he was both too inarticulate and too shy to do so.

Half an hour later, after walking down through the meadows, he fully expected to see Miss Wilkinson waiting for him on the bank of the stream under the willow-tree, where the tea-table, cool with lace cloth, was already laid. But there was no sign of her there or in the greenhouse, where cucumbers were growing on humid vines, or in the kitchen.

Then, to his great surprise, he heard her voice calling him from some distance off and a moment later he saw her twenty yards or so away, paddling in the stream.

"Just remembered I'd seen a bed of watercress yesterday and I thought how nice it would be. Beautifully cool, the water."

As he watched her approaching, legs bare and white above emerald skim of water-weed, the Colonel again experienced the tremor that circumvented his heart like a whisper. This time it was actually touched with pain and there was nothing he could say.

"Last year there was a bed much farther upstream. But I suppose the seeds get carried down."

Miss Wilkinson was fair and pink, almost cherubic, her voice jolly. A dew-lap rather like those seen in ageing dogs hung floppily down on the collar of her cream shantung dress, giving her a look of obese friendliness and charm.

"The kettle's on already," she said. "Sit yourself down while I go in and get my feet dried."

The Colonel, watching her white feet half-running, half-trotting across the lawn, thought again of the surprise she had in store for him and wondered if paddling in the stream was it. No other, he thought, could have had a sharper effect on him.

When she came back, carrying a silver hot water jug and teapot, she laughed quite gaily in reply to his query about the surprise. No: it wasn't paddling in the stream. And she was afraid he would have to wait until after tea before she could tell him, anyway.

"Oh! how stupid of me," she said, abruptly pausing in the act of pouring tea, "I've gone and forgotten the watercress."

"I'll get it, I'll get it," the Colonel said, at once leaping up to go into the house.

"Oh! no, you don't," she said. "Not on your life. My surprise is in there."

Later, drinking tea and munching brown bread and butter and cool sprigs of watercress dipped in salt, the Colonel found it impossible to dwell on the question of the surprise without uneasiness. In an effort to take his mind off the subject he reremarked on how good the sunflowers were this year and what a fine crop of seeds there would be. He fed them to the hens.

"I think it's the sunflowers that give the eggs that deep brown colour," he said.

"You do?" she said. "By the way did you like the pie I made for you?"

"Pie?"

With silent distress the Colonel recalled a pie of morello cherries, baked and bestowed on him the day before yesterday. He had put it into the larder and had forgotten that too.

"It was delicious. I'm saving half of it for supper."

Miss Wilkinson, looking at him rather as dogs sometimes look, head sideways, with a meditative glint in her eye, asked suddenly what he had had for lunch? Not eggs again?

"Eggs are so easy."

"I've told you before. You can't live on eggs all the time," she said. "I've been making pork brawn this morning. Would you care for some of that?"

"Yes, I would. Thank you. I would indeed."

From these trivial discussions on food it seemed to the Colonel that a curious and elusive sense of intimacy sprang up. It was difficult to define but it was almost as if either he or Miss Wilkinson had proposed to each other and had been, in spirit at least, accepted.

This made him so uneasy again that he suddenly said:

"By the way, I don't think I told you. I've given up *The Times*."

"Oh! really. Isn't that rather rash?"

"I don't think so. I'd been considering it for some time actually. You see, one is so busy with the hens and the garden and all that sort of thing that quite often one gets no time to read until ten o'clock. Which is absurd. I thought that from time to time I might perhaps borrow yours?"

"Of course."

The Colonel, thinking that perhaps he was talking too much, sat silent. How pretty the stream looked, he thought. The purple loosestrife had such dignity by the waterside. He must go fishing again one day. The stream held a few trout and in the deeper pools there were chub.

"Are you quite sure you won't feel lost without a paper? I think I should."

"No, no. I don't think so. One gets surfeited anyway with these wretched conferences and ministerial comings and goings and world tension and so on. One wants to be away from it all."

"One mustn't run away from life, nevertheless."

Life was what you made it, the Colonel pointed out. He preferred it as much as possible untrammelled.

Accepting Miss Wilkinson's offer of a third cup of tea and another plate of the delicious watercress he suddenly realised that he was ravenously hungry. There was a round plum cake on the table and his eye kept wandering back to it with the poignant voracity of a boy after a game of football. After a time Miss Wilkinson noticed this and started to cut the cake in readiness.

"I'm thinking of going fishing again very soon," the Colonel said. "If I bag a trout or two perhaps you might care to join me for supper?"

"I should absolutely love to."

It was remarks of such direct intimacy, delivered in a moist, jolly voice, that had the Colonel's heart in its curious whispering state again. In silence he contemplated the almost too pleasant prospect of having Miss Wilkinson to supper. He would try his best to cook the trout nicely, in butter, and not burn them. Perhaps he would also be able to manage a glass of wine.

"I have a beautiful white delphinium in bloom," Miss Wilkinson said. "I want to show it you after tea."

"That isn't the surprise?"

Miss Wilkinson laughed with almost incautious jollity.

"You must forget all about the surprise. You're like a small boy who can't wait for Christmas."

The Colonel apologised for what seemed to be impatience and then followed this with a second apology, saying he was sorry he'd forgotten to ask Miss Wilkinson if she had enjoyed the long visit to her sister.

"Oh! splendidly. It really did me the world of good. One gets sort of ham-strung by one's habits, don't you think? It's good to get away."

To the Colonel her long absence had seemed exactly the opposite. He would like to have told her how much he had missed her. Instead something made him say:

"I picked up a dead gold-finch in the garden this morning. It had fallen among the sea kale. Its yellow wing was open on one of the grey leaves and I thought it was a flower."

"The cat, I suppose?"

"No, no. There was no sign of violence at all."

Away downstream a dove cooed, breaking and yet deepening all the drowsiness of the summer afternoon. What did one want with world affairs, presidential speeches, threats of war and all those things? the Colonel wondered. What had newspapers ever given to the world that could be compared with that one sound, the solo voice of the dove by the waterside?

"No, no. No more tea, thank you. Perhaps another piece of cake, yes. That's excellent, thank you."

The last crumb of cake having been consumed, the Colonel followed Miss Wilkinson into the flower garden to look at the white delphinium. Its snowy grace filled him with an almost ethereal sense of calm. He couldn't have been, he thought, more happy.

"Very beautiful. Most beautiful."

"I'm going to divide it in the spring," Miss Wilkinson said, "and give you a piece."

After a single murmur of acceptance for this blessing the Colonel remained for some moments speechless, another tremor travelling round his heart, this time like the quivering of a tightened wire.

"Well now," Miss Wilkinson said, "I think I might let you see the surprise if you're ready."

He was not only ready but even eager, the Colonel thought.

"I'll lead the way," Miss Wilkinson said.

She led the way into the sitting room, which was beautifully cool and full of the scent of small red carnations. The colonel, who was not even conscious of being a hopelessly untidy person himself, nevertheless was always struck by the pervading neatness, the laundered freshness, of all parts of Miss Wilkinson's house. It was like a little chintz holy-of-holies, always embalmed, always the same.

"Well, what do you say? There it is."

The Colonel, with customary blissful absent-mindedness, stared about the room without being able to note that anything had changed since his last visit there.

"I must say I don't really see anything in the nature of a surprise."

"Oh! you do. Don't be silly."

No, the Colonel had to confess, there was nothing he could see. It was all exactly as he had seen it the last time.

"Over there. In the corner. Of course it's rather a small one. Not as big as my sister's."

It slowly began to reach the blissfully preoccupied cloisters of the Colonel's mind that he was gazing at a television set. A cramping chill went round his heart. For a few unblissful moments he stared hard in front of him, tormented by a sense of being unfairly trapped, with nothing to say.

"My sister gave it to me. She's just bought herself a new one. You see you get so little allowed for an old one in part exchange that it's hardly worth—"

"You mean you've actually got it permanently?"

"Why, yes. Of course."

The Colonel found himself speaking with a voice so constricted that it seemed almost to be disembodied.

"But I always thought you hated those things."

"Well, I suppose there comes a day. I must say it was a bit of a revelation at my sister's. Some of the things one saw were absorbing. For instance there was a programme about a remote Indian tribe in the forests of South America that I found quite marvellous." The Colonel was stiff, remote-eyed, as if not listening. "This tribe was in complete decay. It was actually dying out, corrupted—"

"Corrupted by what? By civilisation my guess would be."

"As a matter of fact they were. For one thing they die like flies from measles."

"Naturally. That," the Colonel said, "is what I am always trying to say."

"Yes, but there are other viewpoints. One comes to realise that."

"The parallel seems to me to be an exact one," the Colonel said.

"I'm afraid I can't agree."

There was now a certain chill, almost an iciness, in the air. The ethereal calm of the afternoon, its emblem the white delphinium, seemed splintered and blackened. The Colonel, though feeling that Miss Wilkinson had acted in some way like a traitor, at the same time had no way of saying so. It was all so callous, he thought, so shockingly out of character. He managed to blurt out:

"I really didn't think you'd come down to this."

"I didn't come down to it, as you so candidly put it. It was simply a gift from my sister. You talk about it as if I'd started taking some sort of horrible drug."

"In a sense you have."

"I'm afraid I disagree again."

"All these things are drugs. Cinemas, radio, television, telephone, even newspapers. That's really why I've given up *The Times*. I thought we always agreed on that?"

"We may have done. At one time. Now we'll have to agree to differ."

"Very well."

A hard lump rose in the Colonel's throat and stuck there. A miserable sense of impotence seized him and kept him stiff, with nothing more to say.

"I might have shown you a few minutes of it and converted you," Miss Wilkinson said. "But the aerial isn't up yet. It's coming this evening."

"I don't think I want to be converted, thank you."

"I hoped you'd like it and perhaps come down in the evenings sometimes and watch."

"Thank you, I shall be perfectly happy in my own way."

"Very well. I'm sorry you're so stubborn about it."

The Colonel was about to say with acidity that he was not

stubborn and then changed his mind and said curtly that he must go. After a painful silence Miss Wilkinson said:

"Well, if you must I'll get the pork brawn."

"I don't think I care for the pork brawn, thank you."

"Just as you like."

At the door of the sitting room the Colonel paused, if anything stiffer than ever, and remarked that if there was something he particularly wanted he would signal her.

"I shan't be answering any signals," Miss Wilkinson said.

"You won't be answering any signals?"

An agony of disbelief went twisting through the Colonel, imposing on him a momentary paralysis. He could only stare.

"No: I shan't be answering any signals."

"Does that mean you won't be speaking to me again?"

"I didn't say that."

"I think it rather sounds like that."

"Then you must go on thinking it sounds like that, that's all."

It was exactly as if Miss Wilkinson had slapped him harshly in the face; it was precisely as if he had proposed and been rudely rejected.

"Good-bye," he said in a cold and impotent voice.

"Good-bye," she said. "I'll see you out."

"There's no need to see me out, thank you. I'll find my way alone."

Back in his own kitchen the Colonel discovered that the eggs had boiled black in the saucepan. He had forgotten to close the door of the stove. Brown smoke was hanging everywhere. Trying absentmindedly to clear up the mess he twice put his sleeve in the jam dish without noticing it and then wiped his sleeve across the tablecloth, uncleared since breakfast-time.

In the garden the dead gold-finch still lay on the silvery leaf of sea kale and he stood staring at it for a long time, stiff-eyed and impotent, unable to think one coherent simple thought.

Finally he went back to the house, took out the signalling flags and went over to the stile. Standing on it, he gave three difficult blasts on the whistle but nothing happened in answer except that one of two men standing on the roof of Miss Wilkinson's house, erecting the television aerial, casually turned his head.

Then he decided to send a signal. The three words he wanted so much to send were "Please forgive me" but after some moments of contemplation he found that he had neither the heart nor the will to raise a flag.

Instead he simply stood immovable by the stile, staring across the meadows in the evening sun. His eyes were blank. They seemed to be groping in immeasurable appeal for something and as if in answer to it the long row of great yellow sunflower faces, the seeds of which were so excellent for the hens, stared back at him, in that wide, laughing, almost mocking way that sunflowers have.

Colonel Julian

Colonel Julian lay in the sun. By pressing down his hands so that the bony knuckles touched the dusty hot lead of the balcony floor he could raise himself up just enough to look through the openings of the stone balustrade to where the deep ring of rhododendrons broke and revealed, across fields of oak-brown corn, the line of the sea.

The balcony was built above the portico of the house, facing southward. Beyond the rhododendrons, quite flowerless now, dark without that Indian glory the Colonel loved, he could see his only gardener cutting with a horse-mower the wild outer fringe of lawn, and he could smell the sweet, light fragrance of it drying in the August heat. The terrace, the gardener, the horse and the sun were almost all that was left to him of his life before the war. Not, he often reflected, that they were very much good to him. He could no longer ride the horse, and the gardener was a witless sort of bounder who abused him to his face and raided his tobacco jar behind his back. That left him only the terrace, and, if he were lucky, the sun. All the rest had long since been given up to what he always called the young Air Force gentlemen. They had long ago invaded the solitude, broken the silence and recoloured, sometimes excitingly, the grey privacy of a house that was, anyway, too large for one old man. All that remained to him now was a single room above the stables, and, by a purely compassionate arrangement, the terrace in the sun. The young men filled all the rest of the place with their eating and drinking, their laughter and their language that he could never quite understand, and he in turn had lain for four years in the sun, whenever there was any sun, and watched the faces of them come and go.

He had not been very lucky with the sun since invasion day. The papers were saying that it was the worst summer for forty years. Cold gales had swept down from the north in June, breaking the oats into shabby and forlorn wreckage and burning the tender leaves of the limes. The Colonel, who felt the cold easily and bitterly, lit the gas-fire in his room in the evenings, or sat on the balcony with his overcoat on and read over and over again the invasion news in the papers. After the first few days there was very little flying and he began to feel depressed by having to look so often at a sky without planes. It seemed as if the cloud was solid, unchanged by turns of wind, and dark over the whole world. Ten-tenths, the boys called it: which seemed a curious sort of arithmetical and more difficult way of saying complete, he thought.

But then he had no knowledge at all of the language of modern war; he had lost touch with its progress; at eighty-three he had fallen a long way behind. The young men who came and talked to him in the garden and even on the balcony talked to him constantly in a language which it seemed to him made no sense at all. He discovered in himself a depressing and uneasy ignorance as they talked of kites and pieces of cake, of a shaky do and a very curious situation in which they informed you that you had had it. The Colonel did not know where all this had sprung from. Language in his day had been rather a pompous affair, perhaps rather puerile, but he felt that at least you could understand it. He did not understand this other at all. He felt sometimes like a small boy left out in the cold, not yet initiated into the secret of the games of older boys.

And yet he liked talking to them. He liked it very much; perhaps more than he cared to say. On the few days when flying began again he found himself alone on the balcony all day in the sun, bored with the remote contents of newspapers, missing the immediate touch that he got from talking with men who perhaps only an hour before had been over the battlefield.

That also was a thing he could not get used to. In his day you went off to war after a series of stern farewells; you lived a life of monastic remoteness somewhere on a damnable plain in India, or you went to the northern hills and were cut off for some months at a time. Or if there were no war you went pig-hunting or you had furlough, and if you liked that sort of thing you arranged something unofficially pleasant in the way of women. You needed the hide of a pig yourself not to be affected by all this, and you did in fact come back with that sort of hide, sunbrown or yellow and as harsh as rind. You looked like a soldier. But nowadays these young fellows flew out and put the fear of God into what they called a gaggle of Wolfers or a bunch of tanks at four-thirty in the afternoon, and at seven they were lying in the hay with a young woman or drinking gin in the local bar. For some reason or other they hadn't any kind of soldierly look about them, either. He had looked almost in vain for a martial type. He sometimes saw instead a touch of almost feminine dreaminess about some of them. They were very quiet sometimes and had long-seeing eyes that seemed to be dreaming in planetary distances. They were boyishly hilarious and laughed fantastically behind quite impossibly unclipped moustaches. There was none of that heroic stuff at all.

He spread out his fingers loosely in the sun. The weather had changed at last. Now he could feel the heat stinging up through his fingers from the lead. It was the sort of heat he loved; it seemed to burn him to the bone. It was now about twelve o'clock and if he were lucky one of the young night-fliers who slept all morning would be waking up now and would come up to talk to him before lunch. The war was going very well at last, and there had arisen another of those curious situations in which the night-fliers now talked of beating the daylights out of Jerry.

He sat for another ten minutes or so alone, listening to the clap-racket of the horse-mower and the soft wind that lifted gently up and down, in slow dark swells, the flat branches of two cedars on the lawn. He felt the sun beating not only into his fingers but down through the closed lids of his eyes, which seemed transparent in the vertical light. Then he heard sounds in the bedroom that opened out on to the balcony and the voice of one of the young men saying "Good morning, sir," and he opened his eyes to see Pallister, one of the night-pilots, standing there quite naked except for a pink-and-white towel round his loins.

"Ah, young fellow," he said.

Pallister danced from one foot to another on the hot lead of the balcony, and then dropped the towel and stood on it. His body was brown all over, a sort of light buttery brown, except for paler islands of skin on the inner flanks of his thighs. The Colonel knew all about those islands. The skin from them had been used to re-cover the burnt lids of the boy's eyes.

The Colonel watched Pallister spread out the towel and then sit on it, cross-legged, like one of the Indian boys the Colonel so clearly remembered. The boy sighed and screwed up his eyes and put on a pair of dark glasses.

"Too hot for you?" the Colonel said.

"I just can't have enough of that sun soak into me," the boy said.

"It's certainly very beautiful," the Colonel said.

He wanted to talk about the war; to get that intimate touch of fire no newspaper ever gave. But Pallister, behind dark glasses, looked remote and anonymous. He was cut off from him, and the Colonel lost for some moments the friendliness of the young face.

But after a time he got used to the dark glasses; he concentrated on the lips of the boy instead. They, too, were friendly, and unlike the eyes had never been burnt out of the shape of youth. They had sometimes a way of looking very cynical that only made them more youthful still.

"Well," the Colonel said, "what is it like over there?"

He supposed he always asked that. He could think of no other way of beginning.

"Oh! It's a bloody ramping mess," the boy said. "Looks like fair-day."

"Even at night?" the Colonel said. He wondered how even the August moon showed this rampant detail.

"Oh! It was light already when I was coming back," the boy said. "There was a bit of a doings."

"Shoot something down?"

"Up," the boy said. "Road stuff. And a Ju.88 down. Piece of cake."

"Tell me about it."

"Oh! They hadn't a clue. It was just a hell of a nice bang on the ground and hell of a nicer bang upstairs," the boy said. "Very smooth do."

The boy grinned as he spoke, and the Colonel got the impression of an idol, darkly eyeless, laughing up into the sun. The severance of the lips from the black-glassed eyes was so complete as to be unreal and in a way almost hideous. The eyes in their unalive darkness were for the Colonel the symbol of the fact that there had been a time, only a summer ago, when the boy had really been eyeless and for many months nearly dead. It had happened that flak over Denmark had hit something in the Mosquito, the Colonel thought perhaps the pyrotechnics, and had driven white whirlwinds of flame down through the aircraft with terrible fury that could not be stopped. It burnt the face of the boy for a few moments as the heat of a blow-lamp burns off the skin of old paint. The boy had heard himself screaming against the death that was coming up to seize him with a terror that made a lacerating shriek throughout the whole of his body. Instantaneously he was dead but alive: the death living and torturous in a second of screaming flame before its hellish extinction of him. He knew in this awful interval what it was to be burning alive; to be dying and to be aware; to be aware and to be quite helpless. The flame leapt up for an awful and final moment of savage agony and slit the light out of his eyes and left the light of his body and the terror of his mind completely dead.

He did not know quite what happened after that. The flame went out into darkness. It seemed never to have happened; there seemed never to have been a flame. He was afterwards told that for a long time he did not utter a sound; but he had a fanciful and private impression of talking the whole time. It was also quite real; an impression of repeating to himself a frenzied catechism; "I can see, I can see, I can see." And then: "I will see, I will see, God! I will see!" Then it appeared that at last he did begin talking and did amazing things in the way of instructing Jackson, his observer, to fly the aircraft. He was reported as being nervously and consciously active over the whole seaward course, and that, among other details, he kept naming the stars. He had again the private and absolute conviction that all this was nonsense. He had never talked at all. He knew that he was not even very good at naming the stars. He was quite certain about these things. And yet it was quite certain also that Jackson had flown the aircraft home and could only have done so under his advice. As he struggled afterwards to get at the truth of the long darkness that had succeeded the catastrophic moment of white flame, in which he was living and yet also dead, he fell back on the simple defence against terror that was its own dissolution. It was just one of those things.

There followed about nine months in hospitals. The Colonel, who was still staring at the boy and trying to get himself into a state when he could talk easily beyond what were always the first moments of embarrassment, knew all about that time. Sometimes the boy talked very well. Even then the Colonel got the impression that, as often as not, he did not talk to him. He lay flat on his back, perfectly naked, outstretched and very brown except for white patches on the inner flanks of his thighs, and simply talked upward to the sun. He talked quite rapidly, giving no other sign of his high-pitched nervousness except that he drummed his fingers restlessly on the lead of the balcony. It might have been, the Colonel thought, that he was sometimes very much afraid. In a laconic and careless sort of way he talked of the miracles they had done to him in hospital. The Colonel, simply by sheer repetition, got to know some part of the surgical language of them: things like scarlet mercurochrome, Tierch grafts, pre-anaesthetic injections and God knew what. He heard how those grafts had left the boy for some time looking like a young cuckoo, his face a mess of puffed sewing that had a foul baldness not yet touched by sun. He had heard of physiotherapy and occupational therapy, and how, at last, the boy had come out of it, less shocking to look at than he had feared, with the fierce light of living in him, and able to see.

Then the miracle of it all had almost been lost. It appeared from the livid language of the boy, who could out-swear a regular army sergeant without effort, that there had been a fool of a psychiatrist who had made the suggestion that he was mentally unfit to fly. It had had a violently opposite effect. It instantly brought to the surface, in a high emotional temperature, all the symptoms of the disease from which the Colonel now knew the boy was suffering. For as the Colonel lay on the terrace day after day and talked to the boy, it seemed to him that the very great differences between war as he had fought it long ago in Northern Indian hills, and as the boy fought it over the fields of France, was not a difference of time, of latitude, of speed or of weapons, but something more simple and more amazing. The Colonel had gone into war as another man might go into business; respectably, steadfastly, following his father in a line of succession. For the boy it was all quite different. Flying was a disease.

He did not know if the boy was aware of that. He had only recently become aware of it himself. You could, of course, suffer from a disease without being aware of it. It was quite certain that it was something not wholly conscious which had sent the boy into a frenzy of antagonism and scheming against all authority until at last authority had finally given way and let him fly once more.

Thinking of this, and then letting it slip away from his mind, the Colonel once again spoke to the boy. What was now happening in France interested him greatly. This war of movement was so fast that he did not know if you could any longer talk of strategy as he had once been taught it. He longed to get a picture of it, fixed and clear, as the boy might have photographed it from the air.

"Tell me about this Seine thrust," he said. "What do you think of it? Do you think it aims at the coast?"

"I never really trouble about what the Brown Jobs are doing," the boy said.

The Colonel was silenced. It was not a very good morning. Once again he was up against some new term he did not understand.

"Brown Jobs?"

"Army."

"Oh!" the Colonel said. "Oh!" He understood now. Of course, apart from the slight contempt it was very apt, very typical.

"Yes, but it's a combined operation," he said. "You are all in it. You depend very much on each other."

"Oh! I know," the boy said: as if he did not know at all.

The Colonel did not know what to say. The astonishing realisation that the boy did not know what was happening on a general scale stupefied him. It seemed an incredible thing. It seemed to arise from a different sort of blindness, not physical, but from the blindness of this intense and narrow passion to fly. To the boy all horizons beyond these narrow limits of vision were closed. His life soared furiously and blindly between.

"Without you," the Colonel said, "the Brown Jobs might never force the issue."

The boy slightly tilted his head, turning towards the Colonel a pair of black sun-glassy lenses, as if to say "Force the issue? What the bloody hell does that mean?"

For a moment the Colonel felt that he did not know what the hell it meant himself. He lay quietly in his chair. Across the garden now the horse-mower was silent. There was no sound except the sea-sound of cedar branches gently lifting and falling on the summer wind. It seemed now to the Colonel that the battle-front, really half an hour's flight to the south, was a million miles away.

"There is no bloody issue except killing Huns," the boy said. "That's all that matters." He looked straight up into the sun.

A certain essence of individual cruelty in this remark quite shocked the Colonel. It startled him so that he lifted himself up in the chair and looked at the boy. In the hot sun the face had a pure and impersonal immobility. The savagery of the remark was quite natural. To the Colonel there seemed a certain absence of ethics in the whole of this careless and calculated attitude of the boy's towards fighting. In his day, the Colonel's, there had been in fighting some sort of—well, he supposed it to be a sort of ethical water-line. You kept above it. The people who sank below the water-line, who made public a private desire to kill the man on the opposite side, were not thought very much of. It was very much like a game, and all the wars in which he had played it were really, beside this one, quite small. They seemed very important then and were quite forgotten now. He supposed perhaps that that was finally the essence of it: the hugeness of the thing. The boy had in his hands, like the rest of his generation, a frightening and enormous power. It was perhaps the greatest power ever given into the hands of the individual in all time.

"Wizard day," the boy said. As suddenly as he spoke he curved up his long legs and outstretched them again, in a slow convulsive movement of pleasure in the sun. "Bloody wizard." he took great breaths of the warm, noontide air and breathed them out again.

The Colonel, startled out of his reminiscence, did not speak, and the boy went on, talking as if to himself:

"Gosh, the trees," the boy said, "and the smell of the bloody hay and the lime trees and all that. After all those months of smelling hospital wards and ether and anæsthetics, Christ, it's good. Did I ever tell you what it was like in Normandy? I mean in the D-minus days."

"No," the Colonel said. He had given up.

"Not the orchards? You could see them all in blossom at night, in the full moon. Miles of them. You know how short the nights are in May. Never quite dark. You could see everything. Every puff of smoke from a train, and the rivers, and the orchards in blossom. Bloody wonderful, Colonel, I tell you. You never saw anything so lovely as the sun coming up and the moon not set and the sky half pink with sunlight and half yellowy with moonlight, and all the colour on the French orchards. I tell you, Colonel, you never saw anything so wonderful."

So much for the passionate, impersonal cruelty of the boy, the Colonel thought. So much for the notion of calculated savagery. It now seemed quite monstrous beside the tenderness of that description of orchards in May. He could see that the boy felt it very deeply and he tried to remember if, so long ago, he too had been touched by anything like that, but he could remember only scarlet rhododenrons, in fantastic cascades, on a wild furlough trek above Darjeeling; how they fell bloodily into rocky spring valleys there and how impressed he had been and how for that reason he had planted them liberally in the garden here. But the glory of them was never quite the same. The scarlet wildness was never renewed. There was something hot and foreign and un-English about them, anyway; not like the orchards, that were so cool and cloudy, like the northern skies. It pleased him very much that the boy liked them. It seemed to make him quite human again.

Then to his dismay the boy got up. He stood quite naked, and took off his glasses and turned away from the sun. His eyes had the oddest appearance of not belonging to the rest of his body. The pale new tissue, not yet merged into the older skin of the face, seemed lividly dead. It seemed to have been grafted there from another person altogether. It aroused the instant and uneasy impression that the boy was two different people.

"Must you?" the Colonel said. "So soon?"

"I'm as hungry as hell," the boy said. "I've got to get dressed and lunch is off at two."

"Well, nice of you to come up," the Colonel said. "I do so appreciate it."

"Can I send you up a can of beer, sir?" the boy said.

"No. No thanks. I don't think so."

"A half-can? The orderly can bring it up."

"No, thank you. Thank you all the same." He did not want to offend the boy. The pilots were very kind to him sometimes like that, sending him up tobacco or chocolate, or a glass of beer. "Perhaps tomorrow. Perhaps we might have a drink together. I should like that."

"Good show," the boy said.

"About this time?" the Colonel said.

"Yeh. I'll get the orderly to bring the beer up."

"I'll wait for you," the Colonel said.

The boy tucked the towel round his loins and hopped over the hot lead of the terrace into the bedroom, calling back over his shoulder something about the Colonel having a sleep, and as if in obedience the Colonel smiled and closed his eyes against the brassy midday light, the only light in which, after many years in the East, he ever felt really warm.

He lay there next day at about the same time, in much the same attitude, waiting for the boy. The strength of the grasses' sweetness had faded a little overnight. He caught it only at odd moments, in brief renewed waves, on the seaward wind. But the branches of the cedars rose and fell with the same slow placidity as the day before, and beyond them, if he raised himself up on his fleshless knuckles, he could again see across brown cornfields to the blue-grey edge of sea.

He waited for just over an hour before deciding to go down into the garden to see if he could find the boy. He was permitted to use the back-stairs, once the servants' stairs, on which now there was always a loathsome smell of stale cooking. He did not like these stairs and he was glad to be out of them, past the back entrance and the heaps of boiler coke, into the garden and the sun.

At eighty-three he walked very slowly, with a sort of deliberate majesty, keeping his head up more by habit than any effort, and it was some time before he could walk far enough across the lawns to find someone to ask about Pallister. Groups of young officers were playing croquet on the farthest lawn, and the knock of balls and the yelling of voices clapped together in the clear air.

Under one of the cedars, in shadow that was almost black, an officer in battledress was lying on the grass with a book. He had Canada on his shoulder.

"Excuse me," the Colonel said.

"Oh! Hullo, sir," the Canadian said. "How've you bin?"

"I was looking for Mr Pallister," the Colonel said. "We were to have a drink together. I thought you might have seen him somewhere."

"I guess he bought it," the Canadian said.

The language that he did not understand left the Colonel without a reply.

"Yeh!" the Canadian said. "I guess he bought it. Over France last night."

Note on the stories, points for discussion and suggestions for further reading

Love in a Wych Elm

This first story of childhood set in Evensford establishes direct links with H.E. Bates's own childhood. The fictional "Evensford" of many of his stories is in fact Rushden, the Northamptonshire town in which he spent his childhood.

H.E. Bates recalls his childhood in the first volume of his autobiography, *The Vanished World*, in which he describes Rushden:

> In structure Rushden is an odd town; in the lateness and rapidity of its development perhaps odder still. Unlike Higham Ferrers it has no ancient history worthy of the name. At the beginning of the nineteenth century it was still a mere village of a few hundred inhabitants; by the end of the century it had become an industrial town of 15,000 people. Its shape ill-suited to bear the scars of jerry-building and the Industrial Revolution, might well have been carved out by a madman gone slightly beserk with a giant bulldozer. It is impossible to get out of the town without going uphill. Hills rise and slant and dive in all directions, some so precipitously that one or two streets are closed to downhill traffic. The miserable little brook that runs through the entire length of it seems to be the central point of magnetism for these many steep streets and alley-ways, which can be wickedly cold in winter and steamily, oppressively hot in summer. The only buildings of any architectural significance in the whole town are the church, with its famous Strainer arch, one of only three in England, and the Hall, which is the setting for a great deal of my novel, *Love for Lydia*. The rest is a palpably dreadful mess of that mixture of blue slate, factory, chapel and that harsh Midland red brick which equally oppresses heart, soul, eye and senses.
>
> Just occasionally you find this dreary pattern relieved by corner facings of that deep beer-brown ironstone which lies near the surface of the Nene and Walland Valleys, and sometimes in the years of my boyhood you would find grapevines growing on the south walls of these older, softer houses of local

stone. But the street in which I was born was wholly of brick, not all red but ranging from plain white at the southern, more respectable end to a shade of dreary dreadful puce-blue at the other. In it were two boot factories and next to one of them I was born. In the street running in at right angles almost opposite to my parents' house stood the factory where my father worked, and immediately over the roof of the pork butcher's opposite us I could see, on winter evenings, the gas-lights of another factory shining greasy-yellow until six o'clock. The geography of the town might indeed have been laid out by some shoe-making dictator who had insisted that for every hundred yards of dwelling houses there should be thirty or forty of factory sandwiched between and then had added the humanitarian proviso that a bake-house and a chapel or two should somehow be tucked in among them. Immediately opposite us there were indeed two bake-houses, both absolutely identical. At the far end of the street was another, with a fourth fifty yards beyond. A fifth, again next door to a factory, and in this case an outdoor beerhouse as well as a bakery, stood at the far end of the street where my father worked. Here, too, within a distance of a few hundred yards were three chapels; and this pattern of house, factory, bake-house and chapel, with here and there little front room sweet-shops, continued all over the town.

Later in his autobiography H. E. Bates describes some of the street games he played in "Grove Street, in which my parents' house faced the gas-lights of the pork-butcher's shop and the two bake-houses". In "Love in a Wych Elm" the story-teller recalls the same scene. It is also interesting to note the similarity between the way in which the narrator is shocked by the revelation, at the end of the story, that Reggie Candleton came from Gas Street and the way in which H. E. Bates remembers social differences between the streets of his own childhood: "The children of Grove Street never dreamed of consorting with Crabb Street, from which we might have been removed by a thousand miles, even though we were not more than two hundred yards apart."

There are, too, marked similarities between the Candleton gardens and those of Rushden Hall. H. E. Bates describes the position of Rushden Hall in modern times as being

extraordinarily incongruous: an oasis of trees and avenues, the chief of which is (unless a rumour of its recent demolition is correct) composed of sixty-three ancient Wych elms, surrounded on all sides by boot factories, nineteenth and twentieth century developments, with all the chapels, bakeries and fish shops I have already described, together with today's supermarkets and coffee bars.

In "Love in a Wych Elm" we read that "Mr Candleton was a strict Sunday morning churchgoer in pin-stripe trousers, bowler hat and spats, and Hilda went with him to sing in the choir". In his autobiography H. E. Bates describes his own father's love of singing in an "age of male-voice choirs, male-voice quartettes and mixed quartettes" and recalls the sound of his "very fine, strong bass voice, the rich warm depth of which I can still hear emerging from the tiers of the chapel choir, of which he was subsequently conductor, like a splendid diapason".

Points for discussion and suggestions for further reading

1 Why do adults often enjoy recalling childhood? Consider the ways in which adults, particularly when together as a family, enjoy talking about the past.

2 The literature of childhood memories is vast and varied. If you haven't already read it, you might enjoy Laurie Lee's *Cider With Rosie*, Lee's account of his childhood and adolescence in a Cotswold village. Poets, in fact, seem particularly skilled in remembering the importance of childhood in their development as artists. Try, for instance, Clifford Dyment's account of his childhood spent in Nottingham and South Wales, *The Railway Game*. This is highly readable, especially the chapter in which Mr Belton, landlord of the rooms in which Clifford and his mother lived in Nottingham, takes him to his den, a den which turns out to be a room full of model railway engines. Here Clifford is introduced to The Railway Game. Dylan Thomas writes about various incidents in his childhood in his *Portrait of the Artist as a Young Dog*. Some of the incidents are, typically, embroidered, but many of the adventures are based on actual happenings. Begin, perhaps, with "The Fight" and "Extraordinary Little Cough". Remember that Dylan Thomas's writing gains greatly from being read aloud. A challengingly difficult, but rewarding, account of childhood, much more sombre than any of the above books, is *Father and Son*, Edmund Gosse's account of his Victorian childhood with fanatically religious parents and the struggle he had to break away from the religious pressures of his home environment.

As an even greater contrast to 'Love in a Wych Elm' one might read Maxim Gorky's *My Childhood,* a vivid, warm, often grim account of his nineteenth-century childhood in Russia. Equally absorbing and divided into short chapters useful to dip into is Tolstoy's *Childhood, Boyhood, Youth.* Tolstoy's book, like Dylan Thomas's, is a mixture of fact and fiction. Like Thomas's *Portrait* it reveals the vital importance of many of the experiences of childhood in the development of the artist. These experiences were a key factor in the development of Wordsworth as a poet, and Wordsworth describes many incidents of his boyhood in the Lake District in an autobiography in verse, *The Prelude.* These incidents can be found, simply narrated in Books 1 and 2 in particular. Try the descriptions of boating on Ullswater and of skating on the frozen lake in Book 1 and the descriptions of riding, rowing and exploring islands in Book 2.

A number of twentieth-century novels give semi-autobiographical accounts of their authors' childhoods. One of the greatest, certainly one of the most readable, is D.H. Lawrence's *Sons and Lovers,* his account of his own uneasy boyhood and adolescence in a Nottinghamshire mining town. Another important novel is James Joyce's *Portrait of the Artist as a Young Man,* an interpretation of Joyce's experiences at boarding school and of his youth in Dublin.

3 "Love in a Wych Elm" explores the delicate stage in a boy's development when he is becoming sexually aware of girls, yet isn't quite able to express this sexual interest in terms of actual understanding of sexual attraction. He noticed that "at thirteen they were filling out"; he was "agreeably and mystically stunned" at Hilda's appearance; he afterwards found Stella "in some unelevating and puzzling way, awkward and flat". In what ways has this story mirrored your own experiences of growing up? In what ways can the reading of literature concerned with personal relationships, particularly between men and women, help us to come to terms with the rather complex problems of our own relationships?

Here are a few ideas for further reading of novels and short stories that explore this stage in moving from the innocence of childhood to the greater knowing and understanding of adolescence:

L.P. Hartley, *The Go-Between*. This is one of the most sensitive studies of the ways in which a child can be an unwitting servant of the adult world and can even be injured by a shock confrontation with the truth about adult relationships. A film based on this novel appeared in 1971.

Graham Greene, "The Basement Room", a short story about the loss of childhood innocence; a small boy is witness to a murder. Filmed as "The Fallen Idol"

Sid Chaplin, short stories: "The Bridge" and "The End of an Age".

Bill Naughton, a short story: "Weaver's Knot" and a novel *One Small Boy*.

Keith Waterhouse, Novel: *There Is A Happy Land*.

4 Discuss the appeal of a family whose home environment is radically different from one's own. The Candleton home was very different from that of the storyteller.

5 "It's nice to have a man's opinion," says Stella. Think of any occasions when you, in your childhood, were regarded as being worthy of giving a "man's opinion" or "a woman's opinion" and think whether these occasions gave you special pleasure.

Let's Play Soldiers

Here is a story of a situation that starts out as a simple piece of childhood play, an acting out of adult conflicts as war games. In the end, like so many childhood games, it enables a child to gain a first inkling of the sombre reality on which they are based.

This story probably also has its origins in H.E. Bates's own Evensford childhood, as another extract from *The Vanished World* suggests:

> Before the sense of destruction made itself fully felt—even a child couldn't escape the eventual insufferable gloom of the holocaust that every morning was reflected in the long columns of the dead, wounded and missing that darkened every newspaper and still more intimately in the little mourning shrines set up in every street with their own lists of agonies and pitiful jam jars of flowers—I went through a period of martial excite-

ment. War suddenly became glorified—or perhaps it would be truer to say that it merely became glamourised.

I am not now absolutely sure how long the war had been in progress when an advance party of billeting officers suddenly descended on the town, chalking what seemed to me to be meaningless sets of numbers and figures on the walls of houses. Soon the town was full of the sound of marching feet, the bang and blare of army bands and the voices of babbling Welshmen. The Royal Welch Fusiliers, disporting their famous black flash behind the tunic collar and their equally famous goat mascot at the head of their marching columns, were a proud regiment. But none of its soldiers could have been prouder than the small boy who positively worshipped at their parades, became a devout follower of route marches far out into the country and would have given his heart for the privilege of blowing a bugle or beating a drum. Mercifully he had never heard of the words cannon-fodder. All was glamour and glory, from the nodding head of the goat to the silvery jugglings of the magnificent drum major.

In "Let's Play Soldiers" "Fred had a peaked khaki cap on, with the badge of the Beds & Bucks Light Infantry on one side and that of the Royal Welch Fusiliers on the other" and we are told that "the goat ate anything you gave it, even cigarettes". As in "Love in a Wych Elm" there are references to Gas Street.

The War referred to in the story is the First World War ("The Great War") of 1914–18. In the story Albie was "in France, fighting the Germans" and the major battle area comprised the grim trenches of France and Flanders. Casualties were huge, often suffered in the battle for a single hill or a few hundred yards of land. Albie was probably "cannon fodder". For instance, at the battle of Arras (9–14 April 1917) British casualties were 142,000, German 85,000. The main success in this battle was the taking of Vimy Ridge by the Canadians. In July 1917, in the battle of the Somme, the British attack failed, and in one day 19,000 were killed, 57,000 were casualties, the greatest loss ever sustained by a British army in a single day. At Ypres (in Flanders) there were three battles, the first in October 1914 accounting for three-quarters of the British casualties up to that point in the war (begun in August 1914), the second in 1915, in which the Germans used gas for the first time, the third in July and August 1917. The final stage of the third battle, at Passchendaele, was named "the battle of the mud". After an exceptionally rainy August men, guns and tanks became bogged down in the Flanders mud.

For a clear account of the political and military history of the First World War you should read Parts 1, 2 and 3 of A.J.P. Taylor's *English History 1914–45* from which the above facts and figures have been taken.

Suggestions for further reading about the First World War

Robert Graves's autobiography *Goodbye to All That* contains his account of his wartime service with the Royal Welch Fusiliers and describes the horrors of trench warfare in France and Flanders from first-hand experience. Siegfried Sassoon's *Memoirs of an Infantry Officer* is a semi-autobiographical account of similar experiences.

The Longman Imprint edition of David Holbrook's novel *Fleshwounds* contains an article by the present writer on "The Modern Writer and War". The article includes extracts from the work of Sassoon, Graves and other writers connected with the Great War.

The considerable amount of poetry produced by the poets who fought in the First World War is well represented in *Poetry of the First World War*. For valuable information about the major war poets you should consult the Times Authors collection *Poets of the First World War*.

Further reading about "War Games"

Alan Sillitoe's excellent short story "The Decline and Fall of Frankie Buller" (in *A Sillitoe Selection*—Longman Imprint books) is a tale, set in Nottingham, of the exploits of a mentally retarded youth whose chief enjoyment in life is to command a gang of local lads in war games.

Cecil Day Lewis's adventure story *The Otterbury Incident* contains a lively account of boys' war games, particularly in the opening chapter "The Ambush in Abbey Lane".

Points for discussion

1 In what ways can children's play, particularly in games involving the imaginative playing-out of real-life situations, help children to come to terms with life? Discuss such games carefully in the light of your own experiences. What experience does the narrator of "Let's Play Soldiers" finally gain after

his war game has ended? Consider particularly the last sentence of the story and its words "afraid of the enemy we had conquered and the soldier I had killed".

2 "He didn't look very dead when we left him but we knew he was." Discuss the ways in which children are able (as adults later cannot so readily) to imagine a situation to be real whilst at the same time accepting that they are play-acting.

3 As with "Love in a Wych Elm", "Let's Play Soldiers" marks a stage in the transition from innocent childhood to the knowing of adolescence. For an example of a ten-year-old boy's encountering of an adult crisis that he's unable to appreciate or understand until he looks back on it a few years later read and talk about Alan Sillitoe's short story "On Saturday Afternoon" published in *A Sillitoe Selection*.

4 Consider how typical of boys is the story-teller's wartime ambition: "There was nothing on earth I wanted more than to be a lance-corporal: except perhaps to kill a soldier." Why do boys like violence? Can the liking be harmlessly worked out of the system? Are these boyhood characteristics used in the later making of "good" soldiers?

5 What must it be like for a mother, father or wife of a man away at the Wars? Give a few thoughts to Mrs Strickland in "Let's Play Soldiers". How does Albie's absence affect her behaviour? You might read and talk about H.E. Bates's very poignant short story "It's Just The Way It Is" which describes the visit of the parents of a dead airman to the Wing Commander of their son's bomber station. This story can be found in the collected *Stories of Flying Officer X*.

Every Bullet Has Its Billet

Like "Let's Play Soldiers" this story is set in England during the First World War. A passage in *The Vanished World* referring to H.E. Bates's childhood during the war may hint at the original happening that eventually provided an idea for this story:

> To our family fell the duty of billeting a young upperclass lieutenant, a great eighteen stone bag of a man, and his petite, pretty wife. Newly married, they too brought glamour to the house. Wining and dining with fellow officers in the dining-room they produced not only an atmosphere of opulence and

aristocracy but also one that until that time had been as foreign to the household as, say, bad language or the smell of opium: the odours of strong drink. It was really a twilight world. While the young lieutenant painfully slogged it out with his men on long route marches, his tender feet unequal to the task of supporting so vast a frame, his attractive little wife sat at home and, after the fashion of the day, painted in water colours. And sometimes, when both were out, I used to creep into their room and lift the lid of the long black tin box and gaze down at the glittering grandeur of an officer's wardrobe, from the finery of mess kit to the flashing gleam of scabbard and sword.

Soon the obese young officer was to be killed in the filth that was Flanders and the babbling Welshmen were to be replaced as cannon-fodder disguised as symbols of glory by men of the Yorkshire and Lancashire Regiment, at whose feet I worshipped with renewed devotion. It was their lot to be massacred in due course in the holocaust of the Dardanelles, far from the pubs and fish-and-chip shops of home. Often I wonder now what the thoughts of the cannon-fodder were, though I knew of no such wondering then. All was still glory: blow, bugles, blow, swing, rifles, swing. As I listened to the music of marching feet I longed, always, to be a soldier.

The young officer billeted on the Bates family was to be killed in the filth that was Flanders. (See the references to Ypres in the editorial material on "Let's Play Soldiers", page 156.) Lieutenant Bronson was killed at the Dardanelles. The attack on the Dardanelles resulted from Turkey's entry to the War on the side of the Germans and its object was the taking of the Gallipoli Peninsula. The successful occupation of Gallipoli would, it was hoped, lead to the capturing of Constantinople. Like many other campaigns in this War the bungling of politicians and generals led to the defeat of the invading army by the Turks and to a dangerous and costly evacuation of the troops from the beaches of Gallipoli. The Gallipoli campaign has been described in detail in a highly readable book by Alan Moorhead simply titled *Gallipoli*.

Points for discussion

1 How does H.E. Bates bring out his undoubted hostility to Mrs Harris in his descriptions of her? What does he describe about her?

2 Other stories in this collection will be found to contain characters who are salesmen. These individuals often appear to display character failings which appear to be connected with their jobs. Consider this aspect of H.E. Bates's characterisation in his study of Mrs Harris: "Years of financial alertness, of swift concentration against the remote chance of mistaking sixpence for a farthing, had left her eyes virtually lidless. Her concentration on money had become a creed."

3 To what extent is Mrs Harris's attitude towards her daughter affected by this background? Note her choice of the name "Irma". Is this tendency of a mother to seek the fulfilment denied to *her* in her *child* a common one? Is it more common where a mother's marriage has been unsatisfactory? (One of the best examples of the child being "the lost self of the woman", as H.E. Bates puts it, is to be found in the attitude of Mrs Morel to her son Paul in D.H Lawrence's novel *Sons and Lovers*. Just as Mrs Harris "saw Irma captured by someone else, taken away from her", so Mrs Morel feels that Miriam "exults" as she takes Paul away from her.)

4 What was the effect of Mrs Harris's attitude on Irma? Can such attitudes produce actions in adolescent children that injure both children and parents? "She was aware of an increasing feeling that it would be nice if it could be proved the other way. Then she wanted it proved the other way" (page 25). For a classic case of this in fiction read Somerset Maugham's short story "The Kite".

5 What influence does the "aristocratic" background of the Bronsons have on Mrs Harris's behaviour? Why is Mrs Harris so sensitive to this?

6 What caused Irma's heroine-worship of Mrs Bronson to develop? To what extent might this have been affected by the virginal Irma's wishing to see herself in Mrs Bronson's sexual role as wife? To what extent might Mrs Harris's jealousy of Irma and of the Bronsons have been sexual in content?

7 Explain why you think the author chose this particular title for the story.

The Station

In "Love in a Wych Elm" a young boy becomes aware of the

sexual attractiveness of a young woman, although he is not able to put his feelings precisely into words. When the boy returns to the young girl Stella at the wych elms on the day after his encounter with the "magnificent figure" of Hilda he thinks that "something about Stella had not quite ripened". Ripeness often tends, in H.E. Bates's writing, to be associated with sexual maturity and in "Love in a Wych Elm" he evokes the atmosphere of "heavy summer days" and "fruit falling with a squashy mellow plop on the grass and paths".

It is a summer night when Albie first visits "The Station" with Spike. The air is "sultry", the woman is "big-shouldered and dark", "her thin white dress was like the silky husk of a seed-pod, just bursting open", she has "ripe breasts". In the garden the first plum she passes to Albie is "soft" and "ripe" and "the ripe skin broke and the juice trickled over his fingers". He becomes "intoxicated by the smell of corn and plums and the night warmth and her very light, constant stroking of his hand".

Other stories in this collection make use of similar symbols. In "The Good Corn" Mortimer makes love to the girl helper on his farm in the summer, when the corn is ripening and when the "bushes of currant were bright with berries that glistened like scarlet pearls from under old lace curtains" (page 91).

Points for discussion

1 Why is it a most important feature of this story that Albie, alongside Spike, appears "boyish, his cheeks smooth and shiny as white cherries, his hair yellow and light" and that the woman is about thirty with "her thin white dress like the silky husk of a seed-pod, just bursting open"?

2 Do you think that the woman behaves as she does towards Albie with every young man who is like Albie?

3 Spike says that "She'll look at you fit to melt your bleedin' heart out, but it don't mean damn all. She wants to make that station a success, that's all. That's why she runs the night shack." What do you make of her after reading this comment and noting her later behaviour? Does she enjoy using her beauty to attract custom, enjoying its effect on people as, one might think, Alice Pypper enjoys using her smile to attract customers, and a man who is not a customer, in the story "The Loved One"? You might look to see if you can find any other similarities between her and Alice Pypper. Or is this something

that many attractive women enjoy?

4 Why might she know intuitively that Albie hasn't got a girl before she asks the question? Why does she go on to ask him questions that she knows will provoke him to take notice of her? And why, perhaps, are we never told her name? Is this significant?

5 Is her behaviour in the garden merely for her own sexual pleasure—a mature, experienced woman enjoying making advances to an innocent youth? Or are her motives more subtle and more compassionate?

6 What would seem to be H.E. Bates's reason for writing this story? Does he excite desire or compassion for the woman? Come back to this point after reading some of the other stories in this collection—after you have looked at the concern H.E. Bates has for unhappily married women in "The Loved One", "Time To Kill" and "The Ox", and the compassion he has for the unfulfilled person in "The Good Corn" and "Mr Penfold". Then give another thought to the woman at "The Station", left behind, "sitting in the dark... the red sign flashing everlastingly out and on, scarlet to darkness, 'The Station' to nothing at all."

Château Bougainvillaea

In "Château Bougainvillaea" H.E. Bates introduces us to a woman who has grave doubts about her future married happiness and who has these doubts confirmed during the course of a single afternoon during a holiday in France with her fiancé. Several of the stories in this collection reveal H.E. Bates's compassion for the unhappily married. Accompanying this compassion there would seem to be an implied concern that marriage, which should lead to complete fulfilment in the relationship between husband and wife and between parents and children, can be an arid, fruitless, unhappy experience. In "The Good Corn" the fruitlessness of the marriage is its childlessness and the compassion and understanding of the wife eventually binds the marriage happily. In "The Ox" the wife is literally a beast of burden, living for her children, her husband mentally unbalanced after the War. In "Time to Kill" Hanson, with time to kill waiting for a train, visits an ex-girl friend and finds her unhappily married to a sour man on an isolated smallholding. In "The Loved One" Alice

Pypper is married to a soulless travelling salesman and her only harmless excursion into romance outside marriage brings tragedy.

So far in this collection it has been the lushness of summer, its ripeness, its sensuousness, that has been stressed in "The Station" and "Love in a Wych Elm". But the French summer and the French landscape of this story have arid qualities which help Louise Bowen perhaps to see the possible aridity of married life with Arthur Keller. "The headland was like a dry purple island *scorched* by the flat heat of the afternoon, cut off from the mainland by a *sand-coloured* tributary of road"—these are the significant opening words. The sea is "*fierce* blue". Even the sun seems to generate hostility and heat the mind: "The *hot*, *crushed-down* sense of security she had felt all afternoon began suddenly to evaporate, *burnt* away from her by the first *explosion* of discontent and then by small restless *flames* of inward anger." The white tables are *blistered*, the shade is *sparse*, the fig trees are *fruitless*. She is reminded of the "hot and arid" place where perhaps "the Gadarene swine had stampeded down". The leaves of acacia and bay are "metallic summer-hard". The solitude is "barren". There is nothing exotic, a bougainvillaea for instance.

Points for discussion

1 In what ways does the "funny thing" about the "many left-handed people staying at one restaurant" bring out Louise's increasing discontent with Arthur?

2 "And there was a good way off from them an herd of many swine feeding. So the devils besought him, saying, If thou cast us out, suffer us to go away into the herd of swine. And he said unto them, Go. And when they were come out, they went into the herd of swine: and, behold, the whole herd of swine ran violently down a steep place into the sea, and perished in the waters. And they that kept them fled, and went their ways into the city, and told every thing, and what was befallen to the possessed of the devils." (St Matthew's Gospel, chapter 8)

"He spake also this parable; A certain man had a fig tree planted in his vineyard; and he came and sought fruit thereon, and found none. Then said he unto the dresser of his vineyard. Behold, these three years I come seeking fruit on this fig tree, and find none: cut it down; why cumbereth it the ground? And he answering said unto him, Lord, let it alone this year also, till I shall dig it about and dung it: And if it bear fruit, well: and if not, then after that thou shalt cut it down." (St Luke's Gospel, chapter 13)

What is it about the place and the climate that reminds Louise of these stories? In what ways do both stories link, symbolically, with Louise's fears of the future with Arthur?

3 Discuss the qualities in Arthur that increasingly grate on Louise. (Later, after reading the stories "Mr Penfold" and "The Loved One", you might consider whether H.E. Bates in some way wonders about the possible adverse effects of being a salesman on the breadth of a person's character and outlook.)

4 In what ways did it seem that Louise's position as a school-teacher had led her into becoming engaged to Arthur? Why is the alternative to marriage to Arthur such a disturbing prospect to Louise? Note the comment towards the end of the story: "It was now herself who walked, Louise Bowen, Standard V girls, certificated, deduct so much for superannuation scheme, tired as after a long day in the crowded chalk-smelling classroom." Discuss this problem—a woman's rather than a man's: faced with the alternatives of a possibly drab career or a possibly drab marriage which would you choose? Alternatively, how would you avoid the pitfalls of either in the first place?

5 Why did the visit to the château help Louise to come to a full realisation that she couldn't go on with Arthur? How does the tour of the Château emphasise their lack of common ground?

6 Now that you have discussed these dilemmas of Louise, think of the reasons why Louise, arriving at the château, "felt only that there ought to be a bougainvillaea". (*Note:* A bougainvillaea is a tropical plant that has its flowers almost concealed by small purple leaves.)

For further reading

Louise, at the end of this story, fears the boredom of the conventional married life in a semi-detached house on an estate. Try to get hold of a copy of David Turner's play *Semi-Detached*, a grimly comic send-up of a group of characters desperately trying to keep up with the Jones's.

Louise also fears the future as the school-teacher of Standard V girls. In D.H. Lawrence's novel *The Rainbow* the young Ursula Brangwen takes her first teaching post at the sort of school that would certainly justify Louise's fears. Ursula's experiences at Brinsley Street School, Ilkeston, are discussed in chapter 13 of *The Rainbow*, and this chapter can be read virtually as a separate, complete story. It contains some of D.H. Lawrence's finest writing and is a memorable picture of what teaching too often has been in the past. Few headmasters in literature are as hateful as Mr Harby. Ursula, in *her* "eternal bougainvillaea afternoons", "dreamed how she would make everything personal and vivid. She would be so *personal.* Teachers were always so hard and impersonal. There was no vivid relationship. She would make everything personal and vivid. She would give herself. She would give, give, give all her great stores of wealth to her children. She would make them *so* happy, and they would prefer her to any teacher on the face of the earth." But Ursula had reckoned without the influence of Mr Harby and the system. Eventually, as D.H. Lawrence recorded:

> It was no matter how she said to herself that school existed no more once she had left it. It existed. It was within her like a dark weight, controlling her movement. It was in vain the highspirited, proud young girl flung off the school and its association with her. She was Miss Brangwen, she was Standard Five teacher, she had her most important being in her work now.

Was this partly what Louise feared?

Time to Kill

"Time to Kill" is an interesting story to follow "Château Bougainvillaea". In "Château Bougainvillaea" Louise becomes increasingly sure that if she marries Arthur she will be unhappy. Hanson, in "Time to Kill", visits an old girlfriend and discovers that she is unhappily married.

There are a number of indications in this story that H.E. Bates is writing about the Evensford area. A single line branch line certainly ran from Wellingborough to Rushden, H.E. Bates's Northamptonshire home town. In *The Vanished World* Bates remembers his first job as an assistant reporter at the newly opened Wellingborough office of *The Northampton Chronicle*, where his salary was ten shillings a week:

> Out of my ten shillings I had of course to pay train fares and this left nothing for lunches or even a cup of tea. As a result I

had to evolve a special method for actual survival. This meant leaving the newspaper office at 12 o'clock midday, running all the way to the Midland Station at Wellingborough, about a mile out of town, and catching the 12.25 to Rushden. This journey, if the fireman didn't misfire with the transfer key to the branch line at the signal box, took seven minutes. Since the return train left at 1.19 this meant that I had to run every inch of the way home, again nearly a mile, gollop the lunch my mother had waiting for me and then run all the way back to the station again, with about a minute to spare. Small wonder that I was thin as a rake and developed no little prowess as a runner.

Other details in the story, "the naked ash trees", the emphasis on the wintery north-east wind that would blow straight across the low plateau to the east of Rushden from the North Sea ("the isolated farm with the sea-winds striking at the poplars"), suggest that the small farm could have been found somewhere on the higher ground on the outskirts of Rushden. And, of course, Hanson, like H.E. Bates, was a local reporter.

Points for discussion

1 The title "Time to Kill" refers to Hanson's time to kill waiting for his main-line train. In what way does it also provide an ironic summing up of the theme of the story?

2 The story of "The Station" is set on a sultry summer night; "Château Bougainvillaea" is located in a parched, arid summer landscape. In what ways is the winter landscape and weather such an ideal reflection of the theme of this story? Note, for instance, the reference to the young woman's "dark, bleak eyes".

3 How do the details of the farm interior that Hanson observes emphasise the sorry condition of the young woman's marriage and in what ways are the details of his memories of their previous friendship in complete contrast?

4 How is it made clear that Hanson's friendship with the girl had been a close one and might indeed have led to their marrying if she hadn't wanted to remain tied to her family and her small town?

5 What aspects of the husband's behaviour would add to

Hanson's sadness in observing the girl's married life?

6 "All the time it appeared to him as if she were about to stop and say something." What might she have wanted to say? Why had her eyes "got into the habit of not looking far"? How might Hanson have reacted had she said something?

7 In "Château Bougainvillaea" Louise had become engaged to Arthur because she felt she must escape from teaching. In "Time to Kill" the girl turned away from the chance of marrying Hanson because she didn't want to escape from the family circle and influence. What are the dangers of both these attitudes as far as a girl's thoughts of marriage are concerned?

The Loved One

In "Time to Kill" the railway branch line led Hanson to the scene of an unhappy marriage. In "The Loved One" Alice Woodman's marriage to James Pypper is far from satisfactory and her tragic, short-lived and wordless romantic acquaintance with a signalman lives and dies to the accompaniment of passing trains.

H.E. Bates spent his boyhood and youth virtually within sound of the main line of the then Midland Railway. This finely engineered line runs from London (St Pancras) to the towns and cities of the East Midlands, Derbyshire, Nottinghamshire and Yorkshire. North of Bedford the line climbs steadily from the Ouse Valley to Sharnbrook Summit before dipping down again to the Nene Valley and through the towns of Wellingborough and Kettering. In steam days the climb to Sharnbrook would create plenty of "speech" from the hard-working engines of both passenger and goods trains. A few lines of *The Vanished World* recall these sounds as H.E. Bates heard them:

> My grandmother's sister, also an excellent cook, especially as I remember it of potatoes, which she always served with a particularly delicious butter sauce, lived a short distance outside the village of Sharnbrook, in a tiny thatched cottage, at the top of a rough stony track, on the edge of a wood. This wood remains, for me, a paradise: crowded in spring with violets, both purple and white, primroses, anemones and later bluebells and pink campion. In high summer its fringes were red with wild strawberries. In June, after the gold of cowslips had faded, the fields on all sides were white with moon daisies

and deeply fragrant with red clover. Not far away the main railway line from London to the North runs up the long escarpment of the river valley and it is still the sound of the great double-engined steam expresses rushing magnificently past, shattering the woodland silence with a thousand echoes, that remains as vividly with me as the sight and sound of flowers and the song of thrush, blackbird and nightingale.

It is interesting to compare this description with the lines from "The Loved One" that speak of "the awakening and stilling and reawakening of many voices in the woods by the passing of the trains".

Points for discussion

1 Have a look at the ways in which H.E. Bates presents James Pypper and his "tireless enthusiasm" for selling. How does he reveal his hostility towards both James Pypper and his salesman's mind? Is there any similarity between Bates's attitude to Pypper in this story and his attitude to Arthur Keller in "Château Bougainvillaea"?

2 Consider the significance of the situation of the house to which Alice and James move—how it somehow reflects qualities in their lives, a house that "stood on high exposed ground", a place of "raw hideousness", surroundings with a "bleak, sour quality of loneliness". Compare this situation with that of the Edwards home in "Time to Kill". Have both couples any thing in common?

3 Discuss the ways in which the presence of a railway in this story adds dramatic effect even before the event of death of the signalman.

4 H.E. Bates's emphasis of particular personal qualities in the main characters of his stories helps a great deal in our understanding of the characters and in our understanding of the story. This aspect of his writing needs looking at closely in "The Loved One":

(a) Note the title "The Loved One" to begin with. Bates stresses that Alice "had a soft loving face" (page 58) . . ." had a warm, contemplative loving face but she did not eat mustard" (page 58) . . . "she would look straight at the shopkeeper with her lovable, candid eyes" (page 59). Her eyes were lovely too, and she used them, together with an appearance of a smile,

"brown almond eyes that seemed to be always on the verge of smiling at something" (page 58), "seeming to smile at the men who drove up the road . . . playing with her ear and smiling at the fresh spring sky". And, in addition, when "she curled her left arm completely over her head, so that she could play softly with the lobe of her right ear" and then stood against the door-post, "the shape of one breast and one arm beautifully exposed, she had an air of serene and disturbing invitation". Thus, in *this* way, she was "the loved one" as far as James Pypper's customers were concerned and her seeming smile and sexy appearance helped to increase sales. Ironically, James Pypper himself, super-salesman, had first been attracted by her "*supposed* smile".

(b) This would indeed be a cynical story if we were to leave it thinking that a "*supposed* smile" had brought death to a signalman. But note how H.E. Bates ensures that we don't think this: "She discovered that she was smiling, really smiling this time" (page 64), "it was now a real smile . . . she felt that nothing could have been more soothing and beautiful than this fully realised moment of her smile . . . ". On the other hand he also tells us that "it was not so much that she was in love as that she herself was the loved one". So—*why* did she beckon him over? Was she more affected by the fact that her *real* smile had made her "the loved one"—for the first time ever? Did she confuse "the emotion of the passing trains" with the feeling that she was *really* falling in love? Was the signalman *ever* "the loved one"? If the signalman hadn't been killed how do you think Alice would have reacted when they met? Would she have tried to develop their acquaintanceship?

For further reading

The dramatic qualities of a railway setting are wonderfully exploited by E. Nesbitt in her unashamedly sentimental story, *The Railway Children* and this story is well worth reading both as a good tale and as a fine example of children's literature that really shows an understanding of children.

A major recommendation here must be Charles Dickens's spine-chilling short story about a signalman whose box is situated in a deep cutting near the mouth of a tunnel and near the site of a bad railway accident—"No. 1 Branch Line: The Signalman".

A number of Thomas Hardy's poems exploit the emotional possibilities of railway settings, particularly "On the Departure

Platform" and "Midnight on the Great Western".

Finally, H.E. Bates himself knew romance in a station waiting room; as he describes in this passage from *The Vanished World*:

> The over-sensitive intimacies of first love demand, as I have already indicated of poetry, a particular kind of secrecy. Any other mundane, time-table ridden, meal-ridden, family-ridden world must be shut out. First love develops in its own sacred, suspended, breathless, often wordless vacuum. It generates, and revels in, its own pain. It has no language of any known syntax or coherence that can express to others outside the vacuum what ecstasy it feels, always believing that others have either not felt it or not in the same way, never pausing to enquire after the fact, as old and inevitable as dawn, that a million others have.
>
> So we began to meet in secret, or what we thought was secret: under dark railway arches, in remote woods, in hayfields, under wet oak trees dripping with rain, in railway carriages and inevitably, when all else failed, in the First Class waiting-room on Platform Number Three. (We chose the First Class waiting room because there were never any First Class passengers.) We deluded ourselves that only the most intimate friends and confidants knew of these things; of course everybody knew. Even the porters at the station knew and occasionally came to spy gleefully on us as we were locked in blind embrace in the First Class waiting room. The masters at school knew. Now, however, I was no longer bombarded in class with sallies of crushing reprimand such as "I see our friend Bates is dreaming again". The approach was more subtle, the sarcasm infinitely heavier. "I see that our friend Bates has his head in the clouds again. No doubt with eyes on something of more pressing importance than the Treaty of Paris". The word "pressing", of course would draw much laughter.

The waiting-room was on Kettering station and the school was Kettering Grammar School.

The Ox

The Thurlow home isn't invitingly situated; it is "exposed and isolated, the wind striking at it from all quarters, it seemed to have no part with the surrounding landscape. Empty ploughed lands, in winter-time, stretched away on all sides in wet steel curves." And outside the house one "stepped into a country of wide horizons" and one could hear "the sound of the wind blowing across the bare land". The farmhouse home of Mrs Edwards in "Time to Kill" also seemed to have no part in the surrounding landscape. Bates compares it to "a forgotten box" left "on the flat land" (page 51). The wind blew there, too, a biting north-easter. The Pyppers' house in "The Loved One" "stood on high exposed ground like a slice cut out of a working-class street" and there was "some bleak, sour quality of loneliness in the surrounding land" (page 61).

Happiness eludes the Thurlows, the Edwards's and the Pyppers, and again it seems that Bates places these characters in dour environments to emphasise the ultimate emptiness of their lives. It would obviously be unreasonable to suggest here that the characters are as they are because of their environment, but it is perhaps reasonable to suggest that a deliberate choice of a location that reflects the mood and events of a story helps to make a story more effective. H.E. Bates could well have used his native Northamptonshire in this way as Thomas Hardy used Dorset and D.H. Lawrence used Nottinghamshire and Derbyshire.

H.E. Bates remembers, in *The Vanished World*, the difficulties that his grandfather had with a smallholding. The land "overlooking the great pastoral width of the Nene valley... was wickedly heavy, impossible to touch in winter, drying out to a surface of cracked concrete in summer, a devilish challenge, year in, year out". But to Bates his boyhood visits to this hard-working grandfather "afforded me the foundation on which all the joys of my childhood, together with all my feeling and love of the countryside is based". Certainly the countryside around Rushden figures a great deal in his writing—one has only to read, for instance, his novel *Love for Lydia*. "The Ox", "Time to Kill", and "The Loved One" have probably grown out of this love for a region full of the "wide horizons" referred to in "The Ox". Look now at a few more lines of description of his grandfather's smallholding, quoted from *The Vanished World*:

> ... but it was really about the little farmyard, with its clucking hens and squealing pigs, that the horizon of my world extended. The crest of the valley here is quite high, wide and open to every searing, soaking wind. On a really clear fine day it was possible here to pick out no less than nine of the church spires for which Northamptonshire is justly famous. Few trees and no great woodlands were there to break the view. Ash, hawthorn

and elm, with here and there a few small oaks, made up the general pattern of trees; the beeches, sweet chestnuts, turkey oaks and whitebeams which I now know and love in the south country were never to be seen.

Points for discussion

1 Mrs Thurlow's relationship to her bicycle "was that of a beast to a cart"; she was "the ox". Discuss the way H.E. Bates makes the bicycle as essential to the story as Mrs Thurlow herself so that the presence of the bicycle continually turns our sympathy to Mrs Thurlow's plight. Why does Mrs Thurlow even dream about her bicycle?

2 Money was Mrs Thurlow's "creed". How does H.E. Bates prove this to be a false creed? Has this story anything in common, as far as Mrs Thurlow's obession with money is concerned, with Arthur in "Château Bougainvillaea" and James Pypper in "The Loved One"? And note, too, that in "Every Bullet Has Its Billet" Bates says that Mrs Harris's "concentration on money had become a creed".

3 Discuss Mrs Thurlow's motives for wanting "to establish a world beyond her own" for her two sons. Why is her ambition probably stronger than most mothers? When you have read "The Maker of Coffins" compare the strength of Mrs Thurlow's feeling for her sons with the elderly mother's feelings for middle-aged son Luther.

4 Talk about all the ways in which Mrs Thurlow is an "ox". Is it her ox-like disposition that enables her to stay sane in the midst of all her troubles? Study, for instance, the comments on her reading of the papers on Sunday afternoons: "But emotionally, as she read, her face showed no impression. It remained ox-like in its impassivity" (page 71). Discuss how suffering can sometimes anaesthetise one so that one ceases to feel.

5 Mrs Thurlow is proud that her boys go to "a secondary school in the town". Education changes their attitude towards home because "having now some standard by which to judge her, they despised her a little". Talk about the problems that can affect both parents and children when parents are uneducated and children receive a good education and go on to higher education. (See the suggestions for reading at the end of this section.)

6 Was the decision of the boys not to go back home a reasonable one—or, alternatively, would it be to their advantage in the long run? Try and put yourself in Mrs Thurlow's situation as she returns to her home alone. What does the future hold for her?

For further reading

For another story, also a sad one, that tells of a mother who deserved a better deal read Bill Naughton's "Cockney Mum" (in the collection of Bill Naughton's stories—*Late Night on Watling Street*).

A very readable account of some of the problems of the educated boy who comes from a working-class home can be found in the section "Scholarship Boy" in Richard Hoggart's book *The Uses of Literacy*. If these problems interest you you might also have a look at Brian Jackson and Dennis Marsden's *Education and the Working Class*—and particularly at the sections "Education: looking back and looking forward", "Looking back on working-class life" and "Our parents and ourselves".

Walter Allen's novel *All In a Lifetime* contains an interesting, authentic account of the role of a mother in a Staffordshire Black Country home in the late nineteenth century: "It was mother, of course, who kept us respectable, who fought, one might almost say, to maintain our status." (See particularly Chapter 6.)

Finally, one of the finest accounts of the tenacious concern of a mother for her sons is to be found in Part I of D.H. Lawrence's novel *Sons and Lovers*, virtually the story of Lawrence's own childhood.

The Good Corn

After the hopelessness of the ending of "The Ox" it is a relief to turn to "The Good Corn", where the loyalty of a wife to a husband combined with a charity and compassion each for each turns a possibly tragic situation into a conclusion of intense happiness.

In "The Ox" Mrs Thurlow has two sons, lives for them, works for them, saves for them and finally loses them. In "The Good Corn" the Mortimer marriage is childless and husband and wife dearly want a child. The irony is made the more bitter because, living on a small farm and raising a few cattle, they are always aware of Mrs Mortimer's sterility, underlined with the arrival of each new calf.

The notes on "The Station" (page 162) have already referred to H.E. Bates's use of symbols in this story and it will be worth while to look at some of the symbolic description in "The Good Corn" before considering the impact of the story as a whole. First of all—the title itself. That H.E. Bates is thinking of the parable of the sower seems certain. There is an interesting reference to this in *The Vanished World* where H.E. Bates is writing about the probability of his father's wishing that he would grow up to be "a minister of the church":

> My father's position may be likened to that of a diligent and dedicated farmer who had tilled his earth industriously and sown his corn with care, only to observe coming up, in due course, a crop of tares.
>
> The good sound corn that had been sown Sunday after Sunday on my dutiful trottings off to Chapel, Sunday School, Prayer Meeting and Bible Class had at last brought forth exactly the opposite of the crop intended. It could not even be argued that some seed had fallen on stony ground, since the ground too had been prepared and nurtured to a condition exactly right for receiving it. In brief I suddenly and dramatically revolted.

(The parable of the sower is to be found in St Matthew's Gospel, chapter 13.)

Seedtime and harvest: these are the ever-present symbols of conception and birth. Bates first introduces us to Mrs Mortimer walking "across the *bare* autumn stubbles" and, significantly, "sometimes she was lovingly leading a calf by the halter". Mortimer feels the urge for children most "in summer when the corn was ready". The girl Elsie arrives in the late spring, at the time of "the greening hedges of hawthorn, and the rising fields of corn". Her ripeness—her fertility, if you like, as contrasted with Mrs Mortimer's sterility—is reflected in the descriptions of the July fruits (page 91). "The thick fingers of the girl were stained red with the juice of currants as she gathered them." It is in the cornfield that Mortimer becomes aware of Elsie's sexual attraction and round about the time of the gathering of the corn Elsie becomes pregnant. Her baby is expected in the spring and thus for the Mortimers the following spring becomes at once a time of birth and a time of rebirth of their hope for the future. The final sight of the new family is in itself a symbolic setting of hedgerows "breaking everywhere with bright new leaf", primroses, cowslips, flowers, "young curved lines of corn".

Points for discussion

1 Think about some of the psychological problems that accompany the inability of a woman to have children. Look carefully at the description of Mrs Mortimer's sense of "duty", at her feeling that "it was a failure in her living" (page 87) and at her grieving at the death of the calf in her arms (page 88).

2 Discuss the doctor's reasons for advising the Mortimers to move and to "grow nothing but corn". Was his advice wise? Why did Mrs Mortimer tell her husband not to "come near" her?

3 Consider carefully the significance of the details of the evening scene in the cornfield when Mortimer and Elsie first look at wheat together (page 92), bearing in mind the references to symbols made previously in these notes.

4 Look at the sensitive and moving scene when Joe tells his wife that he is the father of Elsie's baby. Why did Joe make love to Elsie? Why did his wife say "I'm sorry. It was me. It was my fault."? Would you say that her forgiveness was a triumph over conventional morality, an example of genuine understanding and compassion? What would have been *your* reaction? Will they be happy afterwards?

For further reading

In Bill Naughton's short story "Weaver's Knot" a tough, married foreman's affair with a mill-girl, Hetty, encounters tragedy when Hetty has an accident in the mill and their child is born dead. Like Joe Mortimer, Hambull technically flouts conventional morality but even so he "suffered the loss of a life's hope" and our sympathy goes out to him. (This story appears in the collection *Late Night Om Watling Street.*) The strength of a woman's maternal instinct is revealed in "The Good Corn". For a further example of this strength you should read the account in Margaret Drabble's novel *The Millstone* of Rosamond Stacey's reaction when her baby daughter Octavia has to go back into hospital for a serious and necessary operation. Particularly interesting is her behaviour when she encounters refusals to let her see her baby in hospital after the operation.

Mr Penfold

Points for discussion and suggestions for further reading

1 Look carefully at some of the recurring words that describe Mr Penfold in the opening paragraphs. Is there any suggestion that his job as a travelling draper acts as a repressing influence in itself?

2 Would you agree, as H.E. Bates seems to imply, that Mr Penfold's major failings stem from his being incapable of "understanding an inner meaning" and from his being too shy to enter "into a single great experience"? Can you see anything in common between Mr Penfold and Arthur Keller in "Château Bougainvillaea"?

3 Compare the description of Mr Penfold's August afternoon picking plums with Mrs Armitage (page 99) with the description of Albie's summer evening picking plums with the manageress of "The Station" (page 36). See also the notes on "The Station" on page 162. What is the symbolic significance of the occasion in "Mr Penfold"? Note the reference on page to the "sweet, almost autumnal fragrance of ripe plums".

It is interesting to speculate that the descriptions of lush summer scenes often found in these stories stem from H.E. Bates's own memories of, for instance, a summer visit with his grandfather to the home of an elderly widow at the village of Stanwick, three miles or so from his home at Rushden. After the widow had grumbled to grandfather about the scrumping that was going on H.E. Bates entered the fruit garden. He recalls the moment in *The Vanished World*:

The grass was long and unmown, dissected only by a narrow path along which, in single file, the dogs, in pup or not, waddled like an advance party of brown troopers. Abruptly to the left, there was a sudden drop of twenty or thirty feet into what had once been what my grandfather would have called, and indeed did call "a stun pit". From here, I gathered, had been quarried the stone for both house and garden wall. The calcareous nature of the remaining soil being admirably suited to the growing of fruit, especially stone-fruit, among which apricots demand certain exceptional conditions, the late husband of the old tit, who I gathered had made modest fortune from the invention of some patent lamp or other, had everywhere planted fruit with great prodigality.

The result was that the old tit was now the possessor of a positive forest of fruit that she had no idea what to do with. Hence the presence of my grandfather and I to survey and assess the prospect of harvest. The scene was utterly idyllic. Time had covered the lacerated cliffs of stone with grass and thyme and wild rose and elderberry and odd bushes of hawthorn; above it all rose the many fruit trees in their full bearing and prime, in particular pears of many varieties, Blenheim Orange apples, Worcester Pearmains, Cox's Orange and an apple that my grandfather called "a summerin' apple", on account of its earliness, softness of flesh and inability to keep. This, I fancy, was ready to pick, a pleasant pale yellow in colour, by the end of July, to be followed a little later by that queen of plums I have already mentioned, the squarish apricot-like plum of incomparable flavour always known as the Stanwick Plum (has it died too with the vanished world, I often wonder?) and then in succession the many pears, the russets, the Williams Bon Chretien, Conference and that great lady, Marie Louise.

4 Would you agree that H.E. Bates, in describing Katie's growing up, emphasises in her the qualities that can give an adolescent girl a beauty that is only present in adolescence and the qualities of temperament that are very typical of adolescence? In what ways does the possession of these qualities make it difficult for a person like Mr Penfold to communicate with adolescents? What need is it in Katie that makes her break the ice and lead him into the situation where he is able to begin to communicate with her? How might the situation—and the story—have developed had Mrs Armitage not burst into the room?

5 Compare Katie's admission to Mr Penfold, "She wants to keep me locked in a glass case", with the dilemma of Irma Harris in the story "Every Bullet Has Its Billet".

6 Discuss the use H.E. Bates makes of changes in weather to reflect emotional states in his stories. At the end of this story, for instance, Mr Penfold could feel the rain "spitting on his face and hands out of the strong heavy western wind". See particularly "Time to Kill" and "The Loved One". Writers from rural environments seem more conscious of these relation-

ships in their writings. Read the opening paragraphs of Thomas Hardy's novel *The Woodlanders* to see how the landscape setting merges with the overall mood of the novel.

7 For a contrasting story of urban loneliness for a middle-aged man read Alan Sillitoe's moving story "Uncle Ernest" (available in *A Sillitoe Selection*).

The Maker of Coffins

This story deals with a theme frequently encountered in literature, that of the possessive mother. On the other hand the treatment of the theme in this story is different from usual. Often this theme involves tension: in D.H. Lawrence's *Sons and Lovers*, for instance, Paul's possessive mother makes his intellectually nourishing friendship with Miriam fail. Somerset Maugham's short story "The Kite" is a grim account of a possessive mother's wrecking of her son's marriage. Irma Harris's life is ruined by a possessive, jealous mother in "Every Bullet Has Its Billet". But, in its own strange way, "The Maker of Coffins" is a happy story, well laced with pathos and nostalgia, yet never too cloying. How H.E. Bates achieves this balance is worth looking at.

Points for discussion

1 Consider the probable reasons for the mother's special love and concern for Luther. Note the remark on page 109, "If she was aware of feeling that the enormous body still enshrined the fragile child she did not reveal it."

2 After reading this story try to analyse what it is that makes parents—of any age—enjoy visits from their children—of any age, even when the children, like Luther, are not particularly marvellous. (What evidence is there in the story that Luther has been drinking and is, in fact, a bit of a tippler?) Is it common for parents deliberately to go about hiding their children's shortcomings from themselves. (Will and Lawrence, we note on page 110, "did not approve of Luther, but then, they did not understand him".)

3 What evidence is there that Luther enjoys these Sunday evenings with his mother? Why does he enjoy them?

4 Why does "Robin Adair" probably appeal most as "the old one"? Here are the words of the first verse and the last verse:

What's this dull town to me?
    Robin's not near.
What was't I wished to see?
    What wished to hear?
Where's all the joy and mirth
Made this town heav'n on earth?
Oh! they're all fled with thee,
    Robin Adair.

But now thou'rt cold to me,
    Robin Adair.
But now thou'rt cold to me,
    Robin Adair.
Yet him I lov'd so well
Still in my heart shall dwell,
Oh! I can ne'er forget
    Robin Adair.

Try to get hold of a volume of these old songs. Look at their typical words and listen to their frequently sugary tunes. Why were they so popular at family musical evenings in the days before television and "pop music", do you think? Why couldn't you "beat the old ones" if you were like Luther and his mother?

5 Finally, consider the significance of the title of the story. For instance, do you get any impression from the story as a whole to confirm H.E. Bates's comment towards the end of the story: "She sat ageless and tranquil as if already *embalmed* among the greenery of fern-pots, before a *shroud* of blanketing curtains, under a gas-blue summer sky." Look also at the references to Luther's craftsmanship as a coffin-maker in contrast to his lesser success as an instrumentalist.

The Little Jeweller

The last three stories in the present collection are concerned, in various ways, with elderly people. The "little jeweller", Elisha Peacock, is a lonely man. He lives alone and in the opening paragraphs of the story H.E. Bates introduces us to what must surely be one of the grimmest moments in life, the moment when "Elisha Peacock, after sixty-eight years of tranquil living, had reached the point where he must die in the night, alone, frightened like a child by the silence and the darkness before anyone could reach him or he could get downstairs to the telephone."

Points for discussion and suggestions for further reading

1 Consider the plight of the elderly, alone, in the dead of night, in pain, frightened of dying. Should they be compelled to give up their independence, in their own interests, and be taken either to relatives or to an old people's home? Would you be prepared to give up your independence?

2 We note that Elisha Peacock was not married. He had been wholly devoted to his business. Is *his* loneliness in any way comparable with that of Mr Penfold? Both were salesmen. (See also "Château Bougainvillaea", "The Loved One" and, possibly, "The Station".)

3 Think about the opening words of Francis Bacon's essay "Of Death", written towards the end of the sixteenth century: "Men fear death, as children fear to go in the dark." And then read Graham Greene's macabre story "The End of the Party", about a little boy Francis, who dreamed that he was dead and who didn't want to go to a birthday party because he didn't like playing hide and seek in the dark. He went with his twin brother to the party, and he did play hide and seek. Note H.E. Bates's comment at the end of the first section of this story (page 118) that Mr Peacock's voice was "now very like the voice of a child, crying in trouble and getting no answer".

4 The second section of this story lays emphasis on Mr Peacock's finding that he had "a great need for companionship". Like the fear of illness and death in the night this great need for companionship can be a major issue for both the elderly and the not-so-elderly. Discuss the problems of this need and compare the problems of Mr Peacock with those of Mr Penfold and Mrs Armitage in the story "Mr Penfold".

5 Why does the chandelier constantly disturb Mr Peacock? Why does H.E. Bates emphasise this? Note on page 124 "unless he took a terribly firm hold on himself he must sooner or later leap up in bed and seize the chandelier and smash it to pieces".

6 Discuss the irony of the situation in section III of this story: the lonely man who really needs human relationships find his relatives objectionable and asks for peace and quiet. Why does

he react in this way?

7 Do you think that the action of Mr Peacock's sister and brother-in-law (see section IV of the story) in taking away the flowers is responsible for finally unhinging his mind?

8 Mr Peacock finally breaks in the taxi: "He felt very frightened by the dark confinement of the taxi and suddenly began to shout like a child." Walter Allen's novel *All In a Lifetime* is a moving study of an old man who, in his last years, writes his life story and tries to come to terms with the problems of his old age. In the final pages of this novel Billy Ashted recalls the events of his running away from his son Will's home in a fit of pique; "I was like a small child in a tantrum," he says. Then he describes his journey to the city he knew in his youth, his searching for places that no longer existed and his wanderings until he finally arrived at the home of his sister, "blarting like a baby. . . I cried with relief."

9 In what ways does Mr Peacock's behaviour in hospital reveal that he really has suffered a mental breakdown and thus needs to be in hospital? What does H.E. Bates seem to suggest is lacking at the hospital when he uses such phrases as "The doctor spoke with heavy kindness" and "her eyes. . . contained no hint of understanding. . . they were regarding him instead with a kind of impersonal pity" (page 130)?

Where the Cloud Breaks

Points for discussion and suggestions for further reading

1 In what ways do the opening paragraphs of this story stress the fact that the Colonel is getting past looking after himself and that he needs the help of Miss Wilkinson very much?

2 The Colonel "never wore a watch". Is this an eccentricity of old age? Or is it something more significant? Why does the Colonel own neither television nor radio and why has he stopped taking *The Times*? Try looking at these things through the eyes of an elderly person and consider just why you might react like this. What arguments would you put forward to suggest that the Colonel, of all people, really *needs* a telephone, a wireless and a television?

3 The Colonel "would like to have put this feeling into words of some kind—signalling was child's play by comparison—but he

was both too inarticulate and too shy to do so" (page 134). The Colonel had lived the major part of his life in the man's world of the army. To what extent might this have affected his capacity both to understand his feelings and to express them?

4 Consider the parallels between Colonel Gracie's difficulties in *signalling* his feelings and Mr Penfold's difficulties in *unfolding* his feelings.

5 Discuss the Colonel's reaction to the sitting room *before* he notices the television: "It was like a little chintz holy-of-holies, always embalmed, always the same" (page 138). Why does the Colonel feel that Miss Wilkinson "had acted in some way like a traitor"?

6 What is the effect of H.E. Bates's ending the story as it began, with the Colonel in a mess in the kitchen?

7 Why is the story called "Where the Cloud Breaks"? What is the significance of the delphinium, referred to several times in the story?

8 Are men, generally, less able to cope than women in their old age? For a hopeful view of being "superannuated" read Charles Lamb's essay, "The Superannuated Man"; for a sadder view of a bachelor's loneliness read Charles Lamb's essay "Dream Children"; for a rather terrifying view of the extremes of old age read John Betjeman's poem "The Cottage Hospital" (in *The Collected Poems*). For a comfortable view read the last pages of John Galsworthy's *The Man of Property*—"Interlude"—describing the death of old Jolyon Forsyte, an end unlikely to be experienced in similar happiness by the lonely Colonel Gracie.

Colonel Julian

The final story in this collection is set in the England of 1944. It was the fifth year of the Second World War. On 6 June occurred one of the most decisive events of the whole war—the beginning of the invasion of Normandy, France, by Allied troops. Northern France had been occupied by German forces since 1940 when the British army had been evacuated from the beaches of Dunkirk; 6 June 1944, was known as 'D Day", the first day of the whole invasion the code name of which was "Operation Overlord". The June weather was unfavourably stormy, but despite this 156,000 seaborne and airborne troops, 73,000 American and 83,000 British including Canadian, were successfully carried across the Channel on D-Day. For a precise account of this campaign you should read the sections on "The conquest of Germany" in *A Short History of the Second World War* by Basil Collier, from which book the above statistics are quoted. But for a superbly detailed account of one man's view of D-Day and the Normandy invasion you should read David Holbrook's novel *Flesh Wounds*.

H.E. Bates recalls the stormy June weather in "Colonel Julian": "The papers were saying that it was the worst summer for forty years. Cold gales had swept down from the north in June, breaking the oats into shabby and forlorn wreckage and burning the tender leaves of the limes."

During the war, houses were likely to be requisitioned for military use; Colonel Julian's home was taken over by the R.A.F., as an officers' Mess for the men who flew from a nearby R.A.F. station. H.E. Bates's novel *A Moment in Time* is the story of a teenage girl whose lovely home is similarly taken over by the R.A.F. during 1940, the period of the Battle of Britain, when the famous confrontation between British and German air force fighters resulted in Britain's gaining air supremacy and this in all probability removed the danger of a German military invasion of Britain in 1940. Colonel Julian's house had been taken over in 1940.

Points for discussion and suggestions for further reading

1 In what ways is Colonel Julian similar to, perhaps, and in what ways is he very different from Colonel Gracie in "Where the Cloud Breaks"? How might Colonel Gracie have reacted to living with the R.A.F.?

2 In his preface to a collection of H.E. Bates's short stories entitled *Seven by Five* Henry Miller writes:

"And then there is *this* element which crops up again and again, I find—an obsession with pain. Pain stretched to the breaking point, pain prolonged beyond all seeming endurance. This element is usually called forth in connection with heroic behaviour. Perhaps it is the supreme mark of the hero, this ability to endure pain. With Mr Bates I feel that it goes beyond the point of the heroic; it carries us into some other dimension. Pain takes on the aspects of space and time, a continuum or perpetuum which one finally questions no longer."

For what reasons do you think H.E. Bates describes the boy's burns and injuries at such length? If you read H.E. Bates's novel *Fair Stood the Wind for France* you might consider carefully the amount of detail given to descriptions of Franklin's injury to his arms, an injury which finally necessitates its amputation.

3 Take a look at the use of R.A.F. slang in this story. What are its typical characteristics? For an excellent example of the use of R.A.F. slang as a means of deliberately playing down harrowing incidents read H.E. Bates's short story "No Trouble At All" from his collection *The Stories of Flying Officer X*.

4 Consider the differences between war as the Colonel had known it and war as the boy fights it. Are these differences inevitable in the changed circumstances of war? Does flying tend to develop a different attitude towards war from that of the soldier? Is it, for instance, bound to be more individual because of the loneliness of the combat—particularly in the case of a fighter pilot? Why should flying become a "disease" or "an intense and narrow passion"? For more extended consideration of the flyers' attitudes towards war and towards flying see particularly "The Greatest People in the World", "A Personal War" and "Yours Is the Earth" in *The Stories of Flying Officer X*.

5 Some of the tensest locations during the Second World War must have been the R.A.F. stations when those in the operations room, not to mention all the fellow airmen, waited for the return or non-return of fliers from a bombing mission or a fighter battle. One of the most poignant aspects is brought out at the end of "Colonel Julian"; one either returns to an apparently casual drink on the terrace or one is suddenly dead, or a prisoner, or down in the sea. Other stories by H.E. Bates refer more specifically to these moments: see, in *The Stories of Flying Officer X*, "There's No Future In It", "It's Never in the Papers", "The Young Man From Kalgoorlie", "The Sun Rises Twice" and "No Trouble At All".

Other writings by H. E. Bates

Stories of wartime

These are deliberately listed under the heading "Stories of wartime" rather than "War stories" because H.E. Bates is never merely concerned with the crude actions of war. Take, for instance, his novel *Fair Stood the Wind for France (1944)*. The action takes place in 1942: a Wellington bomber returning home from a mission to Italy crashes over German-occupied France. Its crew finds refuge with a French family living at a mill. The family arrange for the crew to be provided with the necessary papers and assistance to escape across France and regain their freedom. There is plenty of tension and action in the novel. But, more important is the way in which H.E. Bates explores the mental conflict within the characters: how bomber crews really feel beneath the surface talk with its R.A.F. slang: the importance of the personal relationships within the crew: the love and the compassion of human being for human being that can lead members of a family to risk their lives to help their allies to escape. *Fair Stood the Wind for France* is available as a Longman Imprint Book which contains relevant background information on the Second World War, the role of the R.A.F. and the German occupation of France.

The Stories of Flying Officer X (Cape 1952) have already been recommended in connection with the story "Colonel Julian". During the Second World War H.E. Bates wrote a number of stories under the pseudonym of "Flying Officer X". He himself served in the R.A.F. and these stories are inside views of the real dramas of wartime flying and the men who flew, dramas that invariably received no publicity—as the title of one of the stories "It's Never In the Papers" suggests. H.E. Bates was, in fact, the first writer to be commissioned into the armed forces for the special purpose of producing short stories. He eventually rose to the rank of Squadron Leader.

A Moment In Time (Michael Joseph, 1958) looks at flying during the Battle of Britain in 1940 from a woman's angle. Elizabeth's family home is commandeered by the R.A.F. She and her uncle stay on and she becomes more and more emotionally involved in the air battles taking place virtually over her head as her new friends fly off each day. Like *Fair Stood the Wind for France* this novel explores beneath the surface of the physical events of the war, particularly in its study of the way in which Elizabeth's experiences force her to face not the glamour of war but the harsh reality of it: its call for a universal compassion matures her.

The Purple Plain (Michael Joseph, 1947) has as its setting Burma in the Second World War, and it is mainly concerned with a study of the desperate attempts of three members of a crashed aircraft to return to their base. Their enemies, however, are not the hidden soldiers but the difficult terraine, over which two of them must carry the badly injured third member, and the desperately hot weather. Whilst serving in the R.A.F., H.E. Bates visited Burma, India and Japan, and these visits provided the background for "The Jacaranda Tree" (1949) and "The Scarlet Sword" (1951) as well as "The Purple Plain".

The "Uncle Silas" short stories

(*My Uncle Silas*, Cape 1939.) These are rich, earthy, usually comic and often moving short stories that truly come from "the vanished world" described by H.E. Bates in the first part of his autobiography. Remembering a tiny thatched cottage just outside the village of Sharnbrook and a Turk's cap lily in its garden. H.E. Bates reveals, in *The Vanished World*, the original Uncle Silas:

> This scarlet lily is the key that unlocks the world of a certain Joseph Betts, husband of my grandmother's sister. Born in the Hungry Forties, reprobate, rapscallion, crafty as a monkey, liar, gardener of much cunning, drinker of infinite capacity, afflicted with one blood-shot eye that gave him a look of devilish fascination, he is the original of My Uncle Silas, the character whose alcoholic and womanising adventures I was to chronicle in a series of stories some twenty-five years later. Sitting propped by the kitchen door in corduroy trousers and a thick old broad-cloth waistcoat, he was, to a small boy, a figure both compelling and fearsome. An aura of positively Satanic secrecy surrounded his prowess in raising gooseberries big as golf balls, potatoes unmatched for earliness and flavour, peas of unrivalled succulence and most of all the presence of the Turk's Cap lily. As he supped at glasses of home-brewed cowslip and elderberry wine—in spring the kitchen floor would often be yellow with sheets of drying cowslips—I listened to him with

ears cocked and eyes utterly hypnotised. Already he then seemed to me to be venerable, almost patriarchal, a figure from a past even more remote than Hardy's early novels. He was in fact still to ripen to an even greater age, living into his nineties, for ever growing more crafty, devilish and fearsome, so much so that one day when I much later took my future wife to meet him for the first time she was as near-terrified, poor girl, as if I had presented Old Nick himself.

From those golden days at the little cottage by the woodside there stands out one gilded with special splendour: a summer day when my mother, my grandmother, my aunt, my sister and myself arrived there for the wedding of Joe Betts' only son. By the generosity of the local squire a big white marquee had been put up in the little paddock; inside it long trestle tables were filled with cold meats and sandwiches and salads and cakes and beer and wine. Already by the time we arrived Joe was as merry as a boozy cricket; by afternoon he was rollicking; by evening he was prancing with the ladies; by dusk he was drunkenly bawling "We won't go home till morning!—let 'em all come!", the leading jester on an uproarious summer stage. Such was the sharpness of the impression it all made on me that though it was a near quarter of a century before I put it down in a story called "The Wedding" the words practically wrote themselves.

Joe too belongs to a vanished world. His little thatched cottage, so a correspondent writes to tell me, has been pulled down. The world of television, jets and space craft dazzles our generation with new if sometimes near useless wonders, but for myself I would cheerfully exchange it all for that blood-shot eye, the smell of wood-smoke, the scent of bluebells, cowslips, primroses and the Maiden's Blush, the Turk's Cap lily and the voices of nightingales.

Other short stories

The present collection is only a fraction of H.E. Bates's total output of some 600 short stories: each volume reveals stories which become personal favourites. As one who, before he became a full time writer, had direct experience of life as a reporter on a local newspaper, H.E. Bates is well qualified to write about the ethics of sensational journalism. Two stories that explore these ethics disturbingly are "Shot Actress: Full Story" and "Millenium Also

Ran". "Go Lovely Rose" is a story that catches the fears of many a father waiting anxiously for his daughter to return safely, very late at night, in her boy friend's car (available in *Breaking Away* in this Longman Imprint series). "The Blind" is a poignant story of well-meaning but ignorant parents whose faith in a quack doctor brings their daughter only complete blindness. "Elephants Nest In A Rhubarb Tree" is a sensitive study of a boy who grows up retaining the mind of a child. (Worth comparing this with Alan Sillitoe's story "The Decline and Fall of Frankie Buller") "A Flower Piece" is a delicate account of the blend of make-believe and real life in the games of two young girls. These are merely a few personal choices: if you have enjoyed this collection it would be best to "Cut and Come Again"—which in itself is the title of one of H.E. Bates's collections of short stories.

The Larkin Family stories

These are very popular and a number have been adapted for radio, Sir Bernard Miles playing the part of Pa Larkin. In the Larkin books (1960)—*A Breath of French Air* (1959), *When the Green Woods Laugh* (all published by Michael Joseph) and *The Darling Buds of May* (1958) for instance—we are introduced to a happy, broad humoured, vigorous family from the country who have a habit of outwitting and cocking a snook at officialdom with their combined native wits in a series of light situation comedies. Read how the family cope with Mr Charlton, who comes round from the Inspector of Taxes to persuade Pa Larkins to complete his tax return, and how Pa uses his seductive daughter Mariette to take Mr Charlton's mind off his official duties! (This episode can be found in *The Darling Buds of May*).

H.E. Bates and his wife moved into an old granary in a Kent village in 1931 and the Kent countryside has provided the setting for a number of his stories. In an article in the May 1973 edition of *The Illustrated London News* Wilfred De' Ath claims that "there is a good deal of H.E. Bates himself in Pop Larkin, a passionate Englishman, a profound lover of nature, of the sounds and sights of the countryside, of colour, flowers and things sensual; a hater of pomp, pretension and humbug; a lover of children and family life; an occasional breaker of rules, a flouter of conventions."

Love for Lydia (Michael Joseph 1952)

A number of the short stories in the present collection have their origins in H.E. Bates's Northamptonshire and it is worth while to read one of a number of full length novels that have grown out of the "Evensford" region. The novel, "Love for Lydia" is a particularly good example. We *do* know where the germ of the story came from; H.E. Bates describes the occasion, in *The Vanished World*, when "on a dark, cold and dismal evening" he visited Rushden Hall on a reporting assignment:

> It has passed completely from my mind what I had come to interview the Sartoris about, or what they said to me. Two impressions, however, remain unfaded: first, my own incomparable nervousness which, further actuated by the cold, kept me constantly shivering; and secondly the strangest feeling that the shaping Divinity had actually sent me there for a purpose which then appeared to be totally obscure. All that I bore away with me into the freezing blackness of the winter night was, in fact, in no sense real; it was in some sense both haunting and prophetic.
>
> In fact it was not to become real for another thirty years, when that same room became the setting for the first chapters of a novel of mine. But since one room, like one idea, doesn't necessarily make a novel, it was opportune that somewhere about the same time I had had another experience, even briefer but just as singular in its importance. One morning, as I went to catch my morning train, a smart pony-driven gig drew up at the station and out of it got a tallish, dark, proud, aloof young girl in a black cloak lined with scarlet. I had never seen her before and never saw her again. Such a vision was not, in fact, ever to be seen in that town and I surmised, rightly or wrongly, that she came from the Hall.
>
> In the writing of novels there must necessarily be a fusion of negative and positive. In this case the cold, dismal, wintry Hall was the negative; the girl in the scarlet lined cloak, seen for two minutes, was the positive. In fusion, thirty years later, they became *Love for Lydia*.

Bretherton, Bates's boss at the Wellingborough office of the *Northampton Chronicle*, appears in the opening pages of *Love for Lydia*, and Richardson, narrator of *Love for Lydia*, is sent out to the Aspen home to find out something about the late Mr Aspen. Instead he meets Lydia. And two days later Richardson takes Lydia out for the first time, teaching her to skate. On this first date "She appeared that day in a sort of black cloak that was half a mackintosh, half like the kind of garment, cowled over the head, that nuns or nurses wear."

The Vanished World

A great deal of reference has been made in this edition to this first volume of H.E. Bates's autobiography, published in 1969. As well as being one of the best autobiographies of childhood and growing-up to be written in recent years, it is a lively historical and sociological survey of a small East Midlands industrial town and its often remotely rural hinterland over half a century ago. Finally, it gives one the opportunity, always fascinating, to read something of how a now great writer went about his apprentice pieces. It is interesting to read that H.E. Bates soon abandoned local journalism and went to work as a clerk in a warehouse. It was here that he evolved a system of getting most of his warehouse work finished by about nine-thirty each morning so that he could get on, at the age of seventeen, with the writing of his first novel on "the thickest quarto writing pad, in pale blue, that I could find".

> I bore home that massive chunk of writing-paper with a feeling of rare and peculiar excitement in my heart: an emotion arising from a particular sort of anticipation that has since been repeated a thousand times. Talking only the other day to a celebrated painter I discovered that she too had shared, over and over again, the same anticipatory thrill: hers from a blank area of canvas, mine from a naked quarto of paper. What, eventually, is going to illuminate the canvas, what the paper? The question is still, for me, the most exciting one of a writer's life—out of, and by means of, the simplest materials, will come what? The mere fact of not knowing is over and over again responsible for a positive, impossible excitement.

H.E. Bates has published two further volumes of his autobiography, *The Blossoming World* and *The World in Ripeness*. Several titles by H.E. Bates, including some of those mentioned above, are available in Penguin editions.

H.E. Bates died on 31st January 1974.

List of books recommended

Novels

WALTER ALLEN, *All in a Lifetime*, Michael Joseph 1962; Penguin

MARGARET DRABBLE, *The Millstone*, Weidenfeld & Nicolson 1965; Longman Imprint Books

E.M. FORSTER, *Howard's End*, Arnold, 1910; Penguin Modern Classics

JOHN GALSWORTHY, *The Man of Property* [the first part of *The Forsyte Saga*, Heinemann] Penguin

THOMAS HARDY, *The Woodlanders* (1887) Macmillan: Papermac.

L.P. HARTLEY, *The Go-Between*, Hamish Hamilton 1953; Heinemann Modern Novel series

D.H. LAWRENCE, *The Rainbow*, Heinemann 1915; Penguin

C. DAY LEWIS, *The Otterbury Incident*, Heinemann 1948; Heinemann New Windmill series

E. NESBITT, *The Railway Children* (1908); Heinemann New Windmill series

MARK TWAIN, *Huckleberry Finn* (1884); Heinemann New Windmill series

KEITH WATERHOUSE, *There is a Happy Land*, Michael Joseph 1957; Longman Imprint Books

Autobiographies, and autobiographical novels and stories

CLIFFORD DYMENT, *The Railway Game*, Dent 1962

MAXIM GORKY, *My Childhood* (1915) Penguin Classics

EDMUND GOSSE, *Father and Son* (1907); Heinemann; Penguin Modern Classics

DAVID HOLBROOK, *Flesh Wounds*, Methuen 1966; Longman Imprint Books

D.H. LAWRENCE, *Sons and Lovers*, Heinemann 1913; Heinemann Modern Novels series

JAMES JOYCE, *A Portrait of the Artist as a Young Man* (1916); Heinemann Modern Novels series

LAURIE LEE, *Cider With Rosie*, Chatto 1959; Chatto, Queen's Classics

BILL NAUGHTON, *One Small Boy*, MacGibbon & Kee 1957; Longman Imprint Books

SIEGFRIED SASSOON, *Memoirs of an Infantry Officer*, Faber 1930

DYLAN THOMAS, *Portrait of the Artist as a Young Dog*, Dent 1940; Aldine Paperbacks

LEO TOLSTOY, *Childhood, Boyhood, Youth* (1852–56); Penguin Classics

Short stories

SID CHAPLIN, "The Bridge", and "The End of an Age", both in *The Leaping Lad and Other Stories*, Longman Imprint Books

CHARLES DICKENS, "No. 1 Branch Line: The Signalman", in *Short Stories Old and New*, ed. R.W. Jepson, Longman

GRAHAM GREENE, "The End of the Party", and "The Basement Room", both in *21 Stories*, Penguin

SOMERSET MAUGHAM, "The Kite", in *The Kite and Other Stories*, Heinemann New Windmill series

BILL NAUGHTON, "Cockney Mum", and "Weaver's Knot", both in *Late Night on Watling Street*, Longman Imprint Books

ALAN SILLITOE, "The Decline and Fall of Frankie Buller", "Uncle Ernest", and "On Saturday Afternoon", all in *A Sillitoe Selection*, Longman Imprint Books

Plays

DAVID TURNER, "Semi-Detached", French

ARNOLD WESKER, Roots, in *Trilogy*, Cape 1960; Longman HLS Modern Classics

Poems

JOHN BETJEMAN, "The Cottage Hospital", in *Collected Poems*, Murray, 1958

THOMAS HARDY, "On the Departure Platform", and "Midnight on the Great Western", both in *Collected Poems*, 4th edn, Macmillan 1930

WILLIAM WORDSWORTH, *The Prelude*, Books 1 and 2

M. HUSSEY, ed. *Poetry of the First World War*, Longman 1967

M. MARLAND, ed. *The War Poets*, The Times Authors

Essays

FRANCIS BACON, "Of Death"

CHARLES LAMB, "The Superannuated Man" and "Dream Children"

The Bible

St Matthew, chapters 8 and 13
St Luke, chapter 13.

History

BASIL COLLIER, *A Short History of the Second World War*, Collins 1967
ALAN MOOREHEAD, *Gallipoli*, Hamilton, 1956
A.J.P. TAYLOR, *English History 1914–1945*, Oxford University Press 1965

Education

B. JACKSON and D. MARSDEN, *Education and the Working Class*, Routledge 1962; Penguin (Pelican)
RICHARD HOGGART, *The Uses of Literacy*, Chatto 1957; Penguin (Pelican)